CONQUEST
and the Life of
REST

⁓ A Devotional Study of Joshua ⁓

Warren Henderson

All Scripture quotations are from the New King James Version of the Bible, unless otherwise noted. Copyright © 1982 by Thomas Nelson, Inc. Nashville, TN

Conquest and the Life of Rest – A Devotional Study of Joshua
By Warren Henderson
Copyright © 2013

Cover Design by Benjamin Bredeweg

Published by Warren A. Henderson
3769 Indiana Road
Pomona, KS 66076

Perfect Bound ISBN 978-1-939770-20-2
eBook ISBN 978-1-939770-21-9

ORDERING INFORMATION:
Copies of *Conquest and the Life of Rest* are available through
www.amazon.com/shops/*hendersonpublishing* or
www.order@gospelfolio.com (1-800-952-2382)
or various online retailers.

Acknowledgements

Publishing books is a tedious task requiring a number of individuals with various talents. The author greatly appreciates all those who assisted in the publishing of *Conquest and the Land of Rest*. For those requesting no acknowledgment – the Lord knows of your labor. Special thanks to Kathleen Henderson for the immense task of general editing and also to David Lindstrom and Daniel Macy for proofreading assistance.

Other Books by the Author

Afterlife – What Will It Be Like?

Answer the Call – Finding Life's Purpose

Behold the Saviour

Be Angry and Sin Not

Exploring the Pauline Epistles

Forsaken, Forgotten, and Forgiven – A Devotional Study of Jeremiah

Glories Seen & Unseen

Hallowed Be Thy Name – Revering Christ in a Casual World

Hiding God – The Ambition of World Religion

In Search of God – A Quest for Truth

Managing Anger God's Way

Mind Frames – Where Life's Battle Is Won Or Lost

Out of Egypt – A Devotional Study of Exodus

Overcoming Your Bully

Passing the Torch – Mentoring the Next Generation

Revive Us Again – A Devotional Study of Ezra and Nehemiah

Seeds of Destiny – A Devotional Study of Genesis

The Bible: Myth or Divine Truth?

The Fruitful Bough – Affirming Biblical Manhood

The Fruitful Vine – Celebrating Biblical Womanhood

The Olive Plants – Raising Spiritual Children

Your Home the Birthing Place of Heaven

Preface

The last verse of Genesis reads: *"So Joseph died ... and they embalmed him, and he was put in a coffin in Egypt."* This verse reminds us that despite all the wondrous works of God recorded in Genesis, because of sin, man is under a sentence of death in the world, as pictured by Joseph "in a coffin in Egypt." Thankfully, the Bible does not end with the book of Genesis; God's plan of salvation unfolds with more detail in each subsequent book of the Bible.

The Pentateuch, for example, is one continuing storyline which ultimately reaches its typological climax in the subsequent book of Joshua. Notice how the following prepositions form a mini-outline of these six books. In Genesis, sin brought man *down*. In Exodus, he is redeemed by blood and brought *out* of the world. In Leviticus, man is permitted to come *nigh* (but not too near) to God in worship by substitutional sacrifices. In Numbers, man is guided *through* trials and is refined for service. In Deuteronomy, which means "Second Law," man is brought *back* to remember his responsibility to the Lord and the consequences of rebellion. In Joshua, a redeemed people are led by Joshua through the Jordan River *into* victorious living as they seize their promised inheritance.

It was fitting that Moses should die before the Israelites entered the Promised Land (Deut. 34) and that the very next chapter records Joshua's commission to lead the Israelites into Canaan (Josh. 1). Moses brought the Law, which could never bring spiritual life or produce vitality; the Law only condemned the Jews because they could not keep it. Consequently, Law-keeping, which centers in human effort alone, can never result in victorious living, which depends solely on God's infusing power. Joshua pictures Jesus Christ of the New Testament; both of their names mean "Jehovah is salvation" or "Jehovah saves." Israel's trip through the Jordan River symbolizes the reception of the resurrection life of Christ. It is only by this pervading power that a believer can have victory over the enemy, lay hold of spiritual possessions, and please God.

The English words "rest" and "possession" are key words in Joshua. Before we can practically understand the meaning of divine rest, we first must understand how we acquire our divine inheritance. The words "possess," "possessed," and "possession" are found twenty-four times in Joshua and are mainly translated from two Hebrew words *yarash* and *achuzzah.* *Yarash* means "to occupy by expelling the previous tenants," while *achuzzah* conveys the thought of "something (especially land) seized for a possession." Two important lessons are conveyed through the usage of these two Hebrew words.

First, it is observed that *yarash* is found twenty-nine times in Joshua; the only Old Testament book with more occurrences is Deuteronomy. It is translated "to drive out" as well as "to possess." Joshua is the story of God's people relying on His grace to overcome what impedes them from possessing their God-given inheritance. The benefits of that inheritance were only obtained through faithful and obedient acquisition. For Christians, our inheritance is the sum total of the blessings of grace available in Christ, yet our possession of these blessings relates only to that portion we make our own. Hence, conflict is a necessary aspect of a believer's spiritual development and is inevitable on this side of heaven; it is the means of learning Christ and more intimately identifying with Him. The Kingdom of God advances as believers live for Christ, and they are rewarded accordingly – in this sense there is much ground to be gained.

Second, *achuzzah* occurs six times in Joshua; the only Old Testament books with more occurrences are Leviticus and Ezekiel. The usage of this word in Joshua occurs after chapter 20 (i.e., after the land had been seized by the Israelites from the inhabitants and was available for distribution). Believers must co-labor with the Lord to be victorious in spiritual conflict – we war in response to His wherewithal, not our own. Believers must remain active in faith to fully benefit from their spiritual blessings they already have in Christ. Perhaps the following illustration from the game of football will assist our understanding how these two Hebrew words for "possession" relate to each other.

Two opposing teams are in position and nearly motionless at the line of scrimmage. The quarterback calls out a series of numbers and receives the "snap" from the center – this puts the ball into motion and begins the play. A defensive linebacker seeing the handoff from the quarterback to the halfback begins his approach to tackle the halfback or better yet, strip the football from him. He fights hard through several offensive blockers and with a final lunge is able to knock the ball from the halfback's hands to cause a fumble. The linebacker has arduously toiled to obtain this objective (i.e. *yarash*), and though there has been a tangible accomplishment he is not satisfied with just causing the fumble. He must try his best to recover the ball also for his triumph to have continuing value. Consequently, his recent achievement, though thrilling, resulted in more work to be done. The linebacker scrambles for the loose football, scoops it up, and hangs on to it with all his might until the referee blows the whistle to signal that the play is over. The referee verifies that the defense has recovered the fumbled ball for their possession (i.e. *achuzzah*). This illustration vividly captures the mindset believers are to have as they lay hold of their possessions in Christ by co-laboring with Him, and then going on with Him, both benefiting from what they have and being enabled to gain more. In summary, *Yarash* is the inheritance to be possessed (i.e., labored for), while *achuzzah* is a possession we labor to keep and benefit from now. The Israelites strived to obtain the land (their inheritance) and were to continue toiling in faith to secure the life of rest God provided for them.

The Hebrew words *nuwach* and *shaqat* are translated "rest" six times in the book to express the Israelite's overall existence of tranquility and peace, despite the necessity of further personal conflict in the land. This restful quality of life was enjoyed by the two and half tribes who settled in the Eastern Plateau after Moses vanquished the warrior inhabitants (1:13, 15). Seven years later, rest was apprehended by the nation in a general sense after Canaan had been conquered under Joshua's leadership (11:23, 14:15, 21:44, 22:4, 23:1). The inward spiritual tranquility associated with this rest was only realized because the Israelites exercised faith in Jehovah through active conquest. By faith and obedience the land (their inheritance) was possessed; this accomplishment permitted them the opportunity for rest within the land.

Thirty-eight years prior to their entrance into Canaan the Israelites failed to obtain God's rest in the land because of disbelief (Heb. 4:4-6). In Canaan, the Israelites did enter into God's rest, but then failed to secure their inheritance in faith after receiving it. Consequently, the rest Jehovah had for them was never fully realized and, in time, was lost.

Conquest and the Life of Rest

The writer of Hebrews uses their failure as an exhortation, *"Let us therefore be diligent to enter that rest, lest anyone fall according to the same example of disobedience"* (Heb. 4:11-12). The matter of victorious living has not changed; continued faith and obedience ultimately translate into obtaining divine possessions and rest. Labor without faith or faith without labor will never translate into divine conquest and spiritual peace, but will rather conclude in human failure and emotional anxiety.

This is the message conveyed to us in the Hebrew words relating to "possession" and "rest" in the book of Joshua. By faith and obedience God's people entered Canaan – their inheritance. They could not engage in conquest until they entered the land, they could not possess the land without conquest, and they could not enter God's rest in the land without first possessing it. In the Church Age, believers do not labor for a *place* of rest; our rest and inheritance are in a *Person* – *"Christ in heavenly places"* (Eph. 1:3). Thus, Paul could pray for fellow believers, *"The Lord of peace Himself give you peace in every way"* (2 Thess. 3:16) and also share his life's aspiration with them:

> *Not that I have already attained, or am already perfected; but I press on, that I may lay hold of that for which Christ Jesus has also laid hold of me. Brethren, I do not count myself to have apprehended; but one thing I do, forgetting those things which are behind and reaching forward to those things which are ahead, I press toward the goal for the prize of the upward call of God in Christ Jesus* (Phil. 3:12-14).

Christ is the believer's inheritance and resting place. The practical blessing of those present possessions granted the believer in Christ will be experienced through faith and obedience as one engages in active conquest and is enabled to do so by resurrection power.

Conquest and the Life of Rest is a "commentary style" devotional which upholds the glories of Christ while exploring the book of Joshua within the context of the whole of Scripture. As in *Seeds of Destiny* (Genesis), *Out of Egypt* (Exodus), *Forsaken, Forgotten, and Forgiven* (Jeremiah), and *Revive Us Again* (Ezra and Nehemiah), I have endeavored to include in this book some of the principal gleanings from other writers. *Conquest and the Life of Rest* contains dozens of brief devotions. This format allows the reader to use the book either as a daily devotional or as a reference source for deeper study.

Introduction

The Author

Hebrew tradition ascribes Joshua as the author of the book entitled *Joshua* in our Bibles. The Talmud states that he wrote all but the final five verses, which were written by Phinehas the High Priest. The internal evidence suggests that Joshua wrote much of the book (8:32, 24:26), but clearly brief portions that must have been written later are also included: the record of Joshua's death (24:29-30), Caleb's conquest of Hebron (15:13-14), Othneil's conquest of Debir (15:15-19) and the Danites' victory over Leshem (19:47). Joshua was of course an eye-witness to the conquest of Canaan and naturally includes himself among the company of God's people at that time by employing pronouns such as "us" and "we" (e.g., 4:23, 5:1, 6:17, 7:25). The vivid details provided regarding the crossing of the Jordan River and the various battles the Israelites fought and won also suggest that the writer was among the Israelites when these events occurred.

The Date

Internal evidence suggests an early authorship by Joshua, for Rahab was alive at the time of the writing (6:25) and the Jebusites were still dwelling in Jerusalem (15:63). Donald Campbell draws from other Scriptures to affix the date of the Canaan invasion at 1406 BC:

> Key verses in deciding the issue are 1 Kings 6:1 and Judges 11:26. According to 1 Kings 6:1 the Israelites left Egypt 480 years before the fourth year of Solomon, that is, before 966 BC. Adding these figures gives an Exodus date of 1446 BC. The beginning of the Conquest was 40 years later (after the wilderness wanderings) or 1406. The evidence from Judges 11:26 confirms this. Jephthah said the period from the Conquest to his time was 300 years (Judg. 11:26). Adding 140 years to cover the period from Jephthah to the fourth year of Solomon gives a total of 480 years, which agrees with 1 Kings 6:1. ...Since the actual Conquest lasted seven years (Josh. 14:10), the land was probably

occupied about 1399 BC. The book, apart from minor additions, could have been completed soon after that.[1]

It is likely that Joshua concluded his record of the Jewish Conquest between 1400 and 1380 BC.

Outline
Chapters 1-12: The Land Invaded and Conquered
    The Invasion of Canaan (1:1-5:12)
    The Conquest of Canaan (5:13-12:24)

Chapters 13-24: The Land Possessed and Divided
    The Division of the Land (13:1-21:45)
    Conclusion (22:1- 23:33)

The first section of Joshua is alive with divine vigor, as demonstrated by the Israelites as they act in faith and conquer the inhabitants of Canaan. The latter section, generally speaking, is marked by inaction and incomplete obedience; accordingly, it begins with the exhortation, *"there remains very much land yet to be possessed"* (13:1). Inaction in the face of a dangerous enemy spells failure. Consequently, the Canaanites were not completely driven from the land and thus God's possession for His people was marred. Joshua concludes his book with a charge: God's people were to loath idolatry and were not to ally themselves with the remaining pagans which they had failed to drive out of the land.

The Setting
Moses faithfully led the Israelites for forty years as they wandered in the wilderness until the generation who had rebelled against the Lord at Kadesh-barnea had all died. Moses brought God's people as far as the Jordan River before his ministry ended. This was as far as the Law-giver could venture, for God foreknew the Law could not bring one soul into the spiritual blessings associated with Christ in the heavenlies, as symbolized by Canaan. The Law only condemned; it did not provide the spiritual power that comes from being baptized into the resurrected life of Christ. This is why Paul says the Law of Moses had a fading glory and would be replaced by Christ with something more glorious and permanent (2 Cor. 3:6-11). Thus, Joshua, representing the Lord Jesus

Christ, was now poised to lead the Israelites into the Promised Land to conquer and possess all the inheritance that Jehovah has purposed to bestow to His people.

The Symbolism of Canaan and of the Jordan

Some hymns liken physical death to crossing the Jordan and the land of Canaan to heaven, but this is not correct. Redemption brought the Israelites out of Egypt, through the Red Sea, and into the wilderness as a nation, but when each one passed through the Jordan they experienced death, practically and individually. "When one is dead and risen (in spirit)," says John N. Darby, "one enters into the heavenly places (in spirit). For us, death is life. Jordan is not the sign of natural death, because afterwards they meet with fighting. It is death practically, death in us spiritually."[2] William MacDonald explains why Canaan does not represent heaven (speaking of God's peaceful spiritual abode):

> There was conflict in Canaan, whereas there is no conflict in heaven. Actually the land of Canaan pictures our present spiritual inheritance. It is ours, but we must possess it by obeying the Word, claiming the promises, and fighting the good fight of faith."[3]

Warren Wiersbe elaborates on the symbolism of Canaan and then expounds its practical meaning for Christians today:

> What does Canaan represent to us as Christians today? It represents our spiritual inheritance in Christ (Eph. 1:3, 11, 15-23). ... Since Canaan was a place of battles, and even of defeats, it is not a good illustration of heaven! Israel had to cross the river by faith (a picture of the believer as he dies to self and the world, Rom. 6) and claim the inheritance by faith. They had to "step out by faith (Josh. 1:3) and claim the land for themselves, just as believers today must do. Now we understand that the wilderness wanderings represent: the experiences of believers who will not claim their spiritual inheritance in Christ, who doubt God's Word and live in restless unbelief. To be sure, God is with them, as He was with Israel; but they do not enjoy the fullness of God's blessing. They are "out of Egypt" but they are not yet "in Canaan."[4]

Canaan represents all of the believer's inheritance in Christ who is seated in heavenly places (Eph. 1:3; Heb. 1:3). In Christ, believers will find an infinite treasury of spiritual resources which enable them to powerfully represent the Lord while on earth, but these provisions must first be possessed to do so. Certainly, there are future aspects of our inheritance in Christ that believers will enjoy after glorification. For example, believers will rule and reign with Christ once He returns to claim His inheritance and establish His kingdom (2 Tim. 2:12; Rev. 21:7). However, it is not within the scope of this book to consider what we will enjoy with Christ later, but rather to consider the benefit of possessing as much of our inheritance in Christ now.

The Canaan rest for Israel illustrates the spiritual rest we have in Christ when we, by faith, submit to His Word (Heb. 4:11-12). Salvation rest is experienced when we respond in faith to Christ's kind invitation (Matt. 11:28); through His gospel message we obtain peace with God (Rom. 5:1). As we learn of Him and yield to His will (as expressed in His Word), we enjoy the peace of God (Phil. 4:6-8). By faith we enter into God's salvation rest (Heb. 4:3); and by continuing in faith and obedience His rest enters into us.

The Vision

The subject matter of the book of Joshua is closely aligned with that of the epistle to the Ephesians. For the Israelites, the long journey across the desert had come to an end. In the wilderness God had set a table before them and nurtured them, but it was now time to cross the Jordan under a new leader and to enjoy a land flowing with milk and honey.

Israel in the wilderness pictures the believer who is weak and immature, who still struggles with sin – his heart is divided between the Lord and Egypt (the world). The Jews who died in the wilderness picture the carnal-minded Christian (they continue to think about and long for Egypt). The two and one half tribes picture the believer who loves the Lord and fellow believers, but have not fully given themselves over to Him because of their love for worldly things. Those who settled on the east side of the Jordon, represent earthly-minded Christians (i.e. those who are saved, but never enter into the full joy of their salvation and the fullness of the blessing in Christ).

The faithful who crossed the Jordon and settled in the Canaan picture those few believers who enter into the fullness of fellowship with the risen Savior and enjoy the blessings which that fellowship ensures. On the other side, the Israelites would experience the power of God in a practical way as they obeyed the Lord's command to possess the

Introduction

Promised Land by driving out their enemies who dwelt there. It is the same for believers today, as set forth in Ephesians. Although we sojourn on earth, we are to lay hold of the heavenly blessings in Christ and thus possess our "Canaan" here and now.

Through the power of the Holy Spirit, who unites us and seats us with the ascended Christ at the right hand of the majesty on high, we are enabled to both acquire and enjoy that which He alone provides for our conquest. In this way, the books of Joshua and Ephesians are mysteriously joined; F. B. Meyer elaborates:

> The book of Joshua is to the Old Testament what the Epistle to the Ephesians is to the New. The characteristic word of the Ephesians is the heavenlies (1:3, 20, 2:6, 3:10, 6:12). Of course it does not stand for heaven; but for that spiritual experience of oneness with the risen Saviour in His resurrection and exaltation which is the privilege of all the saints, to which, indeed, they have been called, and which is theirs in Him.[5]

> The seven nations of Canaan held the land with strongholds and chariots of iron; though the Lord caused them to be to his people as bread which needs only to be eaten. They came against the invading hosts in all the pride of their vast battalions and the array of their warlike preparations, but at His rebuke they fled, at the voice of His thunder they hastened away. The "heavenly places" also are not removed from the noise of conflict, or free from the presence of foes. Those who are raised to sit there in Christ have to encounter the spiritual hosts of wickedness, principalities and powers of evil. They are conquered foes, but, nevertheless, are terrible to behold, and certain to overcome, unless we are abiding in our great Joshua, who has already vanquished them, and have taken to ourselves the whole armor of God. Thus the land of Canaan and the heavenly places are one.[6]

Canaan is a representation to the Church of the laying hold of heaven's resources in such a way that exalts, on this present earth, our heavenly Joshua. W. Graham Scroggie notes the specific language within the Epistle to the Ephesians to emphasis this point:

> The order is progressive. Entrance must precede conquest, and conquest must precede possession. If it be thought strange that we must fight to rest, it is worthy of our notice that the Epistle to the Ephesians, which is the New Testament counterpart to the Book of Joshua,

emphatically connects rest with conflict. There it is said that we are *"blessed with all spiritual blessings in the heavenlies in Christ,"* that we are *"made to sit together in the heavenlies in Christ Jesus,"* and that it is there, *"in the heavenlies,"* that we are to *"wrestle against principalities, against powers, against the rulers of the darkness of this world, against spiritual wickedness"* (1:3, 2:6, 6:12). This expression, "the heavenlies," which occurs five times in Ephesians, has well been defined as "the sphere of the believer's spiritual experience as identified with Christ" (Scofield). It is the New Testament equivalent of the land of Joshua. We shall understand this if we keep clearly before us two things; first, what every Christian is and has in Christ, from the moment of his conversion; and secondly, what every Christian should become and have in Christ by faith and effort. The first relates to our spiritual standing in Christ, and the second, to our actual state experimentally. ...The entering, and conquering, and possessing, are the translating into experience of all the blessings which are already ours in Christ.[7]

Paul did not pen his letter to the Ephesians in order to convert the world, or to wake the dead, but to reveal the true position of holiness, power, and victory believers have in Christ. So, dear believer, we must humble ourselves before the Lord, and fight the good fight of faith against spiritual wickedness in high places from the highest place in the heavenlies where we are now seated with Christ. Only there can we appropriate every inch of territory that God has bestowed to us to inherit. Why wait until we are in heaven to inherit what we can appreciate now?

Joshua Devotions

Moses, My Servant
Joshua 1:1-2

Joshua commences his book by recounting the Lord's message to him shortly after the death of Moses: *"Moses My servant is dead. Now therefore, arise, go over this Jordan, you and all this people, to the land which I am giving to them – the children of Israel"* (Josh. 1:2). Moses had resolutely guided the Israelites for forty years in the wilderness, during which time he expounded God's Law to them, and brought them safely to the brink of the Jordan River. It was here that the life and the ministry of Moses conclude. Moses died after being permitted to view Canaan from Mount Nebo (Deut. 32:49), and the Lord then buried him in the land of Moab, near Beth-peor (Deut. 34:6).

As previously explained in the introduction to this book, from a typological point of view, it was appropriate for Moses to complete his ministry without entering the Promised Land. Moses brought the Law of God to the Jews to show them their sin (Rom. 3:10-12) and its consequences (Rom. 3:19-20), and to point them to God's means of salvation – Christ (Gal. 3:24). Accordingly, the Law could not justify anyone (Rom. 3:28; Gal. 3:10-11); rather, it ensured God's condemnation (Rom. 4:4). Spiritual strength and blessing cannot be obtained by trying to keep the Law, but only through the One who put Himself under the Law and fulfilled it (Gal. 4:4). *The Christian Friend and Instructor* provides this insight into the typological representation associated with Joshua's commission and its practical benefits for us today:

> Their inheritance could not in any wise be of the law, and thus Moses, as the mediator of the legal system, apart from his own personal failure, could not lead the people over Jordan. It was typically impossible; and hence when he pleaded to be allowed to go over and see the good land that is beyond Jordan, the Lord replied, *"Let it suffice thee; speak no more unto Me of this matter."* Joshua – Israel's savior in this sense – was the chosen vessel for the accomplishment of God's purpose; Joshua, type of Christ in spirit as the Leader of His people in their

conflicts. And surely we may say that Joshua, just because he thus prefigured Christ, sets forth also that God's conflicts cannot be waged, nor the inheritance possessed, except in the power of resurrection.[1]

In type, Joshua pictures the coming of the Lord Jesus Christ in the New Testament to enable believers to live victoriously in Him (i.e., to live out His life). Both the names "Joshua" and "Jesus" mean "God is Salvation." Israel's passage through the Jordan River later in this book represents the believer coming from spiritual helplessness into resurrection power. Consequently, *Joshua* is a continuation of God's dealings with mankind, especially Israel, as initially described in the Pentateuch; therefore, the first verse of Joshua is connected with the previous book of Deuteronomy by a conjunction rendered "and" or "now."

In Deuteronomy, Moses reviewed all of the Law of God a second time with God's covenant people. This would reinforce the idea that Law-keeping could never earn the spectacular blessings that would be theirs in Canaan, for no Jew could keep the Law perfectly. Thankfully, salvation by grace through Christ's work accomplished at Calvary permits the believer access to all spiritual blessings in heavenly places. This enables the Lord to live out His life *within* His Church, while in the dispensation of the Law it enabled God to live *among* His people for the same purpose (i.e., first in the tabernacle and then the temple).

As previously explained, Canaan, in present day application, does not picture God's heavenly and peaceful abode, for the Israelites would be engaged in hard fighting for years to conquer their enemies and lay hold of their God-given possession. The writer of Hebrews affirms that Canaan was not to be the final resting place for the children of Israel: *"For if Joshua had given them rest, then he would not afterward have spoken of another day. There remains therefore a rest for the people of God"* (Heb. 4:8-9). The Greek word translated "rest" in verse 9 is *sabbatismos*, and is only found here in the New Testament. *Sabbatismos* literally means "a keeping of the Sabbath" and speaks of the future "battle-free" rest believers will enjoy with God in heaven. But as in the days of Joshua, the earthly sojourn of faithful believers today will undoubtedly be fraught with conflict (2 Tim. 3:12), but hopefully not against each other (Gal. 5:15). Paul marks out the enemy for Christians:

Finally, my brethren, be strong in the Lord and in the power of His might. Put on the whole armor of God, that you may be able to stand against the wiles of the devil. For we do not wrestle against flesh and blood, but against principalities, against powers, against the rulers of the darkness of this age, against spiritual hosts of wickedness in the heavenly places (Eph. 6:10-12).

If you are a believer reading this book, heaven is still future, which means the battle against principalities and powers is before you now – that is, if you want to live for Christ. Like the Israelites of old, spiritual battles can only be won in the power of the Lord. This means that spiritual warfare is the believer's great opportunity to learn of and lay hold of all his or her spiritual blessings in heavenly places in Christ (Eph. 1:3). This is living the resurrected life of Christ as pictured by Joshua ("God saves") leading the Israelites through the Jordan River and into Canaan to seize their possession.

From a personal standpoint, Moses, a man empowered by the Holy Spirit, exhibited steadfast faithfulness throughout his life, yet he grew in faith as well. When Jehovah first summoned Moses from among the Midianites to deliver His people from bondage and from Egypt, Moses rejected the idea (Ex. 3). He argued that the Israelites would not believe that he was from God, that the Egyptians would not release their slave force, and that, beside all this, he was not an eloquent speaker. A few moments later, after a small demonstration of God's power, Moses surrendered to God's call (Ex. 4).

The New Testament attributes a special honor to Moses' service to the Lord. The Greek word *therapon*, translated as "servant" in Hebrews 3:5, is used to describe the type of servant Moses was. *Therapon* is not the typical word used in the New Testament to describe a servant or a slave; in fact, it is only used in connection with Moses. This word conveys the idea of a voluntary servant who is motivated by devotion for his superior. At first, Moses was hesitant to accept the call of God for his life, but when he did, he did so of his own free will because he loved the Lord.

It was Moses' unwavering faith in Jehovah and his irreproachable character that enabled him to accomplish amazing feats for God. The character of the servant of God is as important as his or her work. The servant of the Lord represents God in character and conduct; neither aspect can be missing from a true testimony of God. As a result of Moses' resolve and leadership, Pharaoh and his armies, the Amalekites, and many other enemies of the Jews were humbled under the power of Jehovah.

At the burning bush, Moses' faith in Jehovah was but in its infancy, but over the strenuous years that followed, his faith in and devotion to Jehovah steadily grew. Joshua referenced this man as "the servant of the Lord" sixteen times in his own book. While living, Moses was spoken of as a servant once (Ex. 14:31), but the title "the servant of the Lord" is not used until after his death (Deut. 34:5).

Moses was not a perfect man, but his life was characterized by faithfulness. Accordingly, after his death, Scripture acknowledges him as "the servant of the Lord." Interestingly, Joshua would be bestowed the same honorary title after his death; he also finished well (24:29). The Lord appreciates those who learn from their mistakes and failures, rise up again in divine grace, and finish the race they are called to run. This was the testimony of both Moses and Joshua, the servants of the Lord.

In verse 2, the Lord commands Joshua to rise up and lead the people over the Jordan and into the land He will give to them. The land belonged to Israel by divine decree and on that basis God commanded them, *"Arise and possess it."* The plain of Jericho was well-watered by the many brooks and streams flowing into the Jordan River and adorned with countless flowers. All the wealth of the Canaanites was before them now for the taking: fields of grain, olive groves, vineyards, wells of water, houses, and cities. Before them was their new home, with all its wealth and delights, the gift of their God who had brought them out of Egypt and through the wilderness. There was only one requisite to the enjoyment of all they saw from the Eastern Plateau west of the Jordan River: they must "Arise" and possess their God-given portion.

Likewise, dear believer, arise and enter into the blessings wherewith God has blessed us in Christ. All things are yours in Christ; arise and enter into this rich land – only there will you experience victorious Christian living and fulfill your divine calling. Paul reminded the believers at Ephesus that they were created by God for His good pleasure and to fulfill His calling for their lives: *"For we are His workmanship, created in Christ Jesus for good works, which God prepared beforehand that we should walk in them"* (Eph. 2:10). May we too be faithful to our calling in Christ and to do those works which God sanctified for us to accomplish even before the foundation of the world was laid. This is the aspiration of all true "servants of the Lord."

Meditation

The prophet Isaiah extends this prophetic declaration to God's people: *"'No weapon formed against you shall prosper, and every tongue which rises against you in judgment you shall condemn. This is the heritage of the servants of the Lord, and their righteousness is from Me,' says the Lord"* (Isa. 54:17). In time, the nation of Israel would misplace this crucial truth and attempt to establish their own righteousness through legalism. Yet, the verse confirms that a believer's righteous standing is imputed from God alone, and that the believer's union with Him ensures that no opposition can overcome His servants until their warring days are done!

Three Calls
Joshua 1:3-9

After acknowledging the faithfulness of Moses, the Lord puts Joshua in charge of leading His people into the Promised Land. In fact, the land allotted to Abraham was quite vast (Gen. 15:19-21); Canaan was merely the first portion to be possessed for an inheritance (vv. 4, 6). God would fulfill his promise to Abraham by giving his descendants the land in stages, as determined by their faithfulness and willingness to conquer and possess it in the years that followed (Deut. 19:8).

Historically speaking, the Jewish people have never fully possessed all that was promised to Abraham. Even during the glorious reigns of Kings David and Solomon, Israel never occupied more than about a tenth (approx. 30,000 square miles) of the land that God bestowed to Abraham according to Genesis 15:18-21.[1] The western boundary of the land was the Mediterranean Sea and the eastern boundary was to be the Euphrates River, which runs through central Iraq today. The land was to extend from the mountains of Lebanon in the north to the southern wilderness. So, although today the nation of Israel is partially back in the Promised Land after buying it back with a sword, so to speak (see Ezek. 38:8), they do not inhabit the full portion God issued Abraham. We understand the literal fulfillment of this promise to be future, after the Jews have turned back to Jesus Christ whom they crucified and have received Him as their Messiah (Zech. 12:10; Rom. 11:26-32). This is one of the strongest evidences to substantiate a pre-millennial Second Advent of Christ to the earth.

H. L. Rossier notes the practical lesson for believers today as marked out by the boundaries of the land God had set aside as a possession for His covenant people.

> The boundaries of the land were a great *desert,* a great *mountain,* a great *river,* and a great *sea.* That is what was to be found outside this fertile country, that on which the people could not or ought not to

tread. Do we not find here the world with all its moral characteristics: its aridity, its power, its prosperity, and its agitation? As to its aridity, Israel had gone through it, only to prove that it had no resource for them, and that the bread from heaven alone could feed them in these solitudes. Such, beloved, is the character of the things which are *not* ours. But Canaan and heaven is ours; Canaan with its warfare no doubt, but its victories; Canaan with the peaceful enjoyment of infinite possessions, resuming themselves in, and concentrating themselves around the person of a risen Christ seated in the glory.[2]

The Jews would be victorious only if they personally seized through God's strength what He had for them. If their lusting caused them to venture beyond the boundaries of their possession (i.e., into the world), they would fall before their enemies.

While God's covenant with Abraham would bestow a special land to his descendants, he was also given a much wider promise: *"in you shall all families of the earth be blessed."* This covenant would have its ultimate fulfillment in the redemptive work of Christ, a descendant of Abraham. In the meantime, Uriah the Hittite, Caleb the Kenizzite, and Tamar and Rahab of the Canaanites are some of the Gentiles who received divine blessing by trusting Abraham's God. Through exercising faith in revealed truth, God is willing to declare the wonders of His grace to anyone, anywhere, and at any time. Paul puts the matter this way: *"For the grace of God that brings salvation hath appeared to all men"* (Titus 2:11) and God *"is long suffering towards us, not willing that any should perish, but that all should come to repentance"* (2 Pet. 3:9). The Canaanites could either oppose Jehovah and His people or humble themselves and worship Him.

The Lord promised Joshua that if he obeyed His command and led His people into Canaan to obtain their inheritance, no one would be able to withstand him. The Lord had stood with Moses for forty years in the wilderness, and now He was extending to Joshua the same promise He made to Moses at the burning bush (Ex. 3:12): *"I will be with you. I will not leave you nor forsake you"* (v. 5). The Lord spoke to Jacob in the same way, saying, *"Return to the land of your fathers and to your family, and I will be with you"* (Gen. 31:3). Whether the child of God is commanded "to come," "to go," or "to return," the same solace of peace is enjoyed – the communion of God's presence. The prophet Jeremiah depended on it (Jer. 1:8), as did Paul (Acts 18:10). For centuries, suffering saints have found comfort in God's abiding presence during the most arduous of times. Living for Christ in a sin-cursed world is challenging, but the believer's calling in Christ is not burdensome because he or she is yoked with the Lord (Matt. 11:28-30). It is through this vital connection that we learn that every victory is the Lord's victory and that without Him we can do nothing (John 15:5)!

It is for this reason that after the Lord commissioned His disciples and opened their understanding of Scripture, He instructed them to wait in Jerusalem for the coming of the Holy Spirit. He, the Comforter, would infuse them with divine power to enable their ministry. Knowledge of their divine calling and their new understanding of Scripture would be of no avail without God's facilitating power.

Similarly, Joshua could have the clearest possible conception of his mission and yet be powerless in the presence of his enemies. Though the right path is made known through the Word of God, it should never be concluded that this path is therefore easy or comfortable to follow. The opposite is true, for the moment God opens His way before His people, all the power of the enemy will be brought to bear to hinder their progress. This is why in his final address to his mentee, Moses challenged Joshua to *"Be strong and of good courage, do not fear nor be afraid of them; for the Lord your God, He is the One who goes with you. He will not leave you nor forsake you"* (Deut. 31:6). Moses had experienced God's faithfulness and abiding presence and encouraged Joshua to do the same.

Hence, the foremost thing impressed on Joshua at this point is *"to be strong and very courageous."* That is to say, when God's will is apprehended by His people, they must also have divine strength and courage to do it, otherwise they will be overcome by the enemy who will oppose them from every possible vantage point. Joshua could therefore not fulfill his divine calling without the power and presence of the Lord, a fact he would experientially learn in chapters 7 and 9.

After affirming His abiding presence, the Lord exhorted Joshua three times with the words: *"Be strong and of good courage"* (vv. 6, 7, 9). These three calls were meant to energize Joshua to action. The context in which the first is found relates to fulfilling his divine calling by leading the Israelites into Canaan to obtain their possession. The second resounds the timeless biblical principle that obedience to God's Word ensures success in God's plan. Finally, the Lord promised His abiding presence if Joshua would step forward in faith. Likewise, if believers are to further the cause of Christ in this wicked world, they must be faithful to their calling, be obedient to God's Word, and with the knowledge of God's abiding presence aggressively engage the enemy with confidence.

Through these three calls, the Lord was addressing Joshua's immediate needs, who undoubtedly felt weak, fearful, and dismayed at the task at hand. To be strong in the Lord meant that Joshua must read God's Word, meditate on it and obey it (v. 8). Only then would he be able to fulfill his calling to conquer and divide the land for an inheritance (vv. 6-7). It is the same principle that governs our usefulness today, for it is through God's Word that the Holy Spirit manifests His fullness as the mighty occupant of our inner man. We should not think that we possess Him; He resides within to possess and control us.

Joshua was commanded not only to know and to obey all the Word of God, but also to meditate on it. With the hustle and bustle of a fast-paced society, many believers are finding that they have no time to meditate on Scripture. But, as H. F. Witherby notes, there is a unique spiritual benefit to the soul that is gained through the meditation of Scripture:

> "Thou shalt meditate" is a distinct call, which should exercise the heart. Spiritually feeding upon the Word, we gain the desired heart-knowledge. There is no hour more profitably spent than that in which the Christian is alone with God over His word, humbly pondering upon God's thoughts in God's presence. A book-learned and a Spirit-taught Christian are very distinct. There may be a knowledge of the truth of the Word, obtained by reading or instruction, where "thou shalt meditate" is but scantily observed. There may be an intellectual grasp of the doctrines and principles of Scripture, and what then? "Knowledge puffeth up!" The Christian, who has learned to enter in secret into God's presence as to knowledge, is necessarily humble and lowly in mind. We say necessarily so, because God's presence ever makes man humble. Truly blessed is the man whose delight is in the law of the Lord, and who meditates therein day and night. *"He shall be like a tree planted by the rivers of water, that brings forth his fruit in his season; his leaf also shall not wither; and whatsoever he doeth shall prosper"* (Ps. 1:3).[3]

If Joshua would act in faith and obedience, the Lord promised to be with him and to prosper all that he endeavored to do (vv. 8-9). Nothing has changed; this is still the means of obtaining divine blessing today, or, as the hymn writer put it, "trust and obey, for there is no other way to be happy in Jesus, but to trust and obey." God commanded – Joshua obeyed – victory was assured. On this point, H. L. Rossier writes:

> *"Have not I commanded thee? Be strong and of a good courage"* (v. 9). What power the assurance of God's mind gives! All indecision as to the path, all terror, all fear of the enemy disappear. Satan cannot harm us; has not God commanded us? Such then are the principles which should govern the heart that would enjoy heavenly things and fight the battles of the Lord. It is blessed to see them stated quite at the beginning of this book, before Israel has taken a single step, in such a way as to place him in possession of well-furbished weapons wherewith to obtain the victory.[4]

After experiencing the faithfulness of God at Jericho, Ai, and Bethel, Joshua would later relay this same message to the Israelites as they engaged an enormous army from Southern Palestine. They were prevailing against their enemies because *"the Lord fought for Israel"* (10:14). Before personally slaying the five captured kings who had commanded the opposition, Joshua exhorted his fellow countrymen: *"Fear not, nor be dismayed, be strong and of good courage: for thus shall the Lord do to all your enemies against whom ye fight"* (10:25). Because Joshua exercised faith in God's Word and obeyed His Law, the Lord worked miraculous feats to extol him before the Israelites and the various people groups who confronted them.

Besides the previous exhortation, the Lord extended Joshua the following conditional promise: *"This Book of the Law shall not depart from your mouth, but you shall meditate in it day and night, that you may observe to do according to all that is written in it. For then you will make your way prosperous, and then you will have good success"* (v. 8). The Lord promised Joshua He would prosper all of his doings, if he meditated on and obeyed His Word. David also understood that this was God's pathway to spiritual blessing and prosperity:

> *Blessed is the man who walks not in the counsel of the ungodly, nor stands in the path of sinners, nor sits in the seat of the scornful; but his delight is in the law of the Lord, and in His law he meditates day and night. He shall be like a tree planted by the rivers of water, that brings forth its fruit in its season, whose leaf also shall not wither; and whatever he does shall prosper* (Ps. 1:1-3).

Joshua Devotions

Likewise, Christians today can prosper against spiritual enemies even as the Israelites did centuries ago against physical foes in Canaan. How is this possible? Believers already have the authority of God to labor with Christ in effecting His will and power, but we must choose to walk with Him in truth (1 Jn. 1:6-7). If we choose to walk the path of darkness and disobedience, we do so alone, for the Lord cannot abide with us there. At such a time, He does not leave us but we, rather, depart from His fellowship. However, if we walk in accordance to revealed truth we will appreciate the Lord's communion, for He has promised: *"I will never leave you nor forsake you"* (Heb. 13:5).

As the writer of Hebrews pondered the blessed solace of the Lord's abiding presence, he concluded: *"So we may boldly say: 'The Lord is my helper; I will not fear. What can man do to me?'"* (Heb. 13:6). Though conscious of his own deficiencies and the difficulties ahead, Joshua knew what his divine calling was and he chose to move forward to do it. When believers know what they have been called to do and yield themselves as a channel of mercy for that cause, they become invincible! May we all "be strong and of good courage" in the Lord!

Meditation

> When through fiery trials thy pathways shall lie,
> My grace, all sufficient, shall be thy supply;
> The flame shall not hurt thee; I only design
> Thy dross to consume, and thy gold to refine.
>
> The soul that on Jesus has leaned for repose,
> I will not, I will not desert to its foes;
> That soul, though all hell should endeavor to shake,
> I'll never, no never, no never forsake.
>
> — John Rippon

The New Commander
Joshua 1:10-19

As Moses neared the end of his ministry, he was concerned lest God's people become wandering sheep without a shepherd, so he asked the Lord to appoint his replacement (Num. 27:15-17). In response to this request, the Lord commanded Moses:

> *"Take Joshua the son of Nun with you, a man in whom is the Spirit, and lay your hand on him; set him before Eleazar the priest and before all the congregation, and inaugurate him in their sight. And you shall give some of your authority to him, that all the congregation of the children of Israel may be obedient. He shall stand before Eleazar the priest, who shall inquire before the Lord for him by the judgment of the Urim. At his word they shall go out, and at his word they shall come in, he and all the children of Israel with him -- all the congregation"* (Num. 27:18-21).

Before Moses died, Joshua was publicly confirmed as his successor both by divine announcement (through Moses) and by the use of the Urim in the hands of the high priest. Moses then laid hands on Joshua to publicly identify him as God's selected leader for the people. From then until the time Moses died, he and Joshua labored together as equals, so that the people would learn to honor and respect Joshua as they had Moses. Joshua chapter one details how Joshua later received the full charge of his previous ordination.

Jehovah had used Moses to redeem the Jews and deliver them from bondage and from Egypt, but He would use Joshua to seize their inheritance in the Promised Land. J. G. Bellett further contrasts the ministries of Moses and Joshua:

> Joshua was to have a great ministry committed to him. He was to lead Israel into the land of their inheritance. He was to witness, as I may express it, the day of glory among the people of God, as Moses had

witnessed the day of grace. He was to be the redeemer of the inheritance, as Moses had been the redeemer of the heir. By him God would perfect what concerned Israel, as by Moses He had begun it. He was to lead Israel into Canaan, as Moses had led them out of Egypt. Beforehand, therefore, we see him constantly with Moses. He attends him; as I may say, the inheritance attends on the heir, or the close of a work on the beginning of it. And this constant abiding at the side of Moses, or waiting upon him, was a shadow cast beforehand of the ministry he was to fulfill, as soon as his day came – for he was to finish, as we have said, what Moses had begun, for Israel; he was to put the inheritance and the heir together.[1]

Joshua's years of serving Moses not only prepared him for his own ministry of leading the Israelites, but also pointed to it. Even before Joshua's confirmation in Numbers 27, we see indications of his future ministry during the years he faithfully served Moses. For example, Joshua first appears in Scripture as a young man leading the attack against the Amalekites in Exodus 17. The scene is glorious: Moses, on the mount, holding up the rod of God over the battlefield, pictures Christ's intercessory power for His people from the throne of grace in heaven. But while Moses intercedes above, Joshua wields the sword victoriously below. This sight portrays Christ's unrestrained power in the believer's life as he or she uses the Word of God (the sword of truth, Heb. 4:12) and fully relies on the strength of the Holy Spirit.

Next, Joshua is seen at the base of Mt. Sinai waiting for Moses to descend with the Word of God; he stood apart from the idolatrous clamor within the camp of Israel (Ex. 32:17). Likewise, in behavior the Lord Jesus was separate from sinners and longed only to do God's will (John 5:30). Joshua would again demonstrate faithfulness when, months after leaving Mt. Sinai behind, he was one of the twelve spies sent into Canaan by Moses on a reconnaissance mission. They brought back a pledge of the fruit of that land which was their promised inheritance. Ten of the spies doubted God's faithfulness, but Joshua, along with Caleb resolutely withstood them (Num. 13 and 14). Much of Joshua's ministry was centered in confronting those who would deny God's faithfulness to His word.

The above events were a foretaste of Joshua's later ministry; he had been chosen by God to subdue the nations of Canaan and then divide their land for an inheritance for His people. As is often the case before one comes into the fullness of his or her divine calling, Joshua's accomplishments cast their shadow beforehand. He was a man of courage, tenacity, conviction, and holiness – a proven leader among his peers. In God's plan, the young Joshua of the wilderness had forty years of preparatory training before becoming the victorious Joshua of the Promised Land.

Having been publicly confirmed by Moses and the High Priest as God's choice for commander, Joshua begins readying the people to pass over the Jordan. His attention is turned to two important matters. First, Joshua commands the officers, who in turn instruct the general populace, to gather supplies. The Lord had provided manna for His people in the wilderness, but that would soon cease; consequently, the Israelites were to gather grain and fruit from the plains of Moab before disembarking for Canaan. It is said the trip would begin in three days (v. 11). It is generally believed by the majority of both Jewish and Christian commentators that the "three days" referred to in verse 11 actually relates to the command issued by Joshua after the spies' return from Jericho (3:2).[2] Perhaps the Israelites began gathering supplies at this time, but it is not likely that they were actually commanded to do so until Joshua 3.

Regardless of when it was first declared, the duration of "three days" relates directly to the prophetic sign the Lord Jesus announced to the sign-seeking Pharisees: *"For as Jonah was three days and three nights in the belly of the great fish, so will the Son of Man be three days and three nights in the heart of the earth"* (Matt. 12:40). It is suggested that this three-day preparation period to enter into Canaan pictures the death, burial, and resurrection of the Lord Jesus Christ. The Jews must wait three days to pass through the Jordan River, representing Christ's death, to experience His resurrection power in Canaan. It would not be sensible to expect the priests to stand in the dry riverbed for three days holding the Ark of God, to picture the "death of Christ" in type. This the three days of preparation accomplish.

The second matter requiring Joshua's attention was to remind the tribes of Reuben, Gad, and the half-tribe of Manasseh that though they had received their requested inheritance east of the Jordan River, they must fulfill their promise to Moses and fight alongside their brethren so that the remaining tribes might obtain their inheritance (vv. 13-14). Only once they had finished conquering Canaan could they return to their homes (v. 15). While it is true that the Eastern Plateau was within the overall boundaries God had bestowed to Abraham and his descendants, it was God's design for them to first possess the heart of that land and secure the one place in all the earth where Jehovah had chosen to place His name – Jerusalem.

Canaan formed a land-bridge with three continents and therefore was the perfect location for Jehovah to dwell among His people and to be a beacon of light to the nations. Therefore, although the whole region was theirs by promise, it was Canaan that was given to Israel to possess at that time. This alone had been the expressed reason they had been delivered from Egypt: to come into and possess Canaan through conquest. Canaan would be God's beachhead in the region for establishing His own name, but the two and a half tribes were more interested in the welfare of their cattle than establishing His name in the land.

Thus, the two and a half tribes, driven by their lust for rich pasture land, instead of the purposes of God, flatly declared to Moses: *"For we will not inherit with them on the other side of the Jordan and beyond, because our inheritance has fallen to us on this eastern side of the Jordan"* (Num. 32:19). When Moses first heard of their intentions, he warned them of again angering Jehovah with a repetition of the same sin of "unbelief" that the ten spies committed some thirty-nine years earlier at Kadesh Barnea. These spies entered the Promised Land, verified that God had brought them to a land flowing with milk and honey, but then discouraged their brethren from venturing in to possess it. The Lord's anger was kindled and He smote the ten spies with a plague and they all died (Num. 14:37). The history lesson served as a warning to the two and a half tribes – doubting the faithfulness of God to keep His promises has severe consequences.

Moses then learned that the two and a half tribes did not object to entering Canaan and laboring with their brethren to conquer it; they just did not want the land God desired to give them for an inheritance. Moses reluctantly agreed to their request, but as we learn later, settling for what is less than God's best has consequences. Eventually we reap what we sow. Unfortunately, these two and a half tribes did not heed Moses' stern warning in this matter: *"Be sure your sin will find you out!"* And a few centuries later they reaped the consequences of their sin – they were invaded and displaced from their possession.

With this said, the response of the two and half-tribes to Joshua's admonition was favorable; they had not forgotten their pledge to Moses and fully intended to honor it. In fact, Joshua placed them at the head of the column – they would be the first wave of Jewish troops into Canaan

(v. 14). Perhaps this is because they were not encumbered with the task of moving families, livestock, and personal belongings as the congregation ambled into the Promised Land.

The enthusiastic response of the strike force was no doubt a mere reflection of the entire encampment's attitude. The Israelites were excited to be finally entering into their inheritance and all pledged loyalty and obedience to their new leader, Joshua. So vigorous was this commitment that they pledged that anyone not honoring it would be put to death (v. 18). It is noted that the people were not promising to follow Joshua blindly, but to submit to him as they had obeyed Moses, who walked according to the Law of God (v. 17).

The people knew that Moses had obeyed the Lord, and the Lord was with Him; they wanted Joshua to lead them in the same manner. The Israelites understood that if the Lord was not with them, they would fall before their enemies. Consequently, the two and a half tribes concluded their answer to Joshua by charging him to *"be strong and of good courage"* (v. 18). Here lies an important principle: sheep are to follow their God-given shepherds, as the shepherds follow the Lord (Heb. 13:17). If shepherds deviate from the teaching of Scripture, they will lack God's blessing and their flocks will suffer, and ultimately God will judge them (Ezek. 34:1-10). In such situations where God's leadership is in clear violation of Scriptural truth, those whom God has placed in their care are in no way liable to follow them, but should rather submit to the higher authority of the Lord (Acts 4:15, 5:19).

Thankfully, Joshua was not such a leader. As we shall see, he was not a perfect man, but one of like passions as you and I. Yet, his zeal for the Lord by this point had already been repeatedly proven: he had led the assault on the Amalekites, he had waited for Moses at Mt. Sinai while the Israelites engaged in idolatry below, and he had withstood the ten spies who confirmed the goodness of Canaan but denied God's ability to give them the land. The path before him was clear; he had been commanded by the sovereign God of the universe to enter into the land by faith, and that he proceeds to do. Such faith dispels the vanquishing power of the enemy, for God is with His people. Indeed, Joshua and Israel were strong and of good courage.

Meditation

The eternal rule held good: faithfulness in a few things is the condition of rule over many things; and the loyalty of a servant is the stepping-stone to the royalty of the throne.

— F. B. Meyer

Rahab's Faith
Joshua 2:1-13

While the Israelites were preparing supplies for their invasion of Canaan, Joshua sent two spies across the Jordan River to do some reconnaissance work. Joshua thought that information gathered by the spies could help formulate a battle plan against the fortified city of Jericho (v. 2). The Lord, however, would use the information gathered by the spies for a different purpose, which had nothing to do with military strategy. The spies were led by the Spirit of God to the only home in Jericho where prepared hearts were to be found. This reminds us that those who act in faith in response to revealed truth do not need to worry about wasting time; God will direct our ministry to the right places and persons. In this instance, the fear of the Lord was to be found in the least likely of places, the home of a harlot named Rahab.

The two spies were directed there for several reasons, the most prominent being Rahab was seeking Jehovah and likewise He was seeking her. Second, strange men meandering into a harlot's house would not normally arouse much suspicion. Third, her house was conveniently located on an outer wall of Jericho which, as we will see, would be the Lord's means of protecting His faithful servants from harm.

Evidently, the disguises worn by the Hebrew spies were not too convincing, as the king of Jericho quickly learned of their arrival and sent men to Rahab's house to arrest them (v. 3). Rahab, realizing the danger these men were in, chose to hide them under stalks of flax located on her rooftop rather than reveal their whereabouts (v. 6). Flax in Palestine grew to more than three feet in height and was as thick as a cane; when laid out to dry it would form a nice canopy to hide under.[1]

Under questioning, she admitted to the king's officers that two men did visit her earlier, but stated she was unaware that they were Hebrew spies (v. 4). Rahab then claimed the spies had already sallied out from Jericho through the front gate just before it was shut for the night; in chicanery she then suggested that the officers should quickly pursue after them (v. 5). Her story must have been persuasive, as the king's officers quickly left the city without searching her home, apparently hoping to catch the spies before they reached the fords of the Jordan, their best escape route back to Shittim (v. 7). Of course, these fleeing phantoms were never found because they were still hidden on Rahab's rooftop.

We were introduced to two groups of people in Joshua 1: the Israelites to whom God had given Canaan, and those in Canaan who would oppose them and be destroyed (1:2-5). In Joshua 2, we are introduced to a third group of people – Gentiles who would yield to God's plan by faith and, consequently, be saved from destruction.

The primary individual mentioned in this latter group is a harlot living in Jericho named Rahab. Through her testimony others within her family would also be preserved from judgment. Scripture informs us that: *"By faith the harlot Rahab did not perish with those who did not believe, when she had received the spies with peace"* (Heb. 11:31). Rahab's faith in the God of the Israelites was demonstrated by helping the Jewish spies avoid capture and escape from Jericho. She let them down by a cord through a window in her home, which was located on the outside wall of the city. F. B. Meyer explains why Rahab, an immoral woman, found grace in the eyes of God:

> Wherever there is a Rahab, who, amid much sin and ignorance, is living up to the truth she has, and longs for more, God will take her hand and lead her to Himself. He discerns a touch on His robe, and stays His footsteps till the one seeking Him is fully healed. A Nathanael beneath the fig-tree, a eunuch in a chariot, a Cornelius praying beside the sea, are not overlooked amid the crowds of careless souls around. They are as jewels on a heap of cinders, which are eagerly espied and taken up, polished, and placed amid the divine regalia.[2]

Clearly Scripture endorses Rahab's faith in these exploits, but how should we understand her acts of lying and disobedience in order to protect the spies? Perhaps recounting the conduct of the brave midwives who refused to obey Pharaoh's command to kill the Hebrew baby boys in Exodus 1 will be helpful in answering this question. Scripture tells us that the midwives rejected Pharaoh's command because they feared God more than they did Pharaoh (Ex. 1:17). Therefore, the Hebrew midwives did not kill the baby boys as they were born. They then lied to Pharaoh

Conquest and the Life of Rest

in order to protect themselves from harm when he called them into question. Though they lied, God honored their faith: *"God dealt well with the midwives ... and He gave them families"* (Ex. 1:20-21).

Similarly, Rahab feared Jehovah and His people more than the king of Jericho and her fellow citizens (v. 11). She thus sided with Jehovah and the Hebrews, rather than those set to war against them (vv. 10-12). In her estimation deceiving the officials in order to prevent the capture of the two spies was an acceptable solution to the situation. Despite the lie, the Lord responded to her faith and rewarded her by sparing her life and the lives of those in her family who would also exercise faith in Jehovah (2:2-3, 6:25). However, this does not mean that God endorsed Rahab's lying. He cannot, for God is holy and He cannot wink at sin, no matter how justifiable it may seem through human reasoning.

Scripture repeatedly shows that God is able to work His will despite human falsehoods. Mistreated Tamar lied to Judah in order to have children. David acted insane before Achish to escape death. Hushai was David's spy in rebel Absalom's court; Absalom received him as a counselor because Absalom believed his lies, then Hushai defeated the counsel of Ahithophel and saved King David's life. These examples are unique circumstances that all flow within the mainstream of messianic current – God's sovereign plan cannot be thwarted by the evil of the enemy, or by the sins of His people. Perhaps this understanding will help resolve any disparity in the reader's mind as to how a righteous God could bless His people despite the lies of men. Is God capable of accomplishing His purposes without human deception? Absolutely! So let us, as He commands, put away all lying (Eph. 4:25) and, if necessary, suffer honestly for saying the truth in love, or in some cases, for saying nothing at all and suffering the consequences with patience.

In summary, God does not condone lying; He is able to work His will without the aid of human deception, but He is also able to maneuver the moral failures of man to accomplish His before determined purposes. Yet sin, no matter how minor in our own eyes, has divine consequences. We should never justify lying with a "the end justifies the means" mentality. Lying does not honor God, and in fact, it demonstrates a lack of complete faith in His Word.

Scripture does not rebuke Rahab for deceiving the local authorities, but rather commends her faith as demonstrated by her care for the Jewish spies. It was not a blind or misplaced faith, but an act of her heart founded in truth. She made a proclamation to the spies, using the term *"we have heard"* in verse 11 which is securely connected by faith to the words *"I know"* in verse 9. Rahab had heard the stories of how the Israelites were delivered from Egypt, and how Jehovah had parted the Red Sea (v. 10). She too had learned of their victories over the Amorites on the eastern side of the Jordan. In fact, this information was common knowledge among her people, and put them in fear and trepidation as they waited for the coming invasion (vv. 9, 11).

Instead of surrendering, the inhabitants of Jericho fortified themselves against the Israelites; they were putting their faith in the bulwarks which they had constructed with their own hands. They believed that their city was impenetrable and could withstand any attack by the Israelites. They were incited by pride to ignore the clear evidence. Rahab humbled herself and took a different approach to the situation – she sided with God and pleaded for mercy. James reminds us that God's extension of mercy has not changed since the days of Rahab: *"God resists the proud, but gives grace to the humble"* (Jas. 4:6); *"Humble yourselves in the sight of the Lord, and He will lift you up"* (Jas. 4:10). Rahab and her family received God's grace; the others in Jericho perished.

By faith, she understood that God's judgment was coming upon the inhabitants of Canaan because He had promised to deliver Canaan to His people (v. 9). Thus, she reckoned that the Israelites were unstoppable and she, by faith, was willing to identify with them, and thus their God, rather than her own people and their gods. Her conclusion was that the God of the Israelites must be the *"God in heaven above and in the earth beneath"* (v. 11). It is for this reason she harbored the spies and then pled for mercy.

J. N. Darby comments on the scene before us and the basis for Rahab's faith:

> One sees here that dread seizes upon God's enemies, as soon as there is a testimony of the Spirit. One characteristic of Rahab's faith is that she identified herself with the people of God before their victories. The faith of Abraham was in God absolutely, whilst the faith of Rahab identified itself with the people of God.[3]

Mulling over their incredible accomplishments, Rahab concluded that the true God must be with the Israelites and so she joins herself with them. James confirms Rahab's act of kindness to the Jewish spies demonstrated the validity of her faith, in the same way that Abraham's offering of Isaac proved Abraham's faith:

> *Was not Abraham our father justified by works when he offered Isaac his son on the altar? Do you see that faith was working together with his works, and by works faith was made perfect? And the Scripture was fulfilled which says, "Abraham believed God, and it was accounted to him for righteousness." And he was called the friend of God. You see then that a man is justified by works, and not by faith only. Likewise, was not Rahab the harlot also justified by works when she received the messengers and sent them out another way?* (Jas. 2:21-25).

Though Abraham had been previously justified by faith (Gen. 15:6), true faith never stands alone – it possesses works of righteousness. Paul summarizes this important matter: *"Therefore we conclude that a man is justified by faith apart from the deeds of the law"* (Rom. 3:28); *"For if Abraham was justified by works, he has something to boast about, but not before God. For what does the Scripture say? 'Abraham believed God, and it was accounted to him for righteousness'"* (Rom. 4:2-3). When sinners act in faith to what God reveals to them, they are accredited a divine standing of righteousness (i.e., they are justified before God); such a reality will be evidenced by good works.

Like Abraham, Rahab the harlot was justified by believing, but demonstrated her faith through works: *"was not Rahab, the harlot, also justified by works when she received the messengers and sent them out another way?"* (Jas. 2:25). In faith, she asked the spies for "a true token" (a sign) of mercy that she could cling to as she awaited the impending fall of Jericho (v. 12). The scarlet thread hanging in her window would be her symbol of hope while she waited and God's pledge of peace when the invasion came.

Meditation

There is an expressive painting by the artist Rossetti called *Found*. There is a wonderful story connected with the painting. A country boy and a country girl fell in love. They pledged their undying commitment to each other, but the girl later fell prey to evil influences and was lured away to the big city. There she sunk into the deep mire of sin. She tried to forget her former life and the one she still loved. The young man, however, remained true to her and continually sought to find her. The painting depicts a day on Blackfriar's Bridge when he, seeing the gaudily-dressed woman, seizes her wrist and tells her of his abiding love for her. The one he was searching for had been *found*![4] God searched and found a lowly harlot in a doomed pagan city to whom to express His love; she responded by faith and her life was never the same!

The Token
Joshua 2:14-24

The Jewish spies instructed Rabah to place the token of her salvation, the scarlet thread, in her window when they invaded the land (v. 18). If they saw the scarlet thread, all those abiding in her house would be spared. If the scarlet thread was missing or, if hung, and her loved ones were departed from the house – the spies would not be responsible for their deaths.

Despite the fact that the spies told her to act once Israel mounted their invasion, and that she knew the spies themselves would be in hiding for three more days before they even returned to the Israelites, she saw no reason to delay the expression of her faith. Rahab hastened to hang the scarlet thread (*tiqvah*) promptly after the spies had been let down by a rope (*chebel*) through her window. As two different Hebrew words are used in the narrative, the thread hung and the rope used to lower the spies were not likely the same.

Rahab was not concerned about the inquiries of others as to its meaning, but rather, wanted the guarantee of her deliverance from death in its proper place. Rahab's faith was again demonstrated through God-honoring action. As a result, a testimony of God's grace hung from her window for all to see. Most ignored the symbol, but some believed her testimony and were saved on the day that divine wrath fell on Jericho.

There are two substitutional qualities contained within the promise of the spies to Rahab. First, the spies confirmed that because Rahab had saved their lives, they would offer to spare hers also: *"Our lives for yours"* (v. 14). F. C. Cook explains this idiom as "a form of oath in which God is in effect invoked to punish them with death if they did not perform their promise to save Rahab's life."[1] Second, scarlet dye was derived in ancient times from crushing a cochineal worm and, thus, Rahab's scarlet thread is a legitimate type of the death of the One who would later say: *"I am a worm and no man"* (Ps. 22:6). The Lord Jesus substituted Himself in the place of the sinner at Calvary; He shed His own blood to provide redemption for all who would desire to be saved.

A similar redemptive picture could be seen on the eve of the Exodus, when God issued instructions to Moses concerning the Passover lamb. On the tenth day of the first month, the head of each Hebrew home was to choose a male lamb, a yearling without any blemishes. Once chosen, it was separated from the sheep and the goats and was watched closely for four days to ensure its fit condition. On the fourteenth day of the first month, the young, tested, unblemished lamb was to be killed in the evening. For the initial Passover, the lamb's blood was to be applied to the doorpost and lintel of the offerer's home in order to spare the life of the firstborn living there.

Some 1500 years later, John the Baptist declared that Jesus Christ was *"the Lamb of God which takes away the sin of the world"* (John 1:29). Paul taught that Christ was the literal fulfillment of the Passover lamb: *"For indeed Christ, our Passover, was sacrificed for us"* (1 Cor. 5:7). In Moses' day, the sprinkling of blood was the visible expression of one's faith and thus averted God's judgment. But this action occurred only because the sprinkler reckoned that Jehovah had spoken the truth and that He could not lie.

Jehovah had promised not to judge the firstborn within the houses marked by lamb's blood. *Security* of salvation would be obtained through the applied blood, but the *assurance* of that salvation would only be enjoyed by trusting in God's Word. A believer who has laid hold of both the security and assurance of salvation enjoys not only the peace with God, but also the peace of God in his or her life. This individual is obedient to God's Word and is characterized by a humble resolve to face each day with confidence, knowing that he or she is secure in Christ. In the same manner, Rahab displayed the scarlet thread as an act of obedience to and confidence in God's Word.

On the eve of the Exodus, the Israelites did not wait until they saw the destroying angel to place lamb's blood upon their doors. Rahab's response was also prompt; the token placed, her soul was safeguarded. The similarity between these two events is astonishing: just as the blood of the paschal lamb on the lintels of the doorposts diverted the judgment of the destroyer, so the scarlet thread suspended from the window of Rahab's house would preserve all who by faith remained within its confines at the time Jericho's walls crumbled.

Rahab's faith was genuine, for true faith does not hesitate, but acts on what it knows to be true. Rahab did not want to take any chances that she might be out of her home or possibly asleep when the invasion occurred. Thus, she immediately proclaimed from her window her desire to be saved from the coming destruction and, in type, the efficacy of Christ's redemptive work which is able to save the most miserable sinner. The scarlet thread would serve as a constant reminder to her of God's promise of her forthcoming deliverance.

Rahab's emphatic appeal for protection convinced the spies that her offer to assist them was genuine and, thus, they committed their own lives into her hands. Rahab knew the surrounding terrain and her own people's probable course of action, so she not only enabled the spies to escape from Jericho, but also instructed them on how to evade capture: *"Get to the mountain, lest the pursuers meet you. Hide there three days, until the pursuers have returned. Afterward you may go your way"* (v. 16). No doubt they were tempted to head east and return to Joshua as soon as possible to deliver their report, but instead they followed Rahab's counsel completely and hid in the hill country less than a mile to the west of Jericho. This terrain is a convolution of limestone cliffs and caves, which provided ample opportunity for concealment. The spies did return safely to the Jewish camp three days later.

Rahab's sincere, but imperfect exploits in caring for the spies should encourage us to be patient with those younger in the faith, who often, desiring to do something for the Lord, do foolish things. In love, let us extend as much breathing room as possible to new converts. At the appropriate time, a word fitly spoken can provide the needed correction and encouragement to hopefully avoid future mishaps.

The spies relayed to Joshua all that had happened to them in Canaan, including their pledge to Rahab. Thirty-nine years earlier, ten of the twelve spies Moses sent to explore the land had exhibited a lack of faith, stating: *"We are not able to go up against the people, for they are stronger than we"* (Num. 13:31). Perhaps Joshua's two spies remembered this, and the fate of the men who delivered the evil report. At any rate, their own account was very different: *"Truly the Lord has delivered all the land into our hands, for indeed all the inhabitants of the country are fainthearted because of us"* (v. 24). The message rallied the Israelites to invade Canaan, and Joshua moved their encampment to the edge of the Jordan River just across from Jericho early the very next morning (3:1).

God used the faith of one pagan harlot, as reported by two witnesses, to stir up the heart of an entire nation to trust Him. Dear believer, what feat might God do through you, if your faith rested solely in Him? Rahab is proof that the Lord is able to work in any circumstance to honor Himself and preserve those who trust Him.

As we ponder the narrative before us, we naturally wonder why Rahab, a harlot entrenched in paganism, was the one to receive God's abundant favor. Could there be anyone less deserving of God's mercy within the doomed city? Probably, but C. I. Scofield explains why Rahab was saved:

> No more unlikely character than Rahab could have been divinely chosen for deliverance from ungodly Jericho. The salvation of Rahab, the harlot, illustrates that even in a doomed city a wicked individual could find grace by turning to God in faith. Those who charge Israel with barbaric cruelty in exterminating the inhabitants of Jericho fail to comprehend that Israel was God's instrument of divine judgment. The people of Jericho, hopelessly depraved (Lev. 18:24-26), had chosen to fight Israel instead of seeking mercy as did Rahab. Those who perished did not believe (Heb. 11:31).[2]

The fact that immoral Rahab, from the lowest social class in society, could be saved meant anyone else could have received mercy also. The grace shown to Rahab was in fact available to all the inhabitants of the land, for God had told Abraham centuries earlier, *"in you shall all families of the earth be blessed"* (Gen. 12:3). Because of Abraham's demonstrated faith, Jehovah granted him the title deed of all the land between the Euphrates River and the Mediterranean Sea. Although Abraham would not come into possession of his full inheritance, his descendants eventually would and, therefore, would also rule over the ten people groups listed in Genesis 15:19-21 (which included the Canaanites, Rahab's people). This meant that as this future prophecy unfolded in time, these people groups would be exposed to the truth of God's plan and would have an opportunity to be blessed through Abraham. It would be necessary to submit by faith, as did Rahab, to God's rule in the matter and to surrender to His people.

What Paul declares in the New Testament was therefore certainly true in the Old Testament as well: *"For the grace of God that brings salvation hath appeared to all men"* (Titus 2:11). The nations mentioned in Genesis 15 were not hopelessly condemned; there was a way of escape for them through faith. By identifying with and honoring Abraham's descendants, the pagan inhabitants of the land could both know and be reconciled with Abraham's God. This was made possible through the covenant promise of God to Abraham, which ultimately had its fulfillment in the redemptive work of Christ. Uriah the Hittite, Caleb the Kenizzite, and Tamar and Rahab of the Canaanites are some of the inhabitants that received divine blessing by trusting Abraham's God.

By faith these Gentiles came to share the enjoyment of the promises in common with God's covenant people throughout the Old Testament. Accordingly, Rahab the harlot, a Gentile, belongs to that large company of saints mentioned by Paul in his letter to the Ephesians, who like most of us were *"once Gentiles in the flesh ... that at that time you were without Christ, being aliens from the commonwealth of Israel and strangers from the covenants of promise, having no hope and without God in the world. But now in Christ Jesus you who once were far off have been brought near by the blood of Christ"* (Eph. 2:11-13). Rahab's faith not only delivered her and her family from destruction, but God also honored her by incorporating her within the lineage that would bring forth the Messiah in years to come (Matt. 1:5). The writer of Hebrews reminds us that *"without faith it is impossible to please Him, for he who comes to God must believe that He is, and that He is a rewarder of those who diligently seek Him"* (Heb. 11:6). Rahab was not exposed to all the divine revelation that you and I have today, but she did respond in faith to that which was revealed to her and God rewarded her richly.

Rahab's peculiar faith took her from being a pagan prostitute in Jericho to the privileged position of being a co-inheritor of a land flowing with milk and honey. She is thus a picture of Christian Gentiles in general, who were not God's people, but through the finished work at Calvary are permitted to share in the unsearchable riches of Christ in heavenly places. Thankfully, we are second benefactors of God's New Covenant which was established with the Jews through the blood of His Son (Eph. 3:6; Heb. 8:8).

Like Rahab, we Gentiles were not God's people, but now we have been brought into the blessings of the Abrahamic Covenant. In this way God has kept His promise to Abraham to bless all the families of the earth (Gen. 12:3). Just as Rahab became part of the commonwealth of Israel, we too have been grafted into the blessings promised Abraham's spiritual descendants (Rom. 11:16-17). These come to us only through our True Joshua – the Lord Jesus Christ.

Meditation

The following story is an example of how God can work in any situation to cause lost sinners to trust in Christ alone for salvation:

> On January 6, 1850, a snowstorm almost crippled the city of Colchester, England; and a teenage boy was unable to get to the church he usually attended. So he made his way to a nearby Primitive Methodist chapel, where an ill-prepared [man] was substituting for the absent preacher. His text was Isaiah 45:22 – *"Look unto Me, and be ye saved, all the ends of the earth."* For many months this young teenager had been miserable and under deep conviction; but though he had been reared in church (both his father and grandfather were preachers), he did not have the assurance of salvation. The unprepared substitute minister did not have much to say, so he kept repeating the text. "A man need not go to college to learn to look," he shouted. "Anyone can look – a child can look!" About that time, he saw the visitor sitting to one side, and he pointed at him and said, "Young man, you look very miserable. Young man, look to Jesus Christ!" The young man did look by faith, and that was how the great preacher Charles Haddon Spurgeon was converted.[3]

The Wonders
Joshua 3:1-10

Divine wisdom had yoked the energy and zeal of a younger Joshua with the wisdom and experience of a seasoned Moses. The wilderness experience was Joshua's training ground; in fact, these two men labored harmoniously for some forty years before their separation at the Jordan River.

As mentioned previously, Joshua leading the people through the Jordan River pictures Christ's effectiveness of bringing those who are positionally justified in Him into the full blessings of resurrection life. In the Red Sea the redeemed were delivered from oppression and sin was judged; however, the passage through the Jordan initiates an ongoing judgment of self and deliverance from self, as the enemy was confronted in faith and obedience.

> My Saviour, Thou hast offered rest;
> Oh, give it then to me;
> The rest of ceasing from myself,
> To find my all in Thee.

W. Graham Scroggie comments further on the different spiritual aspects typified in the crossing of the Red Sea as compared to the Jordan River:

> The order of these passages is important, first the Red Sea, and then the Jordan, and but for the former there could never have been the latter. Historically and geographically the order cannot have been inverted, and spiritually it cannot be. By the passage through the Red Sea the people were separated from a life of bondage in Egypt, and by the passage through the Jordan they were dedicated to a life of blessing in Canaan. The first experience was from something, and the second was to something. In the one case something lay behind them to which they could never return, and in the other case something lay before them

towards which they pressed. The Sea was the way of exit, and the River was a way of entrance.[1]

Israel's trip through the Jordan River represents the spiritual life gained by the believer through experiencing the death of the Old Man and then receiving life in Jesus Christ. The enemy in Canaan can be conquered, but only through resurrection power. The comprehension of this reality would require a progression of learning experiences, including both failures and victories.

After hearing the good report of the two spies, Joshua moved the camp from Shittim to a location near the Jordan River, where they resided three more days, and he issued two commands. The first was relayed through the officers and pertained to how the Israelites would cross the Jordan. The Jews were to be continually watching for the priests to bear up the Ark of the Covenant and move towards the river. As Matthew Henry observes, this introduced the Israelites to a new method of divine guidance than that which they had experienced in the wilderness:

> The people having been directed before to follow the ark are here told that it should *pass before them in to Jordan* (v. 11). Observe, the Ark of the Covenant must be their guide. During the reign of Moses, the cloud was their guide, but now, in Joshua's reign, the ark; both were visible signs of God's presence and presidency, but divine grace under the Mosaic dispensation was wrapped up as in a cloud and covered with a veil, while by Christ, our Joshua, it is revealed in the ark of the covenant unveiled.[2]

When the people saw the priests bear up the Ark of the Covenant, they were to follow systematically, but not closely; a buffer distance of three thousand feet was to be observed. This distance would later become the basis for the Sabbath Day's journey invoked by rabbinical tradition, though the actual distance has been repeatedly increased by Judaism through the centuries. Each tribe was also to choose one man to represent them for a task to be disclosed in the next chapter (v. 12).

The second command came directly from Joshua to all the people on the same day: *"Sanctify yourselves, for tomorrow the Lord will do wonders among you"* (v. 5). In Joshua 2 we were introduced to the token of salvation, the scarlet thread, which represented the redeeming blood of

Conquest and the Life of Rest

Christ. In this chapter we are made aware of upcoming "wonders" associated with crossing the Jordan River on dry ground. As in the crossing of the Red Sea, the events of this chapter visually express the positional oneness that all believers have with Christ in His death, burial and resurrection. H. L. Rossier supplies the following summary of how the positional ramifications of our salvation in Christ are pictured in the Israelites' deliverance from Egypt and their passage through the Rea Sea and through the Jordan River:

> From Egypt up to this, the deliverance of the people is characterized by two great events: the Passover and the Red Sea; and in order to understand the third great event, that is, the crossing of the Jordan, it is well to seize the meaning of the first two. All three are types of the cross of Christ; but its aspects are so rich, so various, so infinite, that we need all these, and many others, in order to comprehend its depth and extent.
>
> The Passover shows us the cross of Christ as a shelter from the judgment of God. ... Now Israel themselves could only be sheltered by the blood of the paschal lamb placed between the people as sinners and God as a Judge who *was against them*. ...The Passover stayed God Himself as a Judge, and set Israel in safety; at the Red Sea God intervenes as a Savior (Ex. 15:2) in favor of His people, who have nothing to do but to look on at their deliverance: *"Stand still and see the salvation of the Lord"* (Ex. 14:13). God, so to speak, acts as if the enemies which were against us, and which we were quite powerless to overcome, were against Him.
>
> We find in this scene [the crossing of the Jordan] a type of death and judgment borne by another, and for us the Lord presents Himself in it. ... Christ endured to the full the horror of death, and felt it alone in the infinite depths of His holy soul. But the people cross the river dryshod. Judgment finds nothing in them, because it has spent itself in death and for us on the person of Christ on the cross [pictured in the Ark being held by the priests]. They come out on the other side safe and sound, and here we have a type not merely of the death of Christ, but also of His resurrection for us.[3]

In Christ, the redeemed have been shielded from divine judgment through blood (as the Israelites were saved from the plague of death in Egypt), they have been delivered from the clutches of the enemy (as the

Israelites were brought safely through the Red Sea), and they are fully identified in the death and resurrection of Christ (as the Israelites passed safely through the Jordan). John N. Darby summarizes that "the Red Sea is death in redemption (Rom. 5; Ex. 14, 15) and the Jordan is the application of death to the individual – spiritual death with Christ."[4]   Paul elaborates on the implications of the latter identification truth in Romans 6.

Positionally speaking, co-crucifixion took place at the cross and became effectual for a believer at his or her conversion. Paul explains, *"Knowing this, that our old man was crucified with Him, that the body of sin might be done away with, that we should no longer be slaves of sin"* (Rom. 6:6). At the cross, the old man – what we were in Adam before salvation, the man who was dominated and controlled by the flesh – that man died with Christ. Paul conveys the practical aspects of this positional truth to the believers at Galatia: *"Those who are Christ's have crucified the flesh with its passions and desires"* (Gal. 5:24). The believer has been positionally crucified with Christ so that his or her flesh nature will lose its controlling influence as he or she matures in Christ. It is not that the flesh nature diminishes in strength, but rather that the Holy Spirit within the believer overpowers it. What originated in the world cannot compete with that which is supernatural; thus, a yielded life cannot be overcome by the flesh nature.

What is the outcome of those who both know and live in awareness of having been sanctified with Christ in death and in resurrection life? They will be privileged to see the power of God at work. For the children of Israel, this took place in several distinct ways, as we see from the narrative. First, Jehovah would magnify Joshua before the Israelites: *"This day I will begin to exalt you in the sight of all Israel"* (v. 7). Likewise, the Father has exalted the Lord Jesus above all authorities and powers to be the Head of His Church (Eph. 1:20-23). Second, the people themselves, whose eyes were steadfastly fixed on the Ark of the Lord, would witness God do the spectacular before them. This would provide evidence of His abiding presence: *"By this you shall know that the living God is among you"* (v. 10). Third, the Jews would grow in faith and in their hope for the future after witnessing God's fulfillment of His promises: *"He will without fail drive out from before you the Canaanites ... Jebusites"* (v. 10). Indeed, the Lord glorified His name by honoring Joshua, abiding with His people, and overcoming their enemies.

Conquest and the Life of Rest

To see Christ exalted, to experience His wondrous resurrection power, to know His abiding presence, and to grow in hopeful expectation of His immutable promises is the privilege of every believer today as well. This is accomplished through practical sanctification, which is more deeply brought before us in Joshua 5 when the topic of circumcision is broached. It suffices here to merely point out that, positionally speaking, the Father saw all believers die with His Son and then rise up with His Son. Christ does not force us to live in light of this truth, but those who do will be vessels of honor fit for His use to honor Him (2 Tim. 2:21).

Meditation

> O Christ, what burdens bowed Thy head! Our load was laid on Thee;
> Thou stoodest in the sinner's stead, didst bear all ill for me.
> A Victim led, Thy blood was shed; now there's no load for me.
>
> For me, Lord Jesus, Thou hast died, and I have died in Thee!
> Thou art risen – my hands are all untied, and now Thou livest in me.
> When purified, made white and tried, Thy glory then for me!
>
> — Anne R. Cousin

Crossing the Jordan
Joshua 3:11-17

What were the *wonders* God would accomplish to magnify Joshua and motivate the Israelites to enter into Canaan and to seize their possession? The priests were to carry the Ark of the Covenant to the brink of the Jordan. After they stepped into the river, God would pile up the waters at the city Adam and permit His people to cross over on dry ground (vv. 15-17). When this occurred, the Jews were to portage the dry riverbed while the priests stood holding the Ark of the Covenant in the channel that remained. After everyone was safely on the other side, the priests would then carry the Ark up the western bank of the Jordan River.

There are two rainy seasons in Israel, the spring and the fall. In the spring, melting snow from the mountains of Lebanon further contributed to the flood conditions. The scene before us occurred at this time; Joshua noted the river was swollen beyond its banks (v. 15). The lower Jordan River, ordinarily confined to less than 100 feet in width, flows through the bottom of a deep valley. In the rainy season, which peaks in mid-April (the timing of the Israelites' crossing), a torrent of water chokes the river's steep banks, forcing it to escape into the lower plains of the valley through which it flows. During this time, the Jordan cannot be forded and swimming across it is very dangerous.[1]

The priests displayed incredible faith in God's word by carrying the Ark directly into a flooding river. Jehovah responded to their obedience by performing one of the greatest miracles recorded in the Bible – holding back the floodwaters of the Jordan River several miles upstream at a place called "Adam" and then drying up the riverbed, so that His people could expediently cross over on dry ground. The location of Adam is only mentioned here in the Bible; it is generally thought to be Tel ed-Damiyeh, which is located about sixteen miles north of the ford across from Jericho.

Conquest and the Life of Rest

After the waters were removed, the priests apparently moved into the deepest part of the dry riverbed and then the Israelites crossed over. Every eye was fixed on the Ark of the Lord that morning, but it likely moved out of sight when the priests went down into the Jordan, as the people were 3000 feet away and the elevation is nearly flat on the east side of the Jordan (declining only 30 feet over a distance of 3000 feet). However, as each one came to the brink of the Jordan and by faith stepped down its banks, the Ark would have become fully visible. It is indeed sobering to ponder the scene before us, for with the eye of faith we understand that the Ark, held in serene stillness below the level of the ground, represents the Lord Jesus Christ's body in the grave. Yet, He is the bridge from death to life and the multitudes passing by (i.e., through Him) enter into Canaan (i.e., the heavenly places).

H. F. Witherby provides this further insight into the work of Christ that is symbolized in the Jordan crossing:

> The Jordan was God's way of power for bringing them into the fullness of their blessings. ... Resurrection power out of death is taught: Christ's passing through death, and His entry into heaven, and God's power in bringing the saints in Christ where Christ is. The miracle was so brought that the river, which is to all a familiar type of death, was banished from sight by the presence of the ark of the covenant of Jehovah. Now, when the soul is occupied with the second Man, the Lord from heaven, power from on high is granted, enabling the eye of faith to see the greatness of His work, His resurrection and His ascension glories, and the sight of Him prevents all barriers from being seen. The work of Christ for His people – the cross, the empty grave, the ascension on high, is one work, the benefits of which are for "all saints," and recognizing His ascension to heaven, the greatness of His work is apprehended.[2]

There is an element of mystery which shrouds the cross of Calvary; man cannot fully comprehend what transpired during those three dark hours preceding the Lord's death. This divine saga was a private matter between God the Father and God the Son and no trespassing upon holy ground would be tolerated. This private scene is typified by the temporary disappearance of the Ark in the Jordan from the Israelites' vantage point. As far as the Israelites could discern from their position eastward, there was a time when the Ark vanished into the depths of the Jordan.

However, as they came by faith to the Jordan, they were able to see the Ark and the priests who bore it, and to personally witness the miracle.

This same pattern of exclusion was evident when Abraham and Isaac ascended the mountain together, after leaving behind the two young men who had assisted them in their three-day journey to Moriah (Gen. 22:6). What was to happen on the mount was a private matter between father and son; no intrusion was permitted.

A few months before Christ's crucifixion, Moses and Elijah suddenly appeared on earth to converse with the Lord, who was gloriously transfigured before them. This interchange likely occurred on a mountain northeast of Galilee. Perhaps they meant to strengthen the Lord Jesus through encouragement to continue bringing glory to His Father by fulfilling His will. Yet, Moses and Elijah are nowhere to be found at Calvary; the Son endured the horrors of Calvary alone.

What did Calvary mean to God the Father? We will never fully know. This is pictured in the way the High Priest under the Law was to compound special spices to create an incense to be placed before the Lord in the Most Holy Place. No one but God was allowed to appreciate its aroma (Num. 30:34-38), and only God the Father can fully appreciate the deep mystery of godliness and sacrifice pertaining to the Lord Jesus (1 Tim. 3:16). Like the Ark's momentary disappearance in the Jordan, the incense also conveys to us the mysterious and exclusive aspects between the Father and Son at Calvary.

The faith of the priests to step into the Jordan River also typifies the confidence the Lord Jesus would have in approaching the cross and death. How could Christ, after suffering for our sins, say, *"Father into Your hands do I commend my Spirit"* (Luke 23:46)? It was because Christ knew the promise of His Father to raise Him up from the dead:

> *And we declare to you glad tidings – that promise which was made to the fathers. God has fulfilled this for us their children, in that He has raised up Jesus. As it is also written in the second Psalm: "You are My Son, Today I have begotten You." And that He raised Him from the dead, no more to return to corruption, He has spoken thus: "I will give you the sure mercies of David." Therefore He also says in another Psalm: "You will not allow Your Holy one to see corruption." For David, after he had served his own generation by the will of God, fell asleep, was buried with his fathers, and saw corruption; but He whom God raised up saw no corruption* (Acts 13:32-38).

Conquest and the Life of Rest

God the Father responded to His Son's obedience just as He had promised; He raised His Son from the dead and then highly exalted Him in heaven (Heb. 1:3). The work of Christ is effectual for everyone who will choose to repent and receive His offer of salvation (Acts 3:19; John 3:16). After an individual dies, there are no second chances, *"for it is appointed unto man once to die and then the judgment"* (Heb. 9:27). If we do not choose life while living, we experience death after dying.

While Old Testament and New Testament saints alike are justified by faith in God's revealed Word, the sins of Old Testament saints were only atoned for (i.e., covered) by animal blood. Through God's forbearance, sin accumulated until it could be dealt with once and for all through the propitiation (i.e., the satisfaction) achieved through Christ's sacrifice (Rom. 3:25). Thus, it is symbolic that the waters of the Jordan piled up at "Adam," the name of the first man, and affected the Jordan River all the way to its termination point – the Dead Sea. Christ's redeeming blood can effectually reach back to Adam, but it only has value to redeem an individual until he or she dies; after that, the eternal destination of the human soul is immutably determined.

In the Jordan, the believer died with Christ (He being our representative), and thus passing through death with Him we are brought into resurrection life on the other side. Accordingly, believers today, like the Israelites before us, stand as trophies of the victory achieved over the raging waters of death. To save us, Christ had to go into death because that is where we were (i.e., we were all dead in trespasses and sins). After His death, Christ then had to come out of death in order to grant us eternal life and confer to us the ability to live for God, as Paul explained: *"That if one died for all, then all died; and He died for all, that those who live should live no longer for themselves, but for Him who died for them and rose again"* (2 Cor. 5:14-15); *"Even when we were dead in trespasses, made us alive together with Christ (by grace you have been saved), and raised us up together, and made us sit together in the heavenly places in Christ Jesus"* (Eph. 2:5-6). Christ died to enter into and rescue us from death that we might live for Him now and with Him forevermore.

The priests bearing the Ark were *"dipped into the brim of the water"* (v. 15). Because the priests obeyed and entered into the water, God responded by bringing them out of the water – He removed the river. The Greek verb translated as "baptize" in the New Testament is *baptizo*, which means "to dip." Part of the Great Commission the Lord entrusted to His disciples was to water baptize those who responded to the gospel message (Matt. 28:19-20). The early Church obeyed this practice (Acts 2:41, 8:37-38, 10:47). Why were the disciples to baptize new converts? Besides the obvious test of obedience to verify an individual's profession (Rom. 10:10), water baptism also symbolizes several identification truths resulting from unification with Christ. During water baptism, death is pictured when an individual is placed under the water and their new life in Christ is depicted when he or she is brought up from beneath the water. The same truth is placed before us in Joshua 3: willingness on our behalf to identify with Christ in death enables believers to experience the power of His life.

The crossing of the Jordan River by the Israelites often brings to mind another event in their history: the crossing of the Red Sea. These two events were very different, however. The Rea Sea passage was at night with the Israelites following their only source of light – the pillar of fire that was leading step by step through the vast darkness and the turbulent sea walled up on either side of them (Ex. 14:22-24). Jehovah brought them safely through the water and delivered them from their oppressors. The crossing of the Jordan River was during daytime hours and God completely removed the water barring them from Canaan. The Israelites had literally miles of dry riverbed over which to pass. Additionally, at the later crossing the entire nation could see the Ark and the miraculous panorama, and each one could choose his or her particular route across the Jordan into Canaan. This would allow over 2 million Jews to flood into Canaan in a short period of time.

In the figurative sense, both crossings are necessary in the believer's spiritual life and are thus connected. This is likely why the Israelites are described as following Moses down into the midst of the Red Sea (Ex. 14:22), but under Joshua's leadership the people *"passed over"* (Josh 3:17) and *"came up out of the Jordan"* (Josh. 4:19). Their passage through the Jordan brought complete separation and fully equipped them to serve the Lord in Canaan.

The Jews had not passed this way before, so the Lord had to lead them across the Jordan. After their passage they would keep the Passover (Josh. 5:10), which speaks of death, the Red Sea denotes victory, the Jordon portrays separation. In each of these, man could do nothing, but trust God; it was His work alone. Whereas the Red Sea hindered the Israelites escape from Egypt, the Jordon prevented their entry into Canaan. Any attempt to cross either by their own ability and strength would have resulted in death, as shown by the destruction of Pharaoh's army in the Red Sea.

Each Jew that crossed over the Jordan was committing to fight against opposing armies and fortifications in order to obtain their inheritance. There was no going back; the river behind them was death, the same as when it had been before them. For the child of God, it is death (i.e., separation from God's fellowship) to turn back from following Him. The Jews had sanctified themselves to walk in the newness of life with Jehovah. It is within the context of sanctification that Paul writes in Romans 6:23: *"For the wages of sin is death, but the gift of God is eternal life in Christ Jesus our Lord."* It is a general statement that is implicitly true for both the believer and the non-believer. For the latter, the meaning is eternal separation in relationship, and for the former it speaks of the loss of divine communion, and all the power, joy, and goodness that accompanies it.

The Israelites would be defeated in Canaan without God's presence and power to confront their enemies. As Christians, what we were in Adam is no more because we are now completely unified with Christ; the "old man" was crucified, thus in Christ, we are dead to our old master – sin (Rom. 6:6, 20). This means we have Christ's life, His resurrection power, as a limitless resource for daily living. Paul understood this truth and thus proclaimed, *"I can do all things through Christ who strengthens me"* (Phil. 4:13). The Lord Jesus told His disciples: *"for without Me you can do nothing"* (John 15:5)! On the eastern side of the Jordan the believer cannot possess that which Christ has secured and longs for us to experience in Canaan. But on the other side, we are able to lay hold of all spiritual blessings in heavenly places by exercising faith.

Through identifying with Christ's death and thus seeking to die daily in light of it, we trade that which is worthless and cannot be kept for that which has eternal value and can never be lost. This is why the Lord Jesus exhorted His disciples:

> *If anyone desires to come after Me, let him deny himself, and take up his cross daily, and follow Me. For whoever desires to save his life will lose it, but whoever loses his life for My sake will save it. For what profit is it to a man if he gains the whole world, and is himself destroyed or lost?* (Luke 9:23-25).

Dear believer, if you are stagnant in your Christian experience, break camp and move beyond the banks of the Jordan to lay hold of all that is yours in Christ. The Lord Jesus not only desired sinners to experience forgiveness of sins and deliverance from hell, He also wanted them to experience His abundant life: *"I have come that they may have life, and that they may have it more abundantly"* (John 10:10). You must lose your own life to enjoy the abundant life that is in Christ alone.

Meditation

> Before the judgment seat of Christ my service will not be judged by how much I have done but by how much of me there is in it.
>
> — A. W. Tozer

The Memorials
Joshua 4:1-13

Joshua describes two signs or memorials in this chapter that are inseparable in meaning. One of the memorials would be erected later that evening at the location of the Israelite campsite (vv. 3, 8). After all the people had crossed the dry riverbed, representatives from each tribe (who had been waiting to cross the river) walked to where the priests were standing, chose a stone, placed it on his shoulder, and carried it up out of the Jordan (vv. 2-5). The other memorial, also constructed of twelve stones from where the priests were standing, was set up at that site by Joshua himself (v. 9). The latter memorial would be covered over by water when Jehovah returned the floodwaters of the Jordan. The former memorial would be a testimony for future generations as to how Jehovah had miraculously ushered His people safely into Canaan (vv. 6-7).

On this point Matthew Henry notes the illustrative tie between the twelve tribal representatives under Joshua's direction and the appointment of the twelve apostles by the Lord Jesus:

> In allusion to this, we may observe that when the Lord Jesus, our Joshua, having overcome the sharpness of death and dried up the Jordan, had opened the kingdom of heaven to all believers, He appointed His twelve apostles according to the number of the tribes of Israel, by the memorial of the gospel to transmit the knowledge of this to remote places and future ages.[1]

Indeed, the stack of twelve stones at Gilgal (located approximately three miles west of the Jordan) would serve as a constant reminder to God's covenant people of their deliverance. To enter into the Jordan River without the Ark of the Covenant would have resulted in death, but to enter into it after the Ark brought life. The stone monument at the entrance of Canaan would serve to recall the magnificent feat God had performed to bring His people into the Promised Land. It was a day that Jehovah wanted future generations to remember and to understand its significance (vv. 6-7).

The twelve stones at Gilgal have a correlation for those of us in the Church Age, who are to remember the One who died for us, was buried, was raised up, and is now glorified in heaven. God desires to memorialize these events, for it is only through these that sinners may come to Christ (1 Cor. 15:3-4), and in each of these believers are identified with Christ. As Paul explains, remembering this divine union admonishes every believer to consider the eternal value of their actions:

For none of us lives to himself, and no one dies to himself. For if we live, we live to the Lord; and if we die, we die to the Lord. Therefore, whether we live or die, we are the Lord's. For to this end Christ died and rose and lived again, that He might be Lord of both the dead and the living (Rom. 14:7-9).

It behooves us to question ourselves before beginning a course of action: I am now one with Christ; would He engage in this behavior?

The Israelites were to erect a memorial at Gilgal to commemorate God's miracle of allowing them to cross the Jordan. The stones would remind the Jews that Jehovah was with them. All the Jews crossed over the Jordan and symbolically passed through death that day. Unfortunately, even with the erected memorial, what Jehovah had accomplished for them lost its meaning in time, for eventually the Jews forsook their God for false gods.

The twelve stones set up in the riverbed by Joshua also have special significance for believers today, for they remind us of death itself and the One who took our place in death – the death we deserved. Once these stones were covered with water again, the monument would be gone from view, except through the eyes of faith. Thus, we are to continue to remember by faith the value of Christ's death. Paul expounds that this is one of the purposes of the Lord's Supper: *"For as often as you eat this bread and drink this cup, you proclaim the Lord's death till He comes"* (1 Cor. 11:26). It is good for God's people in any dispensation to recall to mind the goodness of God, especially through the means He has deemed appropriate in Scripture.

God's word does not give the Church any yearly feasts to commemorate any aspect of the Lord's birth, life, death, or resurrection; rather, the

Conquest and the Life of Rest

Church was to regularly memorialize the Lord Jesus by keeping the Lord's Supper (Luke 22:19-20). The early Church met weekly on Sunday for the Lord's Supper (Acts 20:7) in obedience to the Lord's command to regularly remember Him and to proclaim the value of His death (1 Cor. 11:24-26). Today, much of Christendom is ignoring the command of Scripture and the pattern of the early Church to practice social and religious traditions which ignore Scriptural teaching.

Just as the scarlet thread would have reminded Rahab of the means of her salvation, believers today are also strengthened in their resolve to live for Christ by regularly being reminded of Him through the breaking of the bread. It is hard to lust after an individual, covet another's possessions, or be given to substance abuse if our minds are stayed upon the Lord. Isaiah 26:3 reads, *"You will keep him in perfect peace, whose mind is stayed on You, because he trusts in You."* Perhaps this is why Jehovah instituted so many special days and feasts for the Jews to keep; He wanted their minds to be continually occupied with Him. This would make it more difficult for the Jews to forget their God. Likewise, the Lord gave the Church a remembrance feast called the Lord's Supper the night before He died to aid our recollection and appreciation of His work at Calvary and His moral beauty.

With the priests standing in the dry riverbed holding the precious Ark of the Lord, *"the people hurried and crossed over"* (v. 10). They did not hasten in fear that the waters of the Jordan would overwhelm them, for God was controlling the river, but rather in excitement of entering the land of promise. Perhaps they were also being considerate of the priests who were patiently bearing the Ark on their shoulders. When all had crossed over and Joshua had erected a memorial in the midst of the Jordan, the priests bore the ark up out of the Jordan. The Ark of the Covenant, representing Christ, had been the first into the Jordan and the last to come out (3:17, 4:11). This reminds us that Christ is the *"Alpha and the Omega, the first and last"* (Rev. 1:11); He alone is *"the author and finisher of our faith"* (Heb. 12:2). Our salvation begins and ends with the Lord Jesus Christ. Thus, the Ark remained in the Jordan until all had passed over; likewise, Christ's death brings full salvation to all who will believe.

Forty thousand soldiers from Reuben, Gad, and the half-tribe of Manasseh did traverse the Jordan with their brethren as they promised Moses they would (vv. 12-13). In fact, as they were unencumbered with moving belongings or their families, these entered into Canaan first as a point guard. However, this forty-thousand-man contingency was only a small portion of the available males from the two and a half tribes who settled on the Eastern Plateau; the entire number (i.e., men twenty years of age and higher) as established by Moses just prior to his death was 136,930 (Num. 26:7, 18, 34). The actual total of Jewish men remaining in Gilead (assuming half of the 52,700 men in the tribe of Manasseh settled in Transjordan) would be 110,580. Thus, the 40,000 troops crossing the Jordan represented only 36.2 percent of the adult male population or about 1 out of every 3. Although these were armed for war and prepared to fight, H. L. Rossier surmises that there were two things of which they remained in ignorance of:

> They were ignorant of the value of the land of Canaan, and the value of death. The river did not arrest them when they turned to rejoin their wives, their little ones, and their cattle, who were awaiting them on the opposite shore. The country "on this side" had its attractions for them, whilst the people, who were peacefully in the enjoyment of Canaan, saw with joy that the Jordan was a barrier to separate them from all that which formerly was of any value to them.[2]

Yes, these 40,000 men were fully prepared to cross the Jordan and fulfill their duty, but they were just as prepared to pass back over to enjoy the rich pasture lands of Gilead and Bashan, for they had much cattle (Num. 32:2-33). They would experience the power of Jehovah in confronting the seven nations of Canaan; yet, they could not remain in the place of blessing because of their fascination with temporal things (i.e worldliness). How many believers today are determined to do something for God in Canaan, but have no deliberate desire to remain there because of their personal investments in Gilead? The Lord was dwelling with His people in Gilgal, not in Gilead on the other side of the Jordan. This begs the question, "Were they really on the Lord's side when their hearts were not?" Only the Lord knows the true intentions of men, but as H. F. Witherby reminds us, the Lord desires lifelong commitment in His people and loathes halfhearted service:

> Gilead, we say, was their home, and a Christian is in his life what he is at home. He may go out at times on the warpath, but the true test of his spiritual condition is the character of his inner life. All the time of their wars in Canaan, these forty thousand were fighting for others, not for themselves; and it is a most solemn thing when Christians in spiritual

warfare are, as it were, only auxiliary troops. Genuine Christian soldiers are exceedingly rare; they are soldiers for life. To such everything subserves the one great object – the pleasing of Him who has called us to be soldiers. "Your wives, your little ones, and your cattle," on the east of the river, were the true witnesses of the actual dwelling-place of the forty thousand. Sooner or later these warriors would return home, and not a man of them was a soldier across the Jordan for his lifetime. The wars of the Lord prove men. All God's people must engage in spiritual battle; but, like the forty thousand, numbers fight the fight of faith with the prospect of returning to their ease and enjoyments here. Too few fight on with the object of obtaining victories for God on earth, and think not, dream not, of rest until they shall reach their home in glory.[3]

Because of their determination to dwell apart from the intimate presence of the Lord, these two and a half tribes would be the first of God's covenant people to enter into widespread idolatry and the first to be chastened by military invasion and captivity (1 Chron. 5:25-26). Their testimony serves as a warning to all God's people – the expense of departing from God's presence to obtain worldly satisfaction is too high.

We are people of like passion, and are capable of committing the same costly mistake, trading Gilgal for Gilead. As stated before, may we then be faithful to what both memorials commemorate. The one to be erected at Gilgal (v. 20) reminds us of all the positional wonders that have been accomplished through the death, the resurrection, and the glorification of Christ – we have experienced these with Him. The one buried beneath the waters of death (v. 9) reminds us of the tremendous cost of our salvation – the death of God's only begotten Son, the Lord Jesus Christ. As we continue to consider these memorials, may we choose the conquest of Canaan (i.e., to possess our heavenly inheritance in Christ), rather than dwell in Gilead apart from the Lord's fellowship and power.

Meditation

> When we crossed the river Jordan, in the land we found:
> Wine and oil and milk and honey, richest fruits abound;
> Sparkling fountains, and the showers come upon the ground;
> We are able, Hallelujah! Let God's praise resound.
>
> — Kittie L. Suffield

On That Day
Joshua 4:14-24

Jehovah desired to bring His people into the Promised Land on a particular day – *"the tenth day of the first month"* (v. 19). It was *"on that day"* that God chose to magnify Joshua in the sight of all Israel; accordingly, *"they feared him, as they feared Moses, all the days of his life"* (v. 14). Beyond this accomplishment there are at least three specific reasons why the timing of Israel's crossing into Canaan gleams with sovereign foreknowledge.

First, the Israelites were delivered from Egypt on the first Passover forty years earlier. *Forty* is the number used in Scripture to symbolize a trial or a probationary period of testing. Clearly, Jehovah was showing His full control of all the circumstances that Israel had experienced in the past forty years in order to prepare them for entering the Promised Land. Their time of probationary testing was now complete.

A few centuries later Jeremiah would warn the Jews in Judah for forty years before they were forcibly removed from their land by the Babylonians. God's long-suffering patience was demonstrated during this probationary period also, but ultimately judgment for Judah's relentless idolatry could no longer be delayed. The prophet Ezekiel would personally mark this period of time by laying forty days on his right side, a day for a year to picture God's anguish over Judah's sin (Ezek. 4:7). In summary, the Lord taught His people for forty years to suitably prepare them to enter the Promised Land by faith, and He would later work with them for the same duration of time before ushering them out of it because of their stubborn disobedience.

Second, the Law required the Passover lambs be tested and inspected for four days to ensure their good condition before being sacrificed and roasted on the fourteenth day of the first month in the Jewish calendar (Ex. 12:4-6). The Israelites' entrance into Canaan on the tenth day permitted the Jewish families to set aside a spotless yearling male lamb

Conquest and the Life of Rest

in preparation for keeping the Passover in accordance with the Law of Moses.

Third, no uncircumcised male could eat the Passover (Ex. 12:44). We learn in the next chapter that while the Israelites were in the wilderness, they had not obeyed God's command to circumcise their sons when they were eight days old. A mass circumcision on the tenth or eleventh day would allow some time for healing before the Passover (5:8). God wanted to ensure His people were obedient to this command in order that everyone could enjoy the Passover feast. Jehovah knew exactly what day to bring His people into the Promised Land in order to convey, through biblical numerology, the idea of a completed period of testing, and in order to properly prepare lambs for the Passover and His people for their inheritance. That day was the tenth day of the first month.

The Hebrew word *yowm*, translated "day" in verse 14, appears frequently in the Old Testament; however, only about twenty times is it used in the Hebrew expression that correlates to the English phrase, "on that day." In fact, the location of this phrase here in Joshua 4 is only its fourth occurrence in Scripture and its substitutional meaning is in keeping with the three previous references.

It is first employed in Leviticus 16:3 in reference to the Day of Atonement, when a goat and a bullock would die in the place of the sinner. The phrase "on that day" is then found twice in Numbers 19:6. Here it describes the unusual situation of a Jewish man who wanted to keep the Passover Feast, but had been defiled by a dead body. God informed Moses that the man should keep the Passover, but he must do so on the fourteenth day of the following month. On the first Passover, a lamb took the place of the firstborn in each family. This emphasizes the importance of substitutional death in the mind of God as the only means of justifying sinners (i.e., an innocent must take the place of the guilty). The same truth was shown "on that day" in Joshua 4 when the Ark of the Lord, carried by the priests, conducted the Israelites through the Jordan, thus picturing what was accomplished for the believer by the substitutional death of Christ.

James Vernon McGee further notes two important aspects to remember about the Ark in the Jordan:

> The ark goes before and divides the Jordan River – not the rod of Moses. The ark goes before, carried by the priests. Christ goes before us

through death, but also goes with us through this life. Jordan is typical of Christ's death, not ours [though we, in Him, did die in the positional sense].[1]

Accordingly, God sent forth His Son to the earth at a particular time to eventually be judged as the Sin-bearer on a specific day: *"But when the fullness of the time had come, God sent forth His Son, born of a woman, born under the law, to redeem those who were under the law, that we might receive the adoption as sons"* (Gal. 4:4-5). No one else but the Lord Jesus (as pictured in the Ark) could accomplish what God desired on that day: not Abraham, not Moses, not David. Although we sometimes misapply the meaning of the text in our singing, the Psalmist also writes of this one special day that God had designed to bring life out of death:

I will praise You, for You have answered me, and have become my salvation. The stone which the builders rejected has become the chief cornerstone. This was the Lord's doing; it is marvelous in our eyes. This is the day the Lord has made; we will rejoice and be glad in it (Ps. 118:21-24).

For the redeemed, the day that God judged His Son is a special day to remember, for what God accomplished on that day is truly marvelous and we will rejoice and be glad in it forevermore!

Further application of the expression "on that day" is noted in the preparatory efforts of the people prior to arriving in Canaan. The Israelites spent three days in preparation before crossing the Jordan (3:2), and on the fourth day they were all in Canaan. As explained earlier, this duration of time pictures the Lord Jesus in the tomb (Matt. 12:40). This prophetic "three-day" illustration reoccurs throughout the Old Testament and is first presented in Genesis 22, when it took Abraham three days to reach Moriah. This was the divinely-appointed site to offer up Isaac, Abraham's only son of promise, as a sacrifice (Heb. 11:17). Why did the journey require three days and not two or four? It is because, in Abraham's mind, God's will and command could not be thwarted; thus, Isaac was as good as dead for those three days. After the Lord's crucifixion on Friday, His marred body, stiffened by the chill of death, was laid in a lonely tomb. His body lay lifeless in that dismal place until

Conquest and the Life of Rest

Sunday when He awoke from the slumber of death and was raised up in a glorified body just before dawn.

The typology within Old Testament Scripture arouses our affections and appreciation for the Lord and His redeeming work, now complete. However, F. B. Meyer notes that the Church has been given two specific ordinances in the New Testament to assist her in remembering *"the day the Lord has made"* with reverence and awe:

> We too may often walk along that river, and gaze into those depths. There Jesus lay in death for us, and there we lay Him; and not we only, but all His Church. *"For if one died for all, then all died."* Each time we partake of the Lord's Supper, or behold the rite of baptism administered in the form of immersion, or fall into the ground to die in acts of self-sacrifice and self-dying, we stand with Joshua beside the Jordan, covering the twelve memorial stones.[2]

To stand on the western side of the Jordan and to gaze into its eerie waters each week during the Lord's Supper is a grand privilege of all believers. To associate with the Lord's death and resurrection by obeying His command to be water baptized is equally a wonderful honor. These are reminders of the believer's association with Christ – a matter that you and I should never think lightly of.

That evening, after arriving at Gilgal, Joshua took the twelve stones carried from the riverbed and built a memorial (v. 23). The number "twelve" is the number of governmental perfection in Scripture (e.g., the twelve tribes of Israel and the twelve apostles of the Church), and is used here to speak of Israel as a whole, for a stone was to be taken *"according to the number of the tribes of the children of Israel"* (vv. 5, 8). Indeed, two and a half tribes were determined to settle on the opposite side of the Jordan, but God relates to His covenant people as a collective. Hence, twelve stones were taken from where the Ark had stood in the Jordan and those same twelve stones were erected in Gilgal, the location of the one and only encampment of His people.

The memorial would serve as a public testimony of God's faithfulness to all His people, not just the nine and a half tribes that were committed to obtaining their possession. Later in the book of Joshua, the Lord, through the priest's use of the urim and thummin, divided the common inheritance and designated to each tribe its appropriate reward. On that day, the two and half tribes obtained nothing, except what they had lusted after; in time, what they had desired was lost. Because of their future idolatry, the other nine and a half tribes would also be temporarily removed from their possession through chastening, but later they again occupied their inheritance. This was not the case with the two and a half tribes; however, the enjoyment of their possession will be restored in Christ's future kingdom on earth.

Today, the Lord Jesus views His Church in a similar fashion; while some may not be presently appreciating or benefiting from their spiritual blessings in Christ, in a future day all true believers will. Positionally, all believers died, were buried, were resurrected, and were raised up to sit together with Him in heavenly places. All those who have been born again enjoy the life of Christ. In Him, the Church presently enjoys a unified life and common purpose, and has an undivided inheritance in waiting. In a future day of Christ's kingdom, the inheritance will be divided; crowns and thrones will be designated to individuals in accordance with their faithfulness. H. F. Witherby suggests that any other view of Christ's Church will lead to pride and division:

> Whether some believers, like the two and a half tribes, settle down, in spirit, on the wilderness side of the river, or whether some, like the nine and a half tribes, make, in spirit, the heavenly Canaan their home, faith ever pitches the twelve stones in our Gilgal; for what Christ did in dying for us, He did for all saints. To allow for an instant that there is not "one body" would be to dishonor Christ who is the Head of the body; to assume that some saints are more of the One body than others would be to deny the reality of the One body. Any circle of interests less than that of "all saints" is necessarily sectarian, such interests being confined to a part of God's whole. In what way then is practical oneness to be reached? What is the true power of unity amongst the members of the body of Christ? The Holy Spirit of God, who has formed all saints into the one body of Christ, has but one mind. He cannot think or act contrary to Himself.[3]

After setting up the stones, Joshua again reminded the people, perhaps to eliminate any later confusion, of the significance of the sign just erected and exhorted them to explain its meaning to future generations:

> *When your children ask their fathers in time to come, saying, "What are these stones?" then you shall let your children know, saying, "Israel crossed over this Jordan on dry land;" for the Lord your God*

> *dried up the waters of the Jordan before you until you had crossed over, as the Lord your God did to the Red Sea, which He dried up before us until we had crossed over, that all the peoples of the earth may know the hand of the Lord, that it is mighty, that you may fear the Lord your God forever* (Josh. 4:21-24).

The Lord did not want the Jews to forget what He had accomplished earlier that day. May we also not forget what the monuments at Gilgal and in the midst of the Jordan stand for – a special day of divine judgment in which the Chief Cornerstone was rejected and judged in our place for our sins. The Lord Jesus ventured into death to rescue us from it and through His resurrection brought us into eternal life! The visible stones at Gilgal remind us that it is not enough to acknowledge the identification principle that we are dead and risen with Christ, but rather we must put away the doings of the old man and mortify our members daily – only then can we experience the bliss of heavenly places during our earthly sojourn.

Meditation

> This is the day the Lord hath made;
> He calls the hours His own;
> Let Heaven rejoice, let earth be glad,
> And praise surround the throne.
> Today He rose and left the dead,
> And Satan's empire fell;
> Today the saints His triumphs spread,
> And all His wonders tell.
>
> — Isaac Watts

The Sign of Circumcision
Joshua 5:1-9

The Amorites and Canaanites were aware that the Israelites had camped at Shittim on the eastern side of the Jordan. They were also familiar with their miraculous history leading up to their arrival at that location, including how Jehovah had brought them out of Egypt through the Red Sea. Despite this knowledge, the local populace probably thought they had some time to prepare their defenses and gather supplies, as a flooding Jordan River provided a natural defense barrier against the Jewish invasion force.

The news that Jehovah had dried up the waters of the Jordan River to allow His people to cross safely into Canaan was unnerving. The Jewish beachhead at Gilgal demoralized the Amorites and Canaanites: *"their heart melted; and there was no spirit in them any longer"* (v. 1). Who could possibly stand against the God of the Jews who did such amazing feats and fought victoriously against every foe? Yet, Joshua understood that Jehovah would only be with His people in battle if they were obedient to Him, so he quickly set about the task of circumcising the males born during the forty-year wilderness sojourn.

During the wandering years, the Jews did not obey the circumcision commandment that was first given to Abraham in Genesis 17 (vv. 4-7), and then formally ratified by the Law of Moses at Sinai (Lev. 12:3). Jewish unbelief had kept them from inheriting the Promised Land almost thirty-nine years earlier. During the disciplinary years that followed, much of the operations of God's covenant with them were suspended. In the wilderness, the Jews did not maintain their appointed sign of separation, but nonetheless God ensured their separation by isolating them from pagan influences during their chastisement. Now the previous generation was gone, and a younger new nation would be learning to exercise faith in Jehovah; the seal of God's covenant with them (circumcision) would therefore be demanded. In Canaan, the Israelites had entered into a new experience with God and the first course of action was for them to act upon the known will of God, thus putting away any cause for reproach.

The older men of war had been circumcised in Egypt, but all these had died prior to entering into Canaan (v. 6), except for Joshua and Caleb (the two spies that had years earlier brought back a good scouting report to Moses). The Passover was only a few days away and the Law prohibited any uncircumcised male from taking part in the Passover (Ex. 12:44, 48). In obedience to the Lord's command, Joshua sharpens knives and ensured that all males within the Jewish encampment are circumcised (vv. 2-3). This would allow the men some healing time before the Passover feast (v. 8).

Given their complete vulnerability (i.e. they had no means of escaping an assault on the western bank of the Jordan), the Israelites were exercising complete faith in Jehovah to protect them as the men rested and recuperated from the surgery. Recall that Levi and Simeon, the two sons of Jacob who avenged the rape of their sister Dinah, wiped out an entire village, shortly after the men of Shechem had been circumcised (Gen. 34). Consequently, in their present state, the Israelites were wide-open to attack from their enemies. Regardless, they were trusting in Jehovah and chose to obey His command on the matter. As J. G. Bellett summarizes, Jehovah was well pleased with this step of obedience and promised to begin anew with His people in Canaan:

> But now they have, as it were, revived or reappeared in proper character, and circumcision becomes a needed thing. Canaan was theirs only as they were Jehovah's, and they must wear their token of being His. They are circumcised, and thus become a new people. All is left behind, "the reproach of Egypt" as is here said, "the shame of their youth" as Isaiah says (Isa. 54:4). All is cancelled. "This day," says the Lord to Joshua, when the circumcision of the people had taken place, "have I rolled away the reproach of Egypt from off you." He was beginning anew with His people. ... Israel may now keep the Passover as in the night of their redemption from Egypt (Ex. 12); for the Passover belongs to a circumcised people. For whom God sanctifies... He redeems, and would have His redeemed know and celebrate their redemption (Ex. 12:45).[1]

It was at Gilgal, after their circumcision, that the Lord *"rolled away"* the past reproach of His people (v. 9). While the Jews were in Egypt, they were likely prohibited from circumcising their males, as that was a rite reserved for priests and upper-class citizens. As slaves, they were prevented from settling in the Promised Land. Now all that reproach and shame had been "rolled away." The Hebrew meaning of Gilgal is "rolling away" or "a rolling thing;" thus, the name of their new encampment affirmed God's response to their obedience in circumcision. Gilgal would become the Israeli base of operation for their campaign, their repose in victory or defeat. It was the place of new beginnings with Jehovah and its name would serve to remind them of that fact.

As a continuing sign of God's covenant with Abraham, his descendants were to circumcise their male babies. Circumcision then became the badge of the Jew; it marked them as God's covenant people. However, as Paul explains, circumcision had a deeper spiritual meaning which the Jews did not perceive: *"For he is not a Jew who is one outwardly, nor is circumcision that which is outward in the flesh; but he is a Jew who is one inwardly; and circumcision is that of the heart, in the Spirit, not in the letter; whose praise is not from men but from God"* (Rom. 2:28-29). Symbolically speaking, circumcision speaks of a life that has no confidence in the flesh (Phil. 3:3). To have no confidence in the flesh means to have no glory in it either. This is why the circumcision was to be done with *"sharp knives"* (v. 2). Since circumcision pictures the cutting away of the flesh, this can only be accomplished by the sharp, two-edged sword of the Spirit which is the Word of God. For the believer, this entails self-judgment as each individual contemplates the Word of God and allow the Holy Spirit to practically and personally apply it.

All Christians have been positionally circumcised in Christ (Col. 2:11) and are thus to manifest this inner spiritual reality daily. It is a quality of life that mere physical circumcision and Law-keeping could never accomplish. As James Vernon McGee notes, the Israelites were about to enter the greatest contest of their lives and their flesh must have no part in God's work.

> The old nature is not good. The old nature cannot inherit spiritual blessing. The old nature cannot even enjoy spiritual blessing. The old nature will not like Canaan, nor anything in the heavenlies. ...The circumcision of the children of Israel recognized these facts.[2]

Conquest and the Life of Rest

The victory in Canaan would be God's and He alone would receive the glory.

Jehovah had positionally sanctified His people by bringing them through the Jordan, which symbolically speaks of unifying believers with His Son in death that they might also experience His Life. But as is true in any dispensation, positional sanctification demands practical sanctification. Jehovah could dry up the Jordan to provide safe passage for His people, but He would not circumcise them – they would have to choose to do that themselves. Likewise, living the "circumcised life" is a choice that all believers should exercise.

Paul clarifies why this is necessary by first explaining the believer's position in Christ and then the believer's proper response to that truth: *"Therefore we were buried with Him through baptism into death, that just as Christ was raised from the dead by the glory of the Father, even so we also should walk in newness of life"* (Rom. 6:4). Paul then clarifies what it means to walk in the newness of resurrection life: *"Reckon yourselves to be dead indeed to sin, but alive to God in Christ Jesus our Lord. Therefore do not let sin reign in your mortal body, that you should obey it in its lusts"* (Rom. 6:11-12). It was thus appropriate for the Jews to sanctify themselves after crossing the Jordan River, just as we ought sanctify ourselves after facing what was symbolized by their passage – positionally experiencing the death of Christ in order to practically experience His life.

Practical sanctification occurs in the believer as his or her flesh supernaturally loses its influence; as its control dies out, the likeness of Christ becomes more apparent. The process will be complete at glorification. Accordingly, Paul commands believers in Colossians 3:5 to "mortify" (or put to death) the deeds of the body (i.e., the flesh), and in Romans 13:14 to starve the lusts of the flesh. The goal of these activities is that Christ, and not the nature of the Old Man (i.e., what we were in Adam), is witnessed in the believer's life. All believers were crucified with Christ in order to declare the power of His resurrection in daily life.

Prior to trusting Christ as Lord and Savior, people do not have the ability to please God; in fact, their flesh nature directly opposes God in thought and in deed (Rom. 5:10, 8:7). Paul minces no words on this important point: *"For those who live according to the flesh set their minds on the things of the flesh, but those who live according to the Spirit, the things of the Spirit. For to be carnally minded is death, but to be spiritually minded is life and peace"* (Rom. 8:5-6). The believer needs a new nature that longs to please God and perform His will.

This new nature is received from God at conversion through an act of the Holy Spirit called regeneration: *"But when the kindness and the love of God our Savior toward man appeared, not by works of righteousness which we have done, but according to His mercy He saved us, through the washing of regeneration and renewing of the Holy Spirit"* (Tit. 3:4-5). The Holy Spirit washes us by bringing us to see the wrong in our sinful attitudes and desires. He makes us feel their uncleanness, and leads us to repent of and repudiate them. Peter refers to the new nature received as a divine nature: *"By which have been given to us exceedingly great and precious promises, that through these you may be partakers of the divine nature, having escaped the corruption that is in the world through lust"* (2 Pet. 1:4). Regeneration is the implantation of a new life and a new order of living. This is why a regenerated person is referred to as a "new man" in Colossians 3:10; he or she received a new disposition which is to govern his or her thinking and behavior. This new disposition is God's own nature, which cannot sin (1 Jn. 3:9), though the believer may still sin by ignoring its moral reckoning (1 Jn. 1:9-2:1).

Before the one-time act of regeneration, the believer was spiritually dead, but through rebirth he or she is made spiritually alive! Imagine for a moment a peach seed placed within a coffin containing a rotting corpse. The seed contains life, while the coffin contains nothing but death. In time, the seed will sprout and grow into a fruit-bearing tree. Through the power of the Holy Spirit, God implants life within a repentant sinner; that which was once dead now lives to bear fruit to God (John 15:1-5). Practically speaking, there is no room in our minds to think the way we did before coming to Christ. Given our identity in Christ, we, like the Jews who circumcised themselves after crossing the Jordan, must have no confidence in our flesh as we pursue personal sanctification.

Meditation

> The effective soldier of Christ is girded about with divine realities, he is braced up in that by God's word as to what real blessing is, and his energy for warfare lies in being in the Spirit as to the truth. Power of darkness and spiritual wickedness in heavenly places are the foes, and,

dwelling in heart in the faith of being blessed with all spiritual blessings in the heavenly places in Christ, we fight the enemy in the field he occupies. To slacken the girdle is to give Satan an advantage. Do we give up a single truth God has given us? Or, do we fail in practically putting our own desires to death? – then, by that surrender, spiritual strength departs and courage fails.[3]

— H. F. Witherby

The Divine Captain
Joshua 5:10-15

On the fourteenth day of the first month in the Hebrew calendar, the Jews kept the Passover; it was the second time they had done so since its institution forty years previously (v. 10). Prior to their rebellion at Kadesh Barnea, the Israelites had celebrated the Passover on the first anniversary of their deliverance from Egypt (Num. 9:5). God told them He would discontinue His ongoing provision of manna for them the day after the Passover, as they could now live off the land (vv. 11-12). Though the barley was ready to harvest, they were not allowed to eat of it until its first-fruits had been waved before the Lord (Lev. 23:9-14). This was done on the day after the Sabbath (i.e., the first day of unleavened bread was observed as a Sabbath). For forty years God had set a table for His people in the wilderness; now the Jews were to eat the fruit of the Promised Land into which He had brought them. Tree groves, vineyards, and grain fields all lay before them as God's sustenance for His people. W. Graham Scroggie draws an important distinction between this Passover and its agricultural benefits as compared to previous Passovers:

> After the operation of circumcision, the children of Israel kept the Passover. This feast had not been observed once during the thirty-eight years of wandering in the wilderness; but that being ended, it is again observed. Spiritual revival always unveils the Cross afresh. But what distinguished this Passover from all others that had previously been observed is that from then "the manna ceased," and the people ate of "the old corn of the land." The manna had come down, but the corn came up; and as Christ is the Bread of Life it is not difficult to see Him here in two aspects, first as incarnate, coming down from heaven, and then as risen from the dead, to be the sustenance of His people. In the history "the manna ceased" when the Israelites entered the land, but in the spiritual counterpart we cannot separate the manna from the corn, we cannot separate the incarnate from the risen Christ, for it is the

whole of Christ, incarnate, living, crucified, and living again, Who is the food of His people. We cannot think too much of the crucifixion, but we can and do think sadly too little of the resurrection, the resurrection which is not only a historical event, but also a spiritual power and experience.[1]

The Israelites would no longer eat the manna which came down from heaven in the wilderness, but rather that which spoke of resurrection life coming up from the ground. Thus, Canaan ideally represents our living in the power of our risen Lord.

The remainder of this chapter records an astonishing event in which Joshua is introduced to the Commander in Chief of Israel's army in a private meeting. Joshua was apparently alone when this encounter occurred; perhaps he had privately strolled out of camp on the eve of battle to ponder their situation and to pray for divine enablement. It is during this moment of solitude that the Commander of the Hosts appears to Joshua:

And it came to pass, when Joshua was by Jericho, that he lifted his eyes and looked, and behold, a Man stood opposite him with His sword drawn in His hand. And Joshua went to Him and said to Him, "Are You for us or for our adversaries?" So He said, "No, but as Commander of the army of the Lord I have now come" (Josh. 5:13-14).

Note that the man before Joshua was a warrior and that Joshua was prepared to engage him in battle. However, after the warrior identified himself as the Commander of the Lord's army, Joshua immediately did two things. First, he fell to the ground and worshipped the One who held the drawn sword before him. It is no longer the rod of God in the hands of Moses that wields the power of God, but the Lord Himself executing vengeance with His sword. H. F. Witherby explains the difference in these emblems of power and suggests an application for the believer:

The drawn sword had now taken the place of the outstretched rod. The rod was the emblem of divine guidance and deliverance out of Egypt, but the sword was that of divine guidance and victory in Canaan. No longer were Israel led as a flock; they were henceforth the army sent by God to overthrow the iniquity of Canaan. We greatly mistake Scripture if we confine our testimony to comfort and peace, for therein also are words of judgment and of woe. ... In the hastening day of the Kingdom, when the heavens shall be opened, the Lord, the Faithful and the True, shall smite the nations with the sharp sword which goes out of His mouth (Rev. 19:15, 21). The exceeding terribleness of God's wrath against sin, and the testimony to the judgment Christ will, by His word, execute against sinners, form part of Christian offensive warfare against this world. To render such testimony, we must have our hearts occupied with the revelation of Himself with the drawn sword, and this revelation is received at His feet (Rev. 1:17).[2]

When the outstretched hand of the Lord grips a sword, it can only mean one thing – swift and exact judgment is imminent. May the Lord burden our hearts to compassionately declare to the lost that the Lord's vengeance will fall upon them if they do not repent. When His sword strikes, there will be no mercy, no second chances, and no further opportunity to be saved. A gospel message which extinguishes the fires of hell is a lie of the worst kind.

After Joshua fell to the ground, the next thing he did was to ask the Lord what message He had for him. The Lord responded to Joshua's request by telling him to loosen the shoes from his feet since he was standing on holy ground. By this command, the One speaking to Joshua clearly identified Himself as Jehovah God, and thus was deserving of Joshua's worship. Joshua quickly responded with reverence and obedience (v. 15).

The removal of Joshua's shoes would remind him that his fitness for battle would not be determined by his strength and wit, but by his personal holiness and consecration to the Lord. Just before his death, Paul conveyed this message to his spiritual son in the faith, Timothy. He was exhorted to cleanse himself from any influence of false teaching, to flee youthful lusts, and to pursue righteousness in order to be a vessel of honor fit for God's use (2 Tim. 2:20-22). Likewise, the Lord wanted Joshua to understand that his *cleanness*, not his *cleverness*, would determine the outcome of his labor in Canaan.

The conversation that followed afterwards, if there was one, is not chronicled in Scripture. What is recorded is Joshua's response to the Lord's appearance: He recognized the Lord, worshipped the Lord, wanted to know the will of the Lord, and obeyed the Lord's instructions. This is a good example for all of God's people to follow.

The Lord refers to Himself as the *"Captain of the Hosts of the Lord"* (v. 14; KJV). Terminology associated with high rank clings to the Lord throughout Scripture. The Hebrew word *sar* is rendered "commander" in Joshua 5:14, but translated as "prince" in Isaiah 9:6. Isaiah also refers to the Lord as *"the Prince of Peace"* and *"a leader and commander for the people"* (Isa. 55:4). In the New Testament, the Greek word *archegos* is found only four times and each time speaks of the Lord Jesus: He is the *Prince* of Life (Acts 3:15), a *Prince* (Acts 5:31), the *Captain* of our salvation (Heb. 2:10), and the *Author* of our faith (Heb. 12:2). Without question, the Lord is the highest ranking authority over all His saints and, indeed, the armies of heaven.

How are we to understand the appearance of the Captain of the Hosts to Joshua in relationship to the whole of Scripture? In Old Testament days, when God had a message for a particular person or collective of people, typically He either sent an angel to directly deliver it or He opened the mouth of a prophet to speak it on His behalf. On other occasions, where a direct verbal message was not advantageous, the Lord communicated through dreams and visions to communicate His will or to call His servants into ministry. The prophets Isaiah, Daniel, Ezekiel, and Zechariah all saw and spoke to the Lord through visions. On rare occasions, the Lord Himself ventured into the realm of time and space to appear and speak to someone. These appearances were usually to faithful Old Testament characters central to the working of God's sovereign purposes. The Lord did not normally appear to those who were perishing in unbelief; His encounter with Balaam is thus exceptional.

Some individuals, like Abraham, experienced a variety of divine encounters. The God of Glory met with Abraham in Mesopotamia (Ur) and later appeared to him several times in Canaan (Gen. 12:7, 17:1, 18:1-20; Acts 7:2). According to Genesis 15, God spoke to Abraham through two different visions, and during the second vision God appeared as a *"smoking furnace and burning lamp"* (Gen. 15:13-17). At other times, the Lord spoke to Abraham without coming into his view (Gen 12:1, 13:14, 22:1-2, 11, 15).

When God actually appeared to someone, as in this instance in Joshua 5, the event is referred to as a *theophany*, which means "God appearance." At such times, the Lord usually emerged as a normal-looking man, but on certain occasions He took other forms to accentuate His message. For example, the Lord spoke to Moses from a bush that appeared to be burning (Ex. 3), and to the Israelites from within a pillar of cloud (Ex. 13). The Israelites watched Mount Sinai visibly burn and quake at God's presence, though He Himself was concealed by thick, ominous clouds. Each of these unusual presentations conveyed the holiness of God to those who witnessed the spectacle. Before the burning bush, Moses was instructed to remove his sandals because he stood on holy ground. God, within the pillar of cloud, separated the attacking Egyptians from the Israelites, provided light to God's people but only darkness to their enemies. Later, when God spoke to the Israelites from a thick cloud engulfing Mount Sinai, they were warned that if man or beast set foot on the mountain they would die. This event affirmed God's awesome holiness and Moses' position as spokesperson to the people on His behalf (Ex. 19:9).

Whether in human form or in some unusual depiction, the One appearing was normally referred to as "the Angel of the Lord." The title is unique and should not be confused with the expression "an angel of the Lord," which may refer to the manifestation of one of many holy angels. Contextual observation confirms that appearances of "the Angel of the Lord" were *theophanies*. A theophany is a pre-incarnate visit of the second person of the Godhead to the earth as His Father's messenger. The Lord Jesus stated that no one had ever personally seen God the Father (John 6:46). The Lord also said that anyone who had seen Him had seen the Father (John 14:9). This means that God the Father did not appear to anyone in Old Testament times, but rather the only One who could perfectly represent Him did. For this reason, some refer to these supernatural Old Testament appearances as *Christophanies*, or literally, "Christ appearances." The obvious question is, "If these visits to the earth were made by the Son of God, why does Scripture refer to Him as 'the Angel of the Lord'?"

The English word "angel" is translated from the Hebrew word *malak* or the Greek word *angelos*; both words mean "messenger." The role of the Son in the Trinity is to do the Father's will, and part of that task involves communicating the Father's will to humanity. When the Son does this in the Old Testament, He is referred to as "the Messenger (Angel) of the Lord." Perhaps this is why Jacob referred to the Lord as "the Redeeming Angel" (Gen. 48:16). Similarly, in the New Testament, the Son of God is called the Word (John 1:1; 1 Jn. 1:1); the Son became a man to bring the ultimate message of God to humanity. The Lord Jesus was a living message sojourning on the earth; He was both the message and the messenger of God.

In addition to the title of "the Angel of the Lord," the context of Scripture can be used to identify a theophany, which has the following characteristics. The Angel of the Lord is rightly worshipped as God by others (Judg. 6:18-20). The Angel of the Lord initiates covenants and promises that only God can keep (Gen. 16:10, 22:16-17). In most occurrences, the Angel of the Lord clearly identifies Himself as God (Gen. 31:11-13; Ex. 3:2-6).

There are also New Testament passages which refer to Old Testament appearances in such a way as to verify that the Person of Christ was the one witnessed. For example, Isaiah writes: *"In the year that King Uzziah died, I saw the Lord sitting on a throne, high and lifted up, and the train of His robe filled the temple"* (Isa. 6:1). In the New Testament John refers to Isaiah's vision while explaining that Christ was fulfilling his prophecies:

> *Therefore they could not believe, because Isaiah said again: "He has blinded their eyes and hardened their hearts, lest they should see with their eyes, lest they should understand with their hearts and turn, so that I should heal them." These things Isaiah said when he saw His glory and spoke of Him* (John 12:39-41).

John confirms that the Lord Jesus fulfilled the prophecies of Isaiah, and that the prominent One that Isaiah saw in his glorious vision of God upon His throne was the same One John loved and served – the Lord Jesus Christ.

These temporary visitations of the Son of God to earth are not needed now to make individuals aware of God's will for their lives or to execute justice on wickedness. God's Word is complete (Jude 3) and reveals His will for all believers (Eph. 5:17; 1 Thess. 3:4; 1 Pet. 2:15). The matter of justice will be handled when the Lord Jesus returns to the earth on a future day (John 5:22; Jude 15).

In summary, before His incarnation, the Son of God appeared on earth, usually in human form, to convey specific divine messages to various individuals, and in rare instances to a collective of people. The role of the second person of the Godhead is to do the will of the Father, which necessitates that He declare God's word to humanity. In the Old Testament, this was sometimes accomplished by brief theophanies, but two thousand years ago the Word became flesh in order to dwell among men (John 1:14) and to fully and personally declare the Father's message of salvation. He was the message and the messenger of God, who freely gave His own life for the punishment of humanity's offenses against God. He was raised from the dead and, in a future day, will bodily return to the earth to judge wickedness and to rule and reign forever.

There is no reason for Him to return until that time, as there is no further revelation which man needs to act upon until then. Presently, there is a Man in the glory who waits to appear again on earth and to establish His kingdom. The Lord Jesus cannot abandon His humanity now or in the future to assume different discreet forms as He did in Old Testament days. Though human, His divine character and essence are unchanged; thus, He continues to possess all the power, wisdom, and insight to accomplish whatever the Father desires Him to do! Consequently, the Son of God no longer appears as "the Angel of the Lord," but rather is the incarnate Word of God for all of eternity.

Although the dialogue between the Lord and Joshua after Joshua's shoes were removed, if there was one, is not chronicled in Scripture, Joshua's response to the Lord's appearance is sufficient for us to understand two things. First, Joshua immediately recognized the Lord's authority as Commander in Chief of the army, which meant Joshua himself was not responsible for the outcome of future battles. Second, he worshipped the Captain of the Host as God and, as His servant, pledged prompt obedience to the Lord's instructions. Accordingly, the visit not only encouraged Joshua to attack Jericho, but also brought clarity to the enormous task of conquering Canaan – it was the Lord's work, not Joshua's. F. B Meyer comments on the scene before us and suggests an application for us to consider:

> Thinking much and deeply, Joshua wandered forth alone; and suddenly, *"as he lifted up his eyes and looked, behold, there stood a man over against him, with his sword drawn in his hand."* We need those uplifted eyes. Too often we keep our gaze fixed on the ground, and miss the celestial visions that await us all round.[3]

David would realize this truth years later while fleeing into the wilderness from his rebel son Absalom. While inspecting the huge rock formation he had taken refuge in, he realized what he really needed to ensure his safety: *"Hear my cry, O God; attend to my prayer. From the end of the earth I will cry to You, when my heart is overwhelmed; lead me to the rock that is higher than I. For You have been a shelter for me, a strong tower from the enemy"* (Ps. 61:1-3). David understood that he needed to look beyond his circumstances to the Rock who was higher than the physical one he was hiding in. Thus, he could pray, *"But You, O Lord, are a shield for me, my glory and the one who lifts up my head"* (Ps. 3:3). Joshua chose to be alone while he anxiously contemplated the battle ahead, but the Lord used His own presence to elevate his attention to something that was far more important to consider – the Captain of the Host of God was with him.

While we will not experience a theophany per se, we do well to learn from Joshua's encounter with the Lord. Life's trials will seem much less challenging if we can refocus our thinking on the Lord, for certainly He is able to rule over all our calamities. As Joshua shows us, knowing the Lord and His Word better should enhance our worship, prompt our obedience, and enable us to do the impossible.

Meditation

> Captain of Israel's host, and Guide
> Of all who seek the land above,
> Beneath Thy shadow we abide,
> The cloud of Thy protecting love;
> Our strength, Thy grace; our rule, Thy Word;
> Our end, the glory of the Lord.
> By Thine unerring Spirit led,
> We shall not in the desert stray,
> The light of man's direction need
> Or miss our providential way;
> As far from danger as from fear,
> While Love, almighty Love, is near.

— Charles Wesley

The Conquest of Jericho
Joshua 6:1-20

The mysterious meeting with the Commander of the Hosts concluded as abruptly as it commenced; the narrative records no further details of the conversation between the Lord and Joshua. However, Joshua's encounter with *"the Captain of the Hosts of the Lord"* on the eve of battle would serve to remind him that he merely led the people; the Lord commanded them. He learned the battle was not his, but the Lord's. Certainly, this personal visit would both strengthen Joshua's resolve to move forward and also guard him from debilitating pride in the aftermath of victory.

By faith the Israelites had entered the land, but now found themselves encamped between Jericho, which checked their advance, and the Jordan which blocked their retreat. This was a grave situation strategically, but they had obeyed all that they had been instructed to do and knew not what to do but to wait for further instructions. In the following years, the Israelites would learn that the land of rest would be a land of conflict, and the life of rest would be a life of conflict. Canaan would not be possessed by a single battle, but rather through a long campaign that would require faith, obedience and courage. After the division of the land, their enjoyment of their possession would diminish if they became complacent and compromising. Likewise, contending for the faith is to be a lifelong adventure for all believers today (Jude 3).

The battle plan for the fall of Jericho was apparently conveyed to Joshua in a subsequent meeting, and not during the encounter with the Lord as recorded in Joshua 5 (v. 2). From a human perspective, the revealed strategy seems foolish, but God declared it perfect by incorporating the number seven in its design. Seven was established as God's number of perfection after He completed the creation of the world in six days and declared it perfect on the following day (Gen. 1:1-2:3) and continues to be used in this context throughout the rest of Scripture. Hence, God's plan for conquering Jericho would require seven priests,

Conquest and the Life of Rest

seven trumpets, seven days, and seven circuits around Jericho on the seventh day.

What is known is that the Israelites' miraculous river-crossing prompted the city of Jericho to secure its gates – no one was allowed in or out of the city (v. 1). In so doing, the citizens of Jericho effectively preserved themselves for judgment, for their walls and gates would not prevent the entrance of the Israelites. Jericho was shut up, but not from God's wrath and destruction. In the days of Abraham, the iniquity of the inhabitants of Canaan had not yet reached its full place (Gen. 15:16), but now the unspeakable corruption of the people was developed and the land was going to *"vomit them out"* (Lev. 18:25). God had long-suffered with the people there, not willing that any should perish, but they now had reach such a point in their depravity that the only way that the Canaan could be cleansed was by their utter destruction.

Jericho was a formidable fortress about four miles west of the Jordan River and located at the lower end of a ridge that ran westward some ten to twelve miles. Ai was another fortified city of less stature situated at the other end of this main ascent into the hill country of Canaan. The elevation of ancient Jericho was about eight hundred feet below sea level, while Ai was about twenty-five hundred feet above sea level. Many archeologists have identified Et Tell, meaning "the ruin," as the ancient city of Ai, the name of which means "a heap of ruins."

To have unhindered access to the central highlands of Canaan, these cities must fall. Ai was also located on the main "ridge route" (a natural route running north and south through the highlands). By taking Ai, Bethel, and Jericho, the Israelites would effectively drive a wedge deep into Canaan that would virtually isolate the northern and southern regions from each other.

Archeological evidence would indicate that Jericho was possibly the most fortified city in central Canaan. British archeologist Kathleen Kenyon did excavations of the Jericho ruins from 1952 to 1958. Although she dismissed the timing of the biblical account because certain pottery shards were not found in the part of the city she was examining, her findings pertaining to the wall of Jericho and the destruction of the city are significant:

- The walls were of a type, which made direct assault practically impossible. An approaching enemy first encountered a stone

abutment 11 feet high, back and up from which sloped a 35° plastered scarp reaching to the main wall some 35 vertical feet above.
- The steep, smooth slope prohibited battering the wall by any effective device or building fires to break it.
- An army trying to storm the wall found difficulty in climbing the slope, and ladders to scale it could find no satisfactory footing.[1]

The design of Jericho's two-stage wall meant there was no possibility of taking the city through a direct assault, even if the Israelites would have had the most sophisticated weapons of that era. Despite the fact that their city seemed invincible, the citizens of Jericho were gripped with fear as they put themselves under a blockade. Jehovah referred to their trepidation as a sign to Joshua that He would deliver the city to him (v. 2).

Joshua was a seasoned warrior, but all of his previous experience was in open combat. He had never attacked a fortified city before and the Jews had none of the battlements, such as catapults and battering rams, necessary for this type of confrontation. However, Jehovah would not be including any man-made weapons of war or orthodox military strategy into His battle plan. The Lord explained His plan to Joshua and how the troops were to be deployed. The Jewish soldiers were to walk silently around the city for six consecutive days, and on the seventh day they were to circumnavigate it seven times; when they heard the trumpet sound everyone was to shout, the walls would come tumbling down, and every man was to go straight into the city from the position he found himself (vv. 4-16).

Not only the men of war were going to journey around Jericho a total of thirteen times, but seven priests blowing trumpets were to follow the men of war; the Ark of the Covenant (also carried by priests) would follow the seven priests, and there was also to be a rear guard behind the Ark of the Covenant (vv. 5-6). The priests were to be blasting their *showphars*; these were the trumpets of gladness, the cornets of jubilee (vv. 5, 6, 8, 13). This meant that a demeanor of joy and enthusiasm was to mark the Israelites as they faithfully walked around the walls of Jericho in silence and anticipated their forthcoming triumph. The scene before us is a great example for the Church today. Christians should be characterized by a spirit of joyful expectation as they faithfully serve the Lord and await glorification. For the believer, the voice of the trumpet signals the Lord's coming to take us home (1 Thess. 4:13-18; 1 Cor. 15:51-52).

Another practical lesson for believers can be found in the posting of the Jewish rear guard; often we set up our defenses for where we think the enemy will attack and then allow him to wreak havoc through the unlocked back door. The Israelites were taking no chances; if the enemy ambushed them, the Ark of the Lord would be surrounded by soldiers and protected. They valued the Lord's presence with them and were willing to protect it at all costs. If we value the Lord's communion, we also will be careful not to allow what is evil and defiling through the backdoor of our homes. Satan often pounces on believers as a lion does upon its prey, while at other times he assaults with the subtly of a slithering serpent lurking in the shadows. Accordingly, what often appears innocent or permissible at first may cause the most harm in the end. Let us not be beguiled by Satan from the simplicity that is in Christ (2 Cor. 11:3).

To a military mastermind, the Lord's battle plan would seem quite foolish, but Jericho would not be conquered by human wisdom, but rather by faith as demonstrated through obedience to God's Word. In fact, there is no record of any Israelites protesting Jehovah's invasion plan; they simply did what Joshua told them to do. One can only imagine how this bizarre stratagem affected the fearful citizens of Jericho, as they did not know when and where the Hebrews would strike. It is possible that their soldiers were circling the city on the inside while the Jews ventured around the walls on the outside, hoping to put up their best defense if attacked.

How far were the Israelites marching each day? Although the exact location of Gilgal is not known, it is generally thought to be about three miles westward of the Jordan River along the ford that ran on the north side of Jericho to the river. If this is correct, a distance of one or two miles is all that separated the encampment of the Israelites and Jericho. Archeological evidence indicates that ancient Jericho occupied about eight or nine acres of land and thus would have had a width of about an eighth of a mile and circumference of less than a half mile. It is likely the Israelites kept a minimum of 100 yards from the city's wall to avoid the archer's arrow. This translates into approximately a three-fourths-mile route to encircle the entire city, or about a twenty-minute walk. Thus, it is estimated that on the seventh day the Hebrew army walked between seven and ten miles (or between three and four hours) before shouting and engaging the enemy.

Although each day's proceedings started early in the morning (v. 12), we know the Israelites began their final journey to Jericho on the seventh day at dawn. Walking to the city and around it seven times while carrying weapons must have been tiring, but that was the point. The Lord wanted the people not to rely on their physical strength to conquer the enemy, but rather His. Paul explains why the Lord chooses to work this way to accomplish the spectacular:

But God has chosen the foolish things of the world to put to shame the wise, and God has chosen the weak things of the world to put to shame the things which are mighty; and the base things of the world and the things which are despised God has chosen, and the things which are not, to bring to nothing the things that are, that no flesh should glory in His presence (1 Cor. 1:26-30).

The method that God used to capture Jericho is not reasonable; it doesn't make sense to the logical mind. Yet, this very fact would indeed prove that the walls came down in an unnatural way and that only God could be responsible for it. He would therefore get all the glory for the achievement. This would serve to keep His people humble and to incite fear in the Canaanites. Indeed, the Israelites would learn that the land was a gift from God to be received by faith, not to be conquered through human effort.

Is there any archaeological evidence which would uphold the accuracy of the biblical account of Jericho's fall? Archeologist Kathleen Kenyon confirms the utter devastation of Jericho in her excavation report: *"The destruction was complete. Walls and floors were blackened or reddened by fire, and every room was filled with fallen bricks, timbers, and household utensils; in most rooms the fallen debris was heavily burnt."*[2] She also noted that piles of mud were found at the base of the outer retaining walls (as described previously). Apparently, the outer wall tumbled down the embankment to the base of the outer wall, causing it to collapse also. The resulting debris poured over the outer retaining wall which held back an earthen barrier, which also formed the foundation of the outer wall of the city. In time these bricks dissolved and formed the deposit of mud at the base of the lower outer wall. The debris field just described would have allowed the Israelites to climb straight up into the city as the biblical account declares.

Conquest and the Life of Rest

A leading archaeologist on Jericho is Dr. Bryant Wood. He reviewed Kathleen Kenyon's findings and subsequent evidence from later Jericho digs and supplies the following summary points relating archeology to the scriptural references:

- At the time of the Israelite Conquest, Jericho was heavily fortified, as the Bible implies (Josh. 2:5, 15).
- Piles of mud bricks from the collapsed city wall were found at the base of the tell, verifying that "the wall fell beneath itself" (Josh. 6:20).
- An earthen embankment around the city required the fighters to go "up into the city" (Josh. 6:20).
- Houses were built against a portion of the city wall that did not collapse [a portion of the north wall was found intact], verifying that Rahab's house was built against the city wall (Josh 2:15), and that her house was spared (Josh. 2:14-21; 6:22-23).
- A layer of ash 3-feet thick with burned timbers and debris demonstrates that the Israelites "burned the whole city and everything in it" (Josh. 6:24).
- The destruction occurred at the end of the 15th century BC, precisely the time of the Conquest of Canaan according to the internal chronology of the Bible (I Kgs. 6:1; Judg. 11:26; I Chron. 6:33-37). Many large jars full of charred grain were found in the destroyed buildings. This is a very rare find since, because of its value; grain was normally plundered from a vanquished city. The large amount of grain at Jericho indicates:
  — The harvest had just been taken in (Josh. 2:6; 3:15).
  — The siege was short (seven days, Josh. 6:15).
  — The Israelites did not plunder the city (Josh. 6:18).[3]

Wood's research shows that archaeological evidence matches perfectly with the biblical account of the walls collapsing in Joshua 6. Kathleen Kenyon's excavations of the 1950s had already concluded that the walls of the city had not decayed over time, but rather suffered a massive collapse without rebuilding. After evaluating Kenyon's work and other information, *Time* magazine reported Dr. Wood's conclusion: "The city's walls could have come tumbling down at just the right time to match the biblical account. ... It looks to me as though the biblical stories are correct."[4]

Truth is truth – truth cannot contradict itself; whether it is recorded in Scripture or buried deep in the ground. Archeological evidence has confirmed that ancient Jericho was violently destroyed and then burned. God's Word has wonderfully withstood the test of time and has again been proven trustworthy.

Meditation

>What is the world to me, with all its vaunted pleasure
>When Thou, and Thou alone, Lord Jesus, art my Treasure!
>Thou only, dearest Lord, my soul's Delight shalt be;
>Thou art my Peace, my Rest – What is the world to me?
>
>The world seeks after wealth and all that Mammon offers,
>Yet never is content though gold should fill its coffers.
>I have a higher good, content with it I'll be:
>My Jesus is my Wealth – What is the world to me?
>
>— Georg M. Pfefferkorn

Utter Devastation
Joshua 6:21-27

The narrative records that the Hebrews *"utterly destroyed all that was within the city"* (v. 21) and that apart from the precious metals they *"burned the city with fire, and all that was in it"* (v. 24). Why did Jehovah command that Jericho be completely obliterated? Jericho was the initial city the Israelites would confront and thus a representative of the entire land, which was thoroughly pagan. Thus, Jericho became a symbol of the world, a society apart from Jehovah, and He didn't want His people to have any part of it. Accordingly, not only were Jericho's inhabitants to be wiped out, but all the spoil of the city was to be destroyed (animals, money, clothing, household goods, etc.). Only the gold, silver, bronze, and iron were to be gathered and stored in the Lord's treasury until refining fires could remake the metals into something useful for the Lord (v. 19). Jericho was the first-fruits of their conquering the Land, and the first–fruits always belong to the Lord alone.

As previously mentioned, both archeological evidence and the biblical narrative indicate the Israelites were obedient: they utterly destroyed the people and animals of the city (v. 21) and then burned the city and its spoil, except for the precious metals which were brought before the Lord (v. 24). Only Rahab and her family escaped the total annihilation of Jericho's population.

Although the battle was a complete success, we learn in the next chapter that not all the spoil was destroyed. The spectacular spoils of Jericho successfully tempted Achan to covertly keep two hundred shekels of silver, a wedge of gold, and a Babylonian garment. The gold and silver was the Lord's and the garment should have been burned. His secret sin would tragically affect the entire nation, just as worldliness in believers presently affects the Church negatively.

Worldliness is any sphere in which the Lord Jesus is excluded. The Lord told His disciples the night before He was crucified, *"If the world hates you, you know that it hated Me before it hated you. If you were of* the world, the world would love its own. Yet because you are not of the world, but I chose you out of the world, therefore the world hates you" (John 15:18-19). Because the disciples loved the Lord, they too would experience the world's hatred of Christ through persecution and most in martyrdom.

It is impossible to love the Lord as we should and also adore a satanic system which openly rejects Him. Thus, James likened worldliness to the sin of spiritual adultery: *"Adulterers and adulteresses! Do you not know that friendship with the world is enmity with God? Whoever therefore wants to be a friend of the world makes himself an enemy of God"* (Jas. 4:4). Worldliness is the love of passing things, and things have no eternal value except in how they are used to please God. Worldliness opposes God, and God hates it.

This is why the world generally tolerates religion, but stands in opposition to Jesus Christ and His message. It is why Christ is excluded from conversations, education, professional realms, etc., while it is permissible to speak about any of the world's religions. This is all Satan's doing; he is behind the scenes controlling the various systems of the world, and he despises Christ and those who take His name. Paul properly identifies Satan as *"the god of this age"* (2 Cor. 4:4) and *"the prince of the power of the air"* (Eph. 2:2). The Lord Jesus says on three different occasions that Satan is *"the prince of this world."* The world is Satan's delegated domain, but he must function within the boundaries which God allows.

Worldliness, then, is a system of thinking which is in direct opposition to the teachings of Christ. Erwin Lutzer puts the matter this way: "Worldliness is excluding God from our lives and, therefore, consciously or unconsciously accepting the values of a man-centered society;" he goes on to explain the world's twisted value system: "Worldliness is not only doing what is forbidden but also wishing it were possible to do it. One of its distinctives is mental slavery to illegitimate pleasure. Worldliness twists values by rearranging their price tags."[1] Often our flesh will try to justify the "price tag" of sin, or something that is questionably permissible, while our inner man is sounding the Philippians 4:8 alarm to enjoin us to pursue the best, God-honoring course of action.

Jericho pictures the world and its influences; it was not built in a day, but brick by brick through repetitive action. In the same way, believers erect strongholds in their minds through unchecked lusting and repeatedly giving in to temptation. In time, believers can become imprisoned by the walls of Jericho which they themselves have constructed. At such times we need a supernatural work of God's grace in our lives to bring down the walls and deliver us from physical addictions, emotional bondage, and mental mastery. Paul tells us the means of pulling down such strongholds:

> *For though we walk in the flesh, we do not war according to the flesh. For the weapons of our warfare are not carnal but mighty in God for pulling down strongholds, casting down arguments and every high thing that exalts itself against the knowledge of God, bringing every thought into captivity to the obedience of Christ* (2 Cor. 10:3-5).

Though Paul is speaking to the Corinthians about the threat of being mastered by false teachers, the provision of deliverance he mentions has broader ramifications. Mental strongholds cannot be pulled down by psychological fixes that ignore the spiritual implications of mastery. Ananias became the target of satanic obsession in Acts 5 because of an apparent stronghold of greed and pride that had been built upon in his mind. He responded in the flesh to satanic obsession (the injection of a thought into his mind) in the flesh, and thus lied to the apostles and the Holy Spirit.

A mental stronghold in a believer's mind is much like a spinning merry-go-round, where the circular motion represents the built-up energy of an unconfessed bent. Though Satan does not have the energy to start the merry-go-round spinning (we supply that with un-Christ-like thinking), he can keep it (the stronghold) whirling by suggestions much like a child on the playground continues to grab and pull the bars of the merry-go-round to maintain rotation. However, a child on the playground equipment who drags his or her feet illustrates when the believer resists by renewing his or her mind; the merry-go-round slowly stops until Satan realizes his efforts are futile and departs. Just as the mental stronghold took time to establish, it also requires time to tear down, through repeated obedience to God and resistance of the devil.

John highlights this wonderful principle of deliverance in his first epistle: *"For whatever is born of God overcomes the world. And this is the victory that has overcome the world – our faith. Who is he who overcomes the world, but he who believes that Jesus is the Son of God?"* (1 Jn. 5:4-5). The world will readily supply the bricks and mortar to erect our mental Jerichos, but we are the ones who place the bricks of compromise and spread out the mortar of carnality. Through repeated sensuous reasoning and engagement in deeds of the flesh, the evil stronghold gains strength in our minds. The solution is before us. In faith the Israelites daily marched around Jericho until God miraculously delivered the city into their hands. Jericho did not collapse through carnal weapons of war, but in divine response to the faith of the Israelites as demonstrated through repeated obedience to God's Word. This is the pathway to deliverance from worldliness and to living the sanctified life.

God's message has always been the same to His covenant people concerning the ungodliness of the world: *"[I will] bring them up out of that land"* (Ex. 3:8), *"come unto Me"* (Ex. 32:26), and *"separate yourselves"* (Num. 16:21). The Lord said to His disciples, *"I have chosen you out of the world, therefore the world hates you"* (John 15:19). The cross of Christ has carved out of the world a group of people Christ calls His own. These compose the Church, literally the "called-out company." Accordingly, the Church is consecrated to Him and is to ignore worldly philosophies (Col. 2:8); as a result, the world hates godliness, and God hates worldliness in the believer's life (Jas. 4:4).

The believer must counterbalance the call to holy separation with the call of the Great Commission – *"Go you, therefore, and teach all nations..."* (Matt. 28:19). Where is the symmetry between the Lord's commands to "separate" from the world and to "go" into the world? It is being in the world, but not of the world. A ship is designed to operate in water, but when water floods into the ship, it ceases to behave as intended – it sinks. It is the same with the believer's vessel. It is designed to be in the world as a testimony for God, but when the world gets into the Christian's life – he or she is sunk. The children of darkness are then quite eager to make an open spectacle of the fallen comrade who is thus a "castaway" in Christian service (1 Cor. 9:27). Though failures are not final with God, the consequences to a Christian's testimony can be so devastating that recovery to full ministry is nearly impossible.

Scripture, likewise, speaks of two contrasting means that call the believer's heart out of the world. The first is to set one's mind on things above, and the second is to come to realize that the things of the earth are temporary and shakable. As the writer of Hebrews reminds us, in a coming day, all that is not of the Lord will be removed: *"... removing of those things that are shaken, as of things that are made, that those things which cannot be shaken may remain. Wherefore, we receiving a kingdom which cannot be moved, let us have grace, whereby we may serve God acceptably with reverence and godly fear; for our God is a consuming fire"* (Heb. 12:27-29). The world is nasty and temporal, but heaven is wonderful and eternal. This is why Jehovah demanded that the spoils of Jericho (excluding the metals which could be refined for His use) be utterly destroyed – He wanted His people to be satisfied, not with worldly trinkets, but with Himself.

The Israelites, especially Achan, would learn the hard way the consequences of valuing the trifles of Jericho, which God deemed "accursed" (v. 18), over His inexhaustible provisions. The Hebrew word *cherem* translated "accursed" (the supplied word "things" is implied) literally means "dedicated to be utterly destroyed." It is translated twice as "devoted" in Leviticus 27:28: *"Nevertheless no **devoted** offering that a man may devote to the Lord of all that he has, both man and beast, or the field of his possession, shall be sold or redeemed; every **devoted** offering is most holy to the Lord"* (emphasis added). The *cherem* things were solely the Lord's and were destined for destruction by fire; even the metals would later be melted, refined, and reformed by fire. While the Jews were tasked with this activity, Jehovah would also labor to refine His covenant people, a matter that would require much time and patience.

However, on this particular day, two great victories could be celebrated. First, Jericho had fallen because the Israelites obeyed Jehovah's instructions explicitly. Second, Rahab and her family were delivered from the slaughter because they demonstrated faith by completely obeying the instructions of the spies, who were Jehovah's emissaries. Faith, obedience, and God's blessings walk together hand in hand.

Because of the fear of Jehovah and her faith in Him alone for salvation, Rahab became part of the nation of Israel (v. 25). In Jericho, she was an immoral woman entrenched in paganism, but after being inducted into God's covenant family she was honored by being included in the genealogy of Christ. Salmon of the tribe of Judah took Rahab as his wife (Matt. 1:5). By grace through faith she had been saved from destruction and given a new identity and enriched life to enjoy as an Israelite.

The chapter concludes with two important statements. First, a curse was placed on the ruins of the city by Joshua: any man attempting to fortify Jericho would lose his oldest son when the foundation was laid and if the construction continued his youngest son would die when the gates were set in place. That curse was meant to keep the Benjamites from refortifying Jericho after they settled in that region. It was not until the reign of evil King Ahab over apostate Israel that Hiel the Bethelite attempted to rebuild the walls of Jericho. It cost him the lives of his two sons Abiram and Segub (1 Kgs. 16:34). Although the Jews had dwelt in the area of Jericho before this time, Hiel made the first attempt to restore Jericho as a walled city. No doubt the direct fulfillment of Joshua's five-hundred-year-old curse served as a warning to Ahab that rebellion against God's revealed Word would not be tolerated – stern judgment would come.

In the last statement of the chapter we learn that God magnified His appointed leader Joshua, not only among the Israelites, but also among all the inhabitants of their promised inheritance (v. 27). Unfortunately, the great victory over Jericho (picturing the world) in Joshua 6 would be ruined by a new enemy in Joshua 7, one that caught the Israelites completely by surprise.

Meditation

The world wants service, but Christ says humble yourself and serve others.

The world says save your life, but the Lord says lose your life to gain one worth living.

The world exclaims "live for the moment," but Christians are to live for eternity.

The world says live for self, but the Lord says die to self.

The world is into power, but the Lord uses weak things to confound the mighty.

The world permits greed to rule distribution, but Christians are to give according to need.

The world says acquire wealth, but God says do not seek to be rich.

The world uses money and power to rule, but Christians are to pray and to use Scripture in love.

The world says retaliate and get even, but the Lord says repay evil with good and be forgiving.

The world uses violence, but Christians are to turn the other cheek.

For They Are Few
Joshua 7:1-10

The first Israelite attack in Canaan had been a complete success: Rahab and her family had been saved from the slaughter and Jericho and its other inhabitants were completely decimated without any Jewish fatalities. The only blemish to this great victory is that one Jew named Achan disobeyed the Lord's prohibition against taking spoil from Jericho. As already discussed, Jericho pictures the world and the Israelites were to be consecrated to the Lord and not the world. They were to be solely dependent on Him for direction and provision, and were not to venture into the world for satisfaction or assistance.

Later in this chapter we are told why Achan disobeyed the Lord and *"took of the accursed thing."* The spoil of Jericho was "devoted" to the Lord; it was not for personal benefit. Achan succumbed to lusting and stole what was the Lord's. His trespass was a secret sin which kindled the Lord's anger (v. 1). It is for this reason the chapter unfortunately begins with the conjunction "but" – the victory at Jericho and the defeat at Ai were connected by Achan's sin. It is often true for us that after relishing a great victory for the Lord, one unconfessed sin ushers in the agony of defeat in our next confrontation with the enemy.

Joshua did not know they would not have the Lord's help in attacking Bethel and Ai, two cities directly west of Jericho. In the conquest of Jericho, Jehovah had given specific instructions to Joshua which were obeyed and led to astounding victory. Yet, Joshua did not seek counsel from the Lord, nor did the Lord provide any, before the next battle. This should have been a warning sign to Joshua that something was wrong. Should he not have wondered why the Lord was silent, since He had been so forthright with instructions concerning Jericho? The Lord was grieved by Achan's sin and therefore was not in communion with His people; He would not be with them in battle until the sin had been dealt with and restoration had been achieved.

As Joshua had done before the battle of Jericho, he sent spies to do some reconnaissance work around Bethel and Ai (v. 2). It is significant that Joshua sends them from Jericho, the accursed city, rather than returning to Gilgal, the place where God rolled back the reproach of the people. Gilgal was where Joshua had met with the Lord and received his orders. The devastating defeat at Ai will cause Joshua to return to Gilgal, the proper location to seek the mind of the Lord.

The spies brought back a good report and suggested that because Bethel and Ai were smaller cities than Jericho, only two or three thousand soldiers should be sent to take the cities (v. 3). In their estimation, the opposition *"were few"* and did not require the attention of the entire army. If the construction of Ai was at all correlated with the meaning of its name, "a pile of rubble," the fortifications of the city may have also been much less robust than those of Jericho.

Yet, the basis for the spies' conclusion was flawed, for Jericho had not been overthrown by the Israelites; they merely walked around the wall, shouted, and finished off those who survived the ensuing catastrophe. It had been the Captain of the Host who had knocked the walls down and facilitated the victory. Lest we be too judgmental of the Israelites, let us be honest about our own attitudes; the pride of victory has caused the abasement of many fine Christians as well. We boast of the number of our converts, our ministry statistics, the size of our congregations... numbers, numbers, numbers... do we really believe that the Spirit of God is energizing the work? For God to exalt Himself through our service, we must co-labor with Him in purest humility. He will honor those who do so, but chasten those who rob Him of His rightful glory. The fact is, He could more easily do the work without us, but desires to provide us with the opportunity to express love to Him through selfless service.

Joshua heeded the recommendation of his scouts and committed three thousand troops for the battle without consulting the Lord (v. 4). The Israelites were guilty of overestimating their own strength and underestimating the power of their enemy. They thought that one victory would lead to another and thus minimized the threat that Ai actually posed. It is a dangerous business when God's people measure their enemy by the same ruler with which they sized up their own stature. The Israelites would soon be reminded that it was the Lord who made the difference at Jericho, not the number of Jewish troops!

Conquest and the Life of Rest

Whenever the Lord is eerily quiet in the affairs of His people, that should serve as a warning to stop, listen, and reflect. Joshua did not sense that there was anything wrong and acted on his own initiative; consequently, thirty-six Jews died that day while fleeing from a battle that should have never been fought. The Jewish force, which would have been approximately equal in number to that of the enemy, was soundly driven off by the Canaanites (v. 5). The Jews must have been stunned when they realized, too late, that they did not have the same supernatural vitality against Ai that they did at Jericho. Apparently, the Jewish losses all occurred near some stone quarries while they were fleeing the army of Ai. News of the defeat quickly spread through the camp and disheartened the Israelites.

Joshua was a zealous man for the Lord, but not a perfect man. God was molding him as a leader, while at the same time refining and enabling the Jewish nation to experience His power in conflict. After hearing of the loss at Ai, Joshua tore his clothes and he, with the elders, put dust on their heads and fell down before the Ark of the Lord (v. 6). To humbly come before the Lord to inquire about the defeat would have been an appropriate response, but that was not what followed. Instead, Joshua resorted to accusing God of unfaithfulness to His word and of wanting His people to be destroyed by the Amorites (v. 7). He proceeded to tell the Lord, as if He needed the information, that it would have been better for them to have remained on the eastern side of the Jordan than to have their enemies become emboldened by the Israelites' defeat at Ai. He feared they would band together, surround them, and *"cut off our name from the earth"* (v. 9).

Rather than asking the Lord where he and Israel have failed, Joshua expresses regret for what God had done. Joshua falls into the same trap that ensnared the children of Israel in the wilderness – blaming God for their self-made circumstances. Joshua's foremost concern is for Israel and how this failure will damage their reputation and cause them to appear weak among their enemies. Only at the end, does Joshua reason that such a slaughter would certainly cause Jehovah's name to be blasphemed among the nations. This conclusion prompted Joshua to ask the Lord, *"What will You do for Your great name?"* (v. 9). Joshua would soon learn that it was for the sake of His name that He had inflicted His people with such sorrow. H. F. Witherby explains:

God was acting amongst them for the glory of His great Name. Because of His great Name were their defeat and slaughter. What a heart-searching discovery! To all appearances the defeat of God's people denied the greatness of the Name of their God, but God sets His glory above appearances, His Name is greater than His people's successes; His character is bound up in His Name; His army, His Israel, had sinned. To the natural eye, the sight of men stricken by the hand of their God might indeed awaken the question, "Is God among them?" To the spiritual understanding the truth is evident, that the honor of the great Name of the Lord demands in His people purity and humility, cost what it may.[1]

Jehovah's actions demonstrated that He was more concerned about how His people regarded His name in their conduct than about how much respect He received from pagans who had rejected His grace.

Jehovah informed Joshua that He was not the problem; rather sin in the camp had resulted in this unfortunate defeat (vv. 10-11). Before He could again accompany His people in battle, the sin must be addressed. The defeat at Bethel and Ai represent the ill effects which beset God's people when they rely on their own wisdom and means to resolve their difficulties; just as Jericho represented the world, these cities, especially Ai, symbolize the flesh. Joshua had commanded the people in the flesh; his behavior was not Spirit-led, as further evidenced by his pity-party after their defeat. Like Joshua, each of us must learn to recognize this type of behavior for what it is – the control of the flesh nature rather than that of the inner man. The inner man is to be controlled by the Holy Spirit and He is to rule our thinking. In the Christian life there is no temptation or trial too small that can be overcome in our own strength, for at its core our flesh opposes the things of God (Gal. 5:17). All the resolution in the world cannot cause what is pitifully weak (our flesh) to master what originated with the devil (a rebel nature).

For this reason it is important for a believer to remember what God says about his or her flesh nature. Everything God says about the flesh is negative. In the flesh there is *"no good thing"* (Rom. 7:18). The flesh profits *"nothing"* (John 6:63). A Christian is to put *"no confidence"* in the flesh (Phil. 3:3). He is to make *"no provision"* for the flesh (Rom. 13:14). A person who lives for the flesh is living a negative life, as Charles Ryrie observes:

It [the flesh] refers to our disposition to sin and to oppose or omit God in our lives. The flesh is characterized by works that include lusts and passions (Gal. 5:19-24; I Jn. 2:16); it can enslave (Rom. 7:25); and in it is nothing good (Rom. 7:18). Based on this meaning of the word "flesh," to be carnal means to be characterized by things that belong to the unsaved life (Eph. 2:3).[2]

Consequently, Paul reminds us that the flesh wants to do what it knows it should not do: *"For when we were in the flesh, the sinful passions which were aroused by the law were at work in our members to bear fruit to death"* (Rom. 7:5-6). The flesh, governed by the fallen nature, is never satisfied; it wants more than what is reasonable or lawful. Solomon put it this way: *"The eye is not satisfied with seeing, nor the ear filled with hearing"* (Eccl 1:8). Instead of drinking *"a little wine for [one's] stomach's sake"* (1 Tim 5:23), the flesh longs to be drunk with wine (Eph. 5:18). This is because when a person is drunk, the restraining influence of reason is lost and it becomes easier for the flesh to rule the moment.

Instead of eating what is necessary to maintain a fit body, the flesh engages in gluttony (Prov. 23:21, 28:7). Scripture exhorts us to dress modestly to avert flaunting our bodies before others (1 Tim. 2:9; 1 Pet. 3:3), and not to seek to be the center of attention (Luke 14:8), but the flesh wants to be noticed and admired by others. The marriage covenant protects the sexual relationship between a husband and a wife, but unchecked cravings lead to fornication, which is a great offense against God (1 Thess. 4:3; Eph. 5:5) and against one's own body (1 Cor. 6:18).

Paul spoke of a law within his members (Rom. 7:23) which continued to oppose the law of God in his mind (i.e., his understanding of what God demanded of him). He referred to this nature as the law of sin (Rom. 7:25) and he knew it was an abiding evil presence within himself. There is no need to put a pre-conversion or post-conversion tag to Romans 7; an unregenerate person or a believer not walking in the Spirit will both have this same difficulty that Paul describes. As Paul concedes, this ongoing battle could not be won through natural means:

For I know that in me (that is, in my flesh) nothing good dwells; for to will is present with me, but how to perform what is good I do not find. For the good that I will to do, I do not do; but the evil I will not to do, that I practice. Now if I do what I will not to do, it is no longer I who do it, but sin that dwells in me (Rom. 7:18-20).

However, after conversion Christians should be governed, not by the law of sin within them, but rather by the Spirit of God (Rom. 8:13). Moderation and self-control are a testimony to others that God is the One controlling a believer's actions (Phil. 4:5). Apparently, many in the church at Corinth did not have such a testimony because they were being controlled by their lusting flesh. In the opening verses of 1 Corinthians 3 Paul tells them three times that they are *"carnal."* The normal Greek word translated "flesh" in the New Testament is *sarx*, and Paul uses this word as a modifier (*sarkikos*) to describe their carnal behavior – they were "fleshly." Their flesh was governing their behavior within the assembly and as a result the testimony of the church was suffering.

In summary, though "the flesh" sometimes refers to the human body, it is applied especially in the New Testament Epistles to refer to the fallen, independent nature which allows sin its opportunity within us. Paul states that through the fall of Adam, sin and spiritual death entered the world (Rom. 5:12). Every individual coming from Adam's line is born with Adam's inherited fallen nature (Ps. 51:5, 58:3); that is, we are born sinners and separated from God. This is why John states that those who reject Christ's offer for salvation are already condemned (John 3:19); we are all born in that spiritual condition. John further explains that the *"lusts of the flesh"* within us are not found in God, but are of the world – a system apart from God and under Satan's delegated control (1 Jn. 2:16).

Thankfully, God's work of sanctification begins in the believer's life immediately after he or she answers the call of salvation. God begins to fashion the new believer into a holy vessel and each believer is exhorted to cooperate in the working out of what God is working into his or her life (1 Thess. 5:23; Heb. 13:21). All believers will ultimately be conformed to the moral image of Christ (Rom. 8:29); there is no human choice of involvement in that aspect of sanctification – it is God's will and power that accomplishes this. Yet, there is an ongoing call to each believer to not resist God's working in his or her life, but instead to yield to it by surrendering to Him. God promises to chasten those who choose not to submit to Him in order that they may become broken in disposition before Him and experience sanctification (Heb. 12:6). Consequently, sanctification in a practical sense is happening to every believer, but some are more serious about it than others and, accordingly, will reap the greater blessing of being further refined here and now. The limiting factor in this process is how much we allow our flesh to stand in the way of our progress onward to Christ-likeness.

Joshua and Achan allowed their flesh to control their decision-making. As a result, the first armed conflict by the Israelites against the enemy was a complete disaster, thus proving that there would be no allowance for self-confidence and coveting in the Lord's army. Achan's coveting is discussed in the latter portion of the chapter. Joshua did not consult the Lord and he reasoned that the battle at Jericho was won so easily that only a few Jewish soldiers were required to defeat the cities of Bethel and Ai. He learned that harboring secret sins and being ruled by the flesh have devastating consequences in warfare, a matter we also know all too well. To be successful soldiers of the cross we must adopt a *no sin* and *no self-estimation* mentality in spiritual warfare – for without the Lord we can do nothing!

Meditation

The following true story from 1890 illustrates that we are foolish to think we can control our flesh nature, which is prone to sin – its deeds must be mortified through the power of the Holy Spirit:

> A noted wild beast tamer gave a superb performance in London. As a closing act, he introduced a boa constrictor, 35 feet long, which he handled for 25 years (beginning when it was just two or three years old), and supposed it to be harmless. The curtain rose on an Indian woodland scene. A rustling noise is heard and a huge serpent is seen winding its way through the undergrowth. It stops. Its head is erect. Its bright eyes sparkle. Its whole body seems animated. A man emerged from the heavy foliage. Their eyes meet. The serpent quails before the man. Man is victor.
>
> Under the man's signals and guidance, the serpent performs a series of frightening feats. At another signal, it slowly approaches the man and begins to coil its heavy foils around him. Higher and higher they rise, until man and serpent seem blended into one. Its hideous head is reared above the man. The man gives a little scream and the audience unites in a thunderous applause, but it freezes upon their lips. The trainer's scream was a wail of death agony. Those cold, slimy folds had embraced him for the last time. They had crushed the life out of him. The horror stricken audience heard bone after bone cracked. Man's plaything had become his master.[3]

Sin in the Camp
Joshua 7:10-18

The mighty fortress of Jericho had fallen without a single Jewish casualty, but thirty-six men had died in the bungled attack on the smaller city of Ai (v. 5). As previously described, this was distressing news to Joshua who tore his clothes and fell on his face before the Ark of the Lord. Joshua was joined by the elders and all put dust on their heads; their defeat had sent them to God where they laid themselves low. They were apparently before the Lord for some time, as He did not answer Joshua's bewildering questions and unjust insinuations until evening (v. 6). When God did speak to admonish Joshua, it becomes clear that whining is never appropriate when addressing the One who knows all, sees all, and is in control of all things:

> *Get up! Why do you lie thus on your face? Israel has sinned, and they have also transgressed My covenant which I commanded them. For they have even taken some of the accursed things, and have both stolen and deceived; and they have also put it among their own stuff. Therefore the children of Israel could not stand before their enemies, but turned their backs before their enemies, because they have become doomed to destruction. Neither will I be with you anymore, unless you destroy the accursed from among you. Get up, sanctify the people, and say, "Sanctify yourselves for tomorrow, because thus says the Lord God of Israel: There is an accursed thing in your midst, O Israel; you cannot stand before your enemies until you take away the accursed thing from among you"* (Josh. 7:10-14).

We read in verse 1 that *"the children of Israel committed a trespass in the accursed thing ... and the anger of the Lord was kindled against the children of Israel."* From God's perspective, the sin of one man was the sin of all Israel. H. L. Rossier explains why there are communal repercussions for sin:

> The people might have said: Does that concern us? How could we have known about a hidden thing, and not having known it, how are we responsible? To all that we reply, that God always has the unity of His people before His eyes. He considers individuals as members of one whole, and responsible the one for the other. The suffering and sin of one is the suffering and sin of all, and if it is thus with Israel, how much more so with us, the Church of God, one body united by the Holy Spirit to the Head which is in heaven.[1]

Jehovah informed Joshua that someone in the camp had stolen from the Lord and kept the accursed things which should have been burned (i.e., the garment Achan took ought to have burned with Jericho and the gold and silver should have been set aside to later be refined by fire for God's use). Furthermore, the culprit was continuing to hide his sin by deceiving others in the matter. This record shows that the eye of the Lord was on each and every soldier in His army. Though there were tens of thousands of Hebrews involved in the conflict, the Lord knew all about the one man who took what did not pertain to him. The Lord knew what his hand had clutched, where he hid it, and how his deceitful heart sought to keep the matter a secret.

As the writer of Hebrews announces, it just is not possible to hide anything from the Lord: *"There is no creature hidden from His sight, but all things are naked and open to the eyes of Him to whom we must give account"* (Heb. 4:13). The Lord is omniscient and it is the self-righteous man who thinks he can avoid being seen, being caught, being judged for his sin (Rom. 2:1-4). No one can hide from the Lord or escape His jurisdiction, *"For the eyes of the Lord run to and fro throughout the whole earth, to show Himself strong on behalf of those whose heart is loyal to Him"* (2 Chron. 16:9). Let us therefore be found among this loyal company, rather than hiding in the tent of Achan; the ramifications of divine judgment totally eclipse any temporary satisfaction of sin! As H. F. Witherby explains, an offended God permitted the Israelites to learn this painful lesson at Ai:

> God never alters His principles of government because of His ways of grace. Israel was flushed with the pride of success; therefore He allowed them to find out, by means of their defeat, that He was angry with them, sin being in their midst. They had committed a trespass; they had "deceived a deceit;" they had "sinned," and "dissembled also." Achan, the troubler, was representative of the people; the sin of

one was that of all; the corporate body was affected by the guilt of the unit. Now, as a matter of fact, Christians usually discover the presence of sin among them, which God hates, by the result of His chastening, and too seldom discern it as dear children in His presence, under the gentle eye of His love.[2]

O God, please grant us the spiritual discernment to rightly recognize when the abiding presence of Your dear Son has been lost by sin. Might we continually ponder His warning to us: *"Abide in Me, and I in you. As the branch cannot bear fruit of itself, unless it abides in the vine, neither can you, unless you abide in Me. I am the vine, you are the branches. He who abides in Me, and I in him, bears much fruit; for without Me you can do nothing"* (John 15:4-5). Dear Lord, may Your face shine upon us, and may Your Spirit grieve our hearts when any ill cloud passes between us.

The Lord promised that He would not be with Joshua in battle until the guilty was discovered and judged, and the accursed things removed from the presence of His people (v. 12). The penalty for the offense was to be severe; not only the accursed things, but also the offender and all that pertained to him were to be burned. Moses made it clear that if anyone stole that which had been "devoted" to the Lord, that man would become "devoted" or "accursed" himself, which meant he must be put to death (Deut. 7:26). Achan, by stealing the accursed things became accursed himself. His unchecked lusting destroyed him. This narrative is a good reminder to us that sin destroys and corrupts from the inside. James Vernon McGee relates another example of the same truth:

> An individual can be destroyed from the inside. Alexander the Great was probably the greatest military genius who has moved armies across the pages of history. There has been no one like him. Before the age of thirty-five he had conquered the world, but he died a drunkard. He had conquered the world, but he could not conquer Alexander the Great. There was an enemy within that destroyed him.[3]

The harsh consequences of Achan's sin proved that there is no deception, no lie, and no thief that is compatible with God's character: *"God is light, and in Him is no darkness at all"* (1 Jn. 1:5). The Lord will not, in fact cannot, have any part in our sin. John continues: *"If we say that we have fellowship with Him, and walk in darkness, we lie and do not practice the truth. But if we walk in the light as He is in the light, we have fellowship with one another, and the blood of Jesus Christ His Son cleanses us from all sin"* (1 Jn. 1:6-7). If we want to enjoy communion with God, we must choose the lighted pathway of holiness to reverently venture into the wonders of His presence. He cannot defy His pure character by entering the darkness of sin when we choose to reside there – we must through repentance come out and stand again in the light of His righteousness.

Israel had been victorious at Jericho, a picture of the world, but the people would need to use a different tactic in order to defeat the flesh, as symbolized in Ai. How does Ai represent our flesh nature? First, the strategy for conquering Ai was self-originating; Joshua did not consult Jehovah for counsel. Second, the spies underestimated the strength of the enemy and overestimated the Israelites' ability to overcome them. Third, if Joshua had sought the Lord before the battle of Ai, certainly he would have heard Israel had an *"accursed thing"* among them. Likewise, the flesh naturally boasts of its strength, generally underestimates the pull of sin, and then in willful ignorance pursues its own way without the Lord (Isa. 53:6). While it is true that Achan's sin angered the Lord, the entire camp suffered because His people had attempted to do His work without Him – this is what the flesh is prone to do.

The Israelites wanted to know who in their camp had sinned in order to ensure Jehovah's presence in future battles, so they all obeyed the command to sanctify themselves. To stand before the Lord meant they would have to be set apart from all the defiling influences of the world and the human reasoning of the flesh. The entire nation sought to be purged of the offender, the one who had insulted their God and who had thus compromised all of them in battle.

Joshua was quite eager to rid Israel of that which offended Jehovah, so he began the investigation early the next morning. Phineas, the High Priest, used the Urim and Thummim held within the priestly breastplate to identify the guilty party as the people passed before him and Joshua (Ex. 28:30). Representatives from each tribe, then from each clan of the tribe selected, then from each family of the clan selected, and then finally the individual himself would be identified. The tribe of Judah was chosen, then the Zerahites, then the family of Zabdi, until lastly Achan the son of Carmi was found. The Lord already knew about Achan's sin, but now everyone knew of it and would agree with God concerning its judgment. *"We know that the judgment of God is according to truth against those who practice such things. ... But in accordance with your hardness and your impenitent heart you are treasuring up for yourself wrath in the day of wrath and revelation of the righteous judgment of God, who 'will render to each one according to his deeds'"* (Rom. 2:2, 6-7). The day of divine revelation and vindication had arrived for Achan.

Meditation

> There is nothing in common between the life of heaven and that of the world. It is not a question of prohibition as to using this or that, but of having altogether different tastes, desires, and joys. It is on this account that people imagine Christians are sad, for we do not enjoy the same things: The world does not know our joys; no unrenewed person can comprehend what renders a Christian happy.
>
> — J. N. Darby

Make Confession
Joshua 7:19-26

Joshua implored Achan, having been identified as the offender by Jehovah, to confess his tresspass and not to hide it any longer: *"My son, I beg you, give glory to the Lord God of Israel, and make confession to Him, and tell me now what you have done; do not hide it from me"* (v. 19). Joshua's appeal reminded Achan that God is always glorified when the truth is declared. Achan did choose to glorify God by confessing his sin, rather than denying that God's finger was pointing at him. This must have been a relief to Achan, who had been pretending to be innocent, but secretly was, no doubt, deeply grieved that he had caused the deaths of his fellow brethren.

For Achan to outwardly participate in the destruction of Canaan's stronghold Jericho, which symbolized the world, but then covertly adore its wares in the place God resided with His people was utter hypocrisy. It is a sin easy to commit today. It is deceitful to be outspoken for Christ in Jericho, but then secretly strut about in Babylonian attire in our own homes. If we covet after, engage in, or glorify ourselves with those things upon which God has passed the sentence of fire, are we any different than Achan? The greater our profession of holiness, the more accountable we are to God to uphold the moral excellence of His Son in daily living. God's severe judgment of Achan proves that He is not fooled by superficial consecration.

Achan admitted he sinned against the Lord by taking a beautiful Babylonian garment, two hundred shekels of silver, and a wedge of gold weighing fifty shekels from Jericho (vv. 20-21). Notice the progress of his sin to its full development: Achan "saw;" he "coveted;" and he "took." These were the same three steps leading to death that Eve made when she ate the forbidden fruit in Eden (Gen. 1:6), and the same David tread when he stole Bathsheba, Uriah's wife (2 Sam. 11:1-4). Achan, Eve, and David sinned for the same reason you and I do today; we first think about, then lust after, and then do what is outside the will of God.

Achan lusted for what God said he could not have, and then entered into sin. James puts the matter this way: *"But each one is tempted when he is drawn away by his own desires and enticed. Then, when desire has conceived, it gives birth to sin; and sin, when it is full-grown, brings forth death"* (Jas. 1:14-15). Our bodies are equipped with all kinds of mechanisms to keep us healthy and to procreate, but when we lust for what is beyond the order God has put in place to guide such behaviors, we enter into sin and take the first step towards death – separation from the Lord. This Achan did. There is an insanity to sin as proven by Achan's decision process: where could he wear that fancy Babylonian garment anyway? In reality, he took something he was not supposed to have and which had no practical use.

The garment (perhaps adorned with colorful embroidery work) speaks of self-gratification and self-glorification, while the silver and gold represent man's desire for self-advancement and self-sufficiency. The common denominator is "self." These accursed things were concealed in the ground under the place Achan pitched his tent (v. 21). Joshua sent messengers to investigate the matter and they found all the objects that Achan had described (v. 22). These were set before the Lord and judgment was then pronounced (v. 23).

It was a somber day in the history of Israel and one not soon to be forgotten. Joshua and the children of Israel took Achan, his family, all his belongings, and his animals to the Valley of Achor, or literally "the Valley of Trouble" (v. 24). There representatives from the entire nation stoned the people, and the animals were killed. The gold and silver that Achan stole were buried with him also. Although it was the Lord's, He had no interest in it. The sin was a national sin and was therefore dealt with at a national level; the entire judicial process would serve as a strong warning to all the Israelites as to the consequences of disobedience.

Afterwards everything (including what Achan had wrongly taken from Jericho) was burnt and a huge pile of stones were raised up over what remained as a public testimony to the consequence of sin in the camp (vv. 25-26). By Law, the accursed (devoted) things were the Lord's and destined to be burned – and so they were. Let us remember that God does not reveal an evil among us which He does not require us to remove. The people did so, and the action of corporate discipline on the offender satisfied the Lord and His anger was stayed.

Conquest and the Life of Rest

To us the consequences may seem harsh, for even Achan's children were judged because of their father's sin. However, it is not likely that Achan's family was completely innocent, for surely they knew of what their father was hiding among them and consented to the deception. The rebellious behavior of their family head had influenced the entire family to reject the revealed will of God in the matter. Given the offense and the consequence (the death of thirty-six men), a stern penalty was called for – one that would have a sobering effect on the nation for some time to come. A similar situation occurred in the early days of the Church Age, which when judged also had a purifying effect on God's people. Ananias and Sapphira were struck dead for lying to the Holy Spirit regarding the price they had sold their property for (Acts 5:1-10). The Church was promptly put into remembrance and fear of God's holiness (Acts 5:11). Remembering the holiness of God and His stern judgment of sin should deter His people from putting their hands on what is forbidden.

The narrative of Acts 5 confirms to us that the sin of one member in the Church affects the whole body, for each believer is vitally connected to Christ and to each other in Him. Because of this intimate spiritual tie, F. B. Meyer reminds us that our conduct affects the entire Church today and for some time to come, just as Achan's sin brought tragedy and a lasting impact to the entire Jewish nation:

> One Israelite only had trespassed, and yet it is said, *"The children of Israel* committed a trespass in the devoted thing." Not one of us stands alone; we cannot sin without insensibly affecting the spiritual condition of all our fellows. We cannot grow cold without lowering the temperature of all contiguous hearts. We cannot pass upward without lifting others.[1]

Paul acknowledges this mysterious truth of Church body-life: *"For none of us lives to himself, and no one dies to himself"* (Rom. 14:7); *"And if one member suffers, all the members suffer with it; or if one member is honored, all the members rejoice with it"* (1 Cor. 12:26). Therefore, let us not think, as Achan did, that our personal sins do not have ramifications for others. The choices we make today affect our family members, our local churches, and indeed all the brethren.

Thus, the narrative of Joshua 7 upholds the New Testament teaching that corporate discipline of an erring believer is at times necessary and justified (1 Cor. 5). When a believer continues in willful sin, he or she should be rebuked (1 Tim. 5:20; 2 Tim. 4:2; Tit. 3:10-11). The Lord Jesus supplies an example of this corrective approach in His dealings with the church at Laodicea: *"As many as I love, I rebuke and chasten: be zealous therefore, and repent"* (Rev. 3:19). This church deserved the rebuke of the Lord: their affection for the Lord and their love for their fellow man were lukewarm. A rebuke is a stern warning to the offending party to repent; it should carry the threat of punishment for continued wrong behavior. If people, even elders, continue in sin, they must be stopped. Strong measures are warranted. This disgraceful conduct cannot be tolerated in the church. A public statement of rebuke is in order, and the individual's participation in the Lord's Supper and assembly ministry is not allowed.

Just as the Israelites had to sanctify themselves to stand before the Lord, the local assembly should completely avoid those who have been warned but continue to be disorderly (2 Thess. 3:11, 14, 15), divisive (Rom. 16:17), or factious (Titus 3:10-11). *"Cast out the scorner, and contention will leave; yes, strife and reproach shall cease"* (Prov. 22:10). The purpose of this shunning is to help another person see that he or she is out of fellowship with God, and therefore out of fellowship with His people. This action is motivated by love and not pity; that is, we want to do what is best for the unrepentant individual, not what will ease his or her sorrow. If a professing believer continues in sin, having rejected Biblical reproof and correction, he or she should be excommunicated (1 Cor. 5:11-13). This has the effect of delivering the rebellious into the dominion of Satan for buffeting which may possibly end in death (1 Cor. 5:5; 1 Tim. 1:20). This latter distress of the wayward individual will hopefully result in his or her repentance, forgiveness, and restoration with God and His people.

Church discipline should uphold God's honor, be accomplished per His Word, and be administered in love with the goal of repentance and restoration. As in the case of Joshua 7, corporate discipline should not be administered by an individual, but rather by the whole church body (2 Cor. 2:6) after the elders have rendered a just decision. No impartiality can be tolerated; as we have seen, not even Achan's own children were spared from judgment. Even if an elder or a member of his family is in sin, appropriate action must be taken (1 Tim. 5:20; Jas. 2:1). In all such matters, it is good to remember that if it were not for the grace of God, we could do the exact thing for which others are being corrected (Gal. 6:1-2).

Conquest and the Life of Rest

Beside the offense of disobedience, Achan was guilty of snubbing God for worldly trinkets. God suffers heartbreak when His people desert Him and venture into the world to indulge their flesh. Paul reminds believers that they are the espoused bride of the Lord Jesus (Eph. 5:22-25; 2 Cor. 11:2; Rev. 19:9). If believers could understand in only a small degree Christ's redeeming love, they would not commit spiritual adultery by fraternizing with the world. Why? It is because such behavior grieves the Savior. The ideologies of the world oppose God and God opposes them. Gomer's lovers didn't care for Gomer or about the hurt they were inflicting on Hosea; they used and abused Gomer until the thrill of the moment was gone. This was what the prodigal son learned in Luke 15 – the world gladly exchanges what has worth in God's eyes for temporary thrills and cheap trinkets. Without constraint, the world will rob a person of everything that has true value and leave them nothing but guilt and misery.

The believer may choose to sin, but it is God who chooses the consequences of that sin. Paul warned, *"Do we provoke the Lord to jealousy? Are we stronger than He?"* (1 Cor. 10:22). The Lord has no desire to destroy a rebel child of His, but He has promised to chasten those He loves (Heb. 12:6). Whether we will be hurt by or helped by the Lord is our choice. Either with the painful rod or the comforting staff, God will lead His people heavenward. The number of regrets we have after arriving there will depend on how well we walked in step with God throughout the course of our lives.

Another important lesson we can learn from Joshua 7 is that, like Achan, we compound our sin by hiding it. There is a stark difference between true repentance and being sorry for getting caught. Achan's confession does not seem to stem from personal guilt and remorse for offending God, but rather seems to be prompted by the persistent pursuit of authority to find out the truth. It is the same pattern that our first parents exhibited after sinning in Eden; their initial response was to hide from God. Ever since that loathsome event, humanity has been denying God's authority and trying to hide from the associated responsibility.

After Lucifer rebelled against God (Isa. 14:12-15), he injected his own proud and selfish spirit into the world (1 Jn. 2:16). This independent thinking and rebel spirit then caused humanity to fall. Consequently, there are now two authority structures in the world, and they stand completely opposed to one another. God's authority is supreme, while Satan's authority is tolerated within boundaries, until God's purposes have been served. God allows Satan to test man's moral resolve. Believers are to serve God in all things and it is understood that the various authority structures He has placed over us are for the purpose of teaching us to submit to Him. Thus, we honor God by obeying those He has placed in authority over us; compliance is rendered to win, not the esteem of men, but the approval of God (Col. 3:22-23).

The Lord Jesus' example of honoring authority is quite evident in Scripture and serves as an excellent pattern to follow. In all His actions, He did His Father's will (John 5:20), for He could only do the things that pleased His Father (John 8:29). Concerning the Lord's submission to parental authority, Luke informs us that *"He went down with them [His parents], and...was subject unto them"* (Luke 2:51). Until the Lord received new "marching orders," He remained under the God-ordained authority of His parents. This serves as a good example for all to follow. Godly authority is like a funnel; if we remain in proper alignment with it, God's blessings will flow down through that funnel to us. If we rebel against His order, we place ourselves under Satan's authority and lose the communion with and blessings of God – the believer will not be able to please the Lord while under Satan's sway.

Achan listened to the rebel voice within his members and removed himself from the blessing of God's authority. He had been enticed by the world and his carnal appetite responded to it. Joshua had acted in human wisdom apart from the expressed will of God. The lesson to be learned from this chapter is that God takes no pleasure in what is accomplished apart from His will and His power. Paul put the matter this way: *"Because the carnal mind is enmity against God; for it is not subject to the law of God, nor indeed can be. So then, those who are in the flesh cannot please God"* (Rom. 8:7-8). Whether our flesh responds to temptation to stray outside of God's will or presumptuously acts in its own strength and wisdom apart from Him, the result is the same – He is grieved and His chastening hand is invoked and, sadly, all believers are affected by it.

Although Israel learned from this experience and would never suffer another military defeat, Joshua would repeat his error of chapter seven again in chapter nine. The consequences of this mistake would hamper the nation's commitment to follow Jehovah for centuries to come. As Achan and Joshua learned, the wages of sin is death, and to be separated from the goodness of God is very costly.

Conquest and the Life of Rest

Meditation

> He is no fool who gives what he cannot keep to gain what he cannot lose.
>
> — Jim Elliot

> Sin is the dare of God's justice, the rape of His mercy, the jeer of His patience, the slight of His power, and the contempt of His love.
>
> — John Bunyan

Take All the People
Joshua 8:1-11

The Israelites, especially their new leader Joshua, were discouraged after their sound defeat at Ai and the sobering judgment of Achan and his family. Mere days earlier they had triumphantly crossed over the Jordan River into the Promised Land, had expectantly marched around the fortress of Jericho, and then witnessed its destruction. Now that the offense had been dealt with, the Lord was ready to accompany His people again into battle and assist them to lay hold of their inheritance. The Lord first sought to revive the heart of Joshua with a message of reassurance: *"Do not be afraid, nor be dismayed; take all the people of war with you, and arise, go up to Ai. See, I have given into your hand the king of Ai, his people, his city, and his land"* (Josh. 8:1). Donald Campbell notes why this particular message would have renewed Joshua's resolve to resume the conquest of Canaan:

> When Joshua heard God's words of encouragement, his heart quickened, for these were the same words Moses spoke in Kadesh Barnea when he sent out the 12 spies (Deut. 1:21). They were also the words Moses said to Joshua 40 years later when he was turning the reins of the leadership over to the younger man (Deut. 31:8). And Joshua heard them again when God spoke to him just after the death of Moses (Josh. 1:9). Now at this crucial time in Joshua's life it was good to be reminded and reassured that God was ready to lead if Joshua were ready to listen to *His* plan, which he was.[1]

Indeed, Joshua was willing to completely heed God's plan. Because Ai was a smaller city than Jericho, Joshua had previously thought three thousand soldiers would be more than sufficient to conquer it. However, without Jehovah's presence and assistance, Joshua quickly learned that the enemy was formidable, especially when his countrymen were pressing the offensive position. The Lord's ingenious plan for defeating these cities did not include a frontal assault, but rather would involve all the men of war in various roles. Previously, division and loss of power had resulted from self-confidence and unchecked lusting, but unity and consecration had been restored after Achan was judged and Joshua was reproved. Now, God's people would work together as one unit and in full cooperation and association with the Lord. This course of action throughout biblical history has always resulted in miraculous feats being accomplished by the Lord's people for God's exaltation.

For example, Nehemiah realized the necessity of involving all the people in the work of rebuilding the wall about Jerusalem, for the task was enormous. So he sought the cooperation of the people and committed himself to co-labor with them: *"Let us rise up and build"* (Neh. 2:18). Unity of purpose enabled the Lord's people to stand as one with Him and be unconquerable.

Moses also highlighted the importance of unity and working with God: *"How could one chase a thousand, and two put ten thousand to flight, unless their Rock had sold them, and the Lord had surrendered them?"* (Deut. 32:30). God can use one man to defeat a thousand foes, but two men fighting as one with the Lord can defeat ten thousand! Holiness had been restored to the camp after Achan's sin had been judged now; the Lord sought to unify all His people in purpose. Accordingly, the Lord told Joshua, *"Do not be afraid, nor be dismayed; take all the people of war with you, and arise, go up to Ai"* (v. 1). Whether it is to arise and build or to arise and conquer, God's people have greater wherewithal when they work together, rather than as individuals, with the Lord.

The first six chapters of Acts indicate that the early Church was successful in evangelism when there was unity and Christ-mindedness among the disciples. When there were division and factions within the church, their testimony was marred, the Spirit was quenched, and fruitfulness ceased. The lesson for us all is to lay hold of the mind of Christ. This will bring unity to the Church, which will then have only one goal, to *"do all to the glory of God"* (1 Cor. 10:31). On the eve of His suffering, the Lord repeatedly acknowledged in His prayer in John 17 the inseparable link between unity and the display of the glory of God:

> *I do not pray for these alone, but also for those who will believe in Me through their word; that they all may be one, as You, Father, are in Me, and I in You; that they also may be one in Us, that the world may believe that You sent Me. And the glory which You gave Me I have*

given them, that they may be one just as We are one: I in them, and You in Me; that they may be made perfect in one, and that the world may know that You have sent Me, and have loved them as You have loved Me (John 17:20-23).

When the Church is unified, the glory of God is displayed in it for all to see. Peaceful unity among men is not a naturally occurring phenomenon, so when it does transpire the world takes notice. The lost are prompted to consider what they see and by the grace of God some will be won to Christ! It is absolutely necessary for a local assembly to be of one accord before they can properly exhibit Christ to their neighborhoods. If there is disunity in the church, the work of the Holy Spirit is concentrated within the house of God in order to remove the rubble of pride, hypocrisy, willful sin, and doctrinal error. When the flesh-controlled operations of Ai are removed from the local assembly, then Spirit-controlled saints will rise up together and be more than conquerors for the glory of God.

The tactic to take Ai and Bethel was different that the strategy that decimated Jericho, just as it is true that the battle tactic for overcoming the flesh is different than for gaining victory over the world. John declares that those who have been born again overcome the world by faith, as they submit to God's Word: *"For whatever is born of God overcomes the world. And this is the victory that has overcome the world – our faith"* (1 Jn. 5:4). By faith we reject God-denying secular philosophies and human traditions, rather than be ruined by them (Col. 2:8). However, victory over the flesh is achieved through a different means: identifying with Christ in His death and in His life (Rom. 6:1-10), not strengthening the flesh nature by engaging in its deeds (Col. 3:5), and through the power of the Holy Spirit mortifying desires that are outside of God's will for us (Rom. 8:13) and strengthening the inner man (Eph. 3:16). In fact, we have no power over our flesh nature which opposes the things of God; only the Holy Spirit can control this internal "bully" with which we constantly wrestle. James Vernon McGee colorfully puts the matter this way:

> My friend, you and I cannot control the flesh. Only the Spirit of God can do that. The tragedy is that thousands are trying to control and eradicate it in their own strength. You might as well take a gallon of French perfume out to the barnyard, pour it on a pile of manure, and

expect to make it into a sand pile in which your children might play. You cannot improve and control this thing we know as the flesh or the sin nature. God says you cannot. Only the Holy Spirit can control it.[2]

If a believer feeds upon the world's delights, the flesh nature will be strengthened to oppose God, but if the believer feeds on the manna from heaven (i.e., Christ and His Word), the power of the Spirit of God is sufficient to overcome any solicitation to sin (1 Cor. 10:13). Each day's battle is won or lost based upon what nature has been strengthened through the nourishment it has received. As Peter acknowledges, a healthy diet consists of avoiding what will hinder spiritual growth and consuming that which promotes it: *"Beloved, I beg you as sojourners and pilgrims, abstain from fleshly lusts which war against the soul"* (1 Pet. 2:11); *"Therefore, laying aside all malice, all deceit, hypocrisy, envy, and all evil speaking, as newborn babes, desire the pure milk of the word, that you may grow thereby"* (1 Pet. 2:1-2). Physically, we are what we eat, but spiritually speaking, we are what we muse on (Prov. 23:7).

Engaging in behavior motivated by the flesh strengthens the flesh's hold on an individual's mind. However, feeding on the Word of God stimulates spiritual growth within our inner man. Since doing the deeds of the flesh fortifies the flesh to oppose God, these behaviors must be put aside in order to feed on God's Word; a believer cannot feed the flesh and the inner man at the same time. The one the believer chooses to strengthen will determine whether he or she is victorious in Christ or whether disdain is brought upon Christ's name. The motto, then, of the Christian life is that *"in all these things we are more than conquerors through Him that loved us"* (Rom. 8:37).

Just as believers are to confront worldliness and the lusts of their flesh differently, the battle plan used at Jericho would not be effective at Ai. At Jericho, the Lord brought the walls down and the Israelites engaged in a direct assault on the city. However, Joshua was to incorporate their previous failure at Ai as part of the strategy to conquer both Bethel and Ai together. God promised to give Joshua victory if he followed His directions (v. 1). Another marked difference between the battles of Jericho and Ai was that while the inhabitants of Ai were to be slain, the spoils of the cities would be for the people (v. 2). H. L. Rossier observes an important practical application for Christian diligence by contrasting the battles of Jericho and Ai:

With regard to Gilgal and the learning of ourselves, it might seem that when once this point in the soul's history is reached, self ought to be done with, but in reality this is only practically realized in the measure that one *keeps* at Gilgal. How little did the people know themselves after the victory of Jericho! Though God had taken a thousand pains to prove to them that all was of Him in the victory, what self-sufficiency, what forgetfulness they show in attempting to face the enemy without Him! Flight and trouble are the result, and when they resume the offensive, their path becomes difficult, laborious, and full of complications, thus exposing to their view their own weakness, which had been already made apparent to the enemy in their defeat. They have to retrace their steps, forced afresh to the discovery of themselves, but it will now be a lesson learnt through grace with Christ and not with Satan. Notice in Joshua 8 how complicated everything becomes, through not having followed the simple path of faith. The soul, humbled, finds itself once more with God, and His presence with it, but the consequences of a carnal walk remain; and although God can ultimately use these for their blessing, the path has no longer the simplicity of the early days of faith. It is a very simple path, for, to the believer who follows God's guidance in human dependence on His word, victory is assured.[3]

Joshua did adhere to Jehovah's instructions. He involved all the men of war, sending 30,000 of them by night to the west side of Ai to lie in wait for the ambush the next day (vv. 3-8). The main ridge ran just south of Ai, angling northwestward to Bethel. As Ai was slightly below this ridge, these troops could have hidden in the many projecting rock formations existing on the southwestern side of the ridge. Early the following morning Joshua departed from Gilgal with the remaining troops and the elders of Israel and took up a position north of Ai across a valley (vv. 10-11, 13). This was a 12 to 15-mile ascent from Gilgal, so it is not likely that Joshua arrived at the location until mid-afternoon. Joshua then secretly placed 5,000 of these troops between Ai and Bethel (possibly in the deep ravine that lies between these two locations). Bethel was the smaller of the two cities and situated about three miles to the northwest of Ai (v. 12). Although we are not specifically told how this contingency of troops was used, it is assumed that they would deal with any reinforcements sent from Bethel to assist the army of Ai in battle. The Jews would thus ambush the troops coming from Bethel and then return to capture the unguarded city.

Conquest and the Life of Rest

    That night Joshua took his main force south into the valley between their newly established campsite and Ai (v. 13). The king of Ai noticed this movement and mustered together his forces to meet Joshua in battle early the next morning (v. 14). The plan was not to fully engage the enemy, but rather to taunt them into an open battle, faking a retreat in order to draw all the forces out of the cities after them. As we read on, we discover this is exactly what happened. When self-reliance was removed from Joshua's leadership, the Lord was able to accomplish the impossible through him.

Meditation

> There was a day I died, utterly died, died to George Muller, his opinions, preferences, tastes, and will – died to the world, its approval or blame – even of my brethren and friends. Since then I have studied only to show myself approved unto God.
>
> — George Muller

The Ambush
Joshua 8:12-29

It is doubtful that the king of Ai would have committed all his troops to sally out after the Hebrews had not the Canaanites' previous engagement been a triumph. The king of Ai rightly represents the propensity of the flesh to do what is unreasonable and to be enslaved by habit-forming behaviors. All the inhabitants of Ai numbered 12,000, which means it did not likely have an army numbering more than 3,000 able soldiers. According to Numbers 26:51, there were 601,730 Jewish men who were twenty years of age or older who came out of the wilderness, although approximately 97,000 of these adult men (those from the two and a half tribes settling east of the Jordan River) did not enter into Canaan (Num. 26:7-34; Josh. 4:13). This meant that Joshua was commanding an army of more than half a million troops and, as directed by the Lord, he brought all of them to the battlefront (v. 11). Statistically speaking, the army of Ai was out-numbered 168 to 1.

Given the previous spectacular Hebrew victories, which the citizens of Ai knew about, only insane reasoning and pride would have prompted the king of Ai to leave his fortifications and confront such an overwhelming force. As epitomized in this pagan king, the flesh wants what it cannot have, and it does not think reasonably about the consequences of obtaining what it wants. Despite the safe confines of a walled city and being greatly outnumbered, the king of Ai defies all logic and does the idiotic – he orders his army to leave the city. Perhaps he was thinking that he had beaten back the Jews before, so he was sure he could do it again despite the army being 168 times larger than it was on the first encounter.

Besides Ai and its king, the Old Testament employs several other symbols to depict the opposition of the flesh nature against God: Ishmael (or the Ishmaelites) and Esau (or the Amalekites) are prime examples. These types are to assist us in better understanding the flesh's opposition towards God, and how much He loathes it.

Concerning Ishmael, Paul reminds the Galatians of two births in the Old Testament with important spiritual implications, that of Isaac and that of Ishmael. God had promised Abraham and Sarah, Abraham's wife, a natural son after he arrived in Canaan. However, after some ten years with no child, Sarah convinced him to take her handmaiden Hagar as a concubine in order to provide a son for Abraham on her behalf. In a moment of weakness, Abraham obeyed the voice of his wife, rather than trusting the promise of God, and Ishmael was conceived in Hagar through human effort. Genesis 21 records that Sarah later bore Abraham a son and nursed him in her old age, just as God had promised. Paul uses Isaac and Ishmael in Galatians 4 to allegorically depict how one is loosened from fleshly bondage. In that chapter, Paul uses Isaac to represent Christ and Ishmael as a symbol of the flesh:

*For it is written that Abraham had two sons: the one by a bondwoman, the other by a freewoman. But he who was of the bondwoman was **born according to the flesh**, and he of the freewoman through promise, which things are symbolic* (Gal. 4:22-24, emphasis added).

Ishmael represents the ability of the flesh, while Isaac portrays the strength of the Spirit. Paul confirms this analogy in Galatians 4:29: *"But, as he who was born according to the flesh* [Ishmael] *then persecuted him who was born according to the Spirit* [Isaac], *even so it is now."* God's miracle solution to a barren couple's problem was not Ishmael changed; it was Isaac born. God demonstrates the same activity in the regeneration of the believer (Tit. 3:5) – God's miracle solution to a barren life is eternal life through rebirth, not a "makeover" of the old nature, which is putrid to God. Ishmael was the son of a bondwoman (a slave), illustrating that, naturally, we are slaves to sin with no hope of deliverance.

Regeneration, however, implants life (the very divine nature of God) within those earthen vessels who accept His offer of salvation through Christ (Jn. 1:12-13). No spiritual rebirth means no spiritual life, no spiritual fruit for God, and no heaven to enjoy (Jn. 3:3). The birth of Isaac did not improve Ishmael, but it did bring out his hidden opposition to the child of promise begotten by God. Just as salvation by works is in opposition to grace, the flesh nature is in opposition to the spirit nature, which is only begotten of God (Rom. 7:21-23). The two natures within the believer war with each other. Thus, God's begotten children must live by faith according to the new nature and not according to the flesh, for there is absolutely nothing in the flesh that pleases God (Rom. 7:18).

The new nature of the believer received at regeneration cannot sin (1 Jn. 3:9) and therefore continually wars against the flesh nature: *"For the flesh lusts against the Spirit, and the Spirit against the flesh; and these are contrary to one another, so that you do not do the things that you wish"* (Gal. 5:17). There is nothing in the old nature that can please God (Rom. 8:8) – only when our vessels are under God's control do we have the capacity to please Him.

Scripture contains other illustrations of the flesh. For example, Amalek was the grandson of profane Esau, *"who for one morsel of food sold his birthright"* (Heb. 12:16). Consequently, both Esau and Amalek are used in Scripture to picture lusting flesh which continues to war against God's people. The Amalekites attacked the straggling Israelites who were weak and weary in the flesh after leaving Egypt (Deut. 25:17-18). This is often when the flesh gains a victory over God's people: just after a major victory when they are exhausted. We see this was the case for Joshua, who acted in the flesh after the great victory at Jericho.

The children of Israel had experienced separation and cleansing from that which defiled them; they were now ready to be used as Jehovah's agency against Ai and Bethel. This time they would not advance in human wisdom and in their own strength, but in faith and in accordance with Jehovah's plan and with His power. Human reasoning and fleshly vigor were to have no part in God's operation.

The Lord desires that the same pattern be followed in the Church Age. Until an individual experiences regeneration and receives the Holy Spirit, the flesh nature is uncontrollable (Rom. 8:2-4). Even after regeneration, a child of God cannot righteously serve the Lord with sin in his or her heart. Sins in our flesh must supernaturally be put to death *"because they that are in the flesh cannot please God"* (Rom. 8:8). This truth was shown to us by the judgment (the death of thirty-six men) that befell the Israelites when they attacked Ai in their own strength and wisdom. Achan's sin affected the entire nation, but the loss of life at Ai would have been avoided if Joshua would have sought counsel from the Lord, instead of proceeding without Him. One cannot rightly exercise the power of God without being under His moral authority (Luke 7:6-9). Both carnal appetites, as seen in Achan's life, and self-motivated behavior, as exhibited by Joshua, must be brought under the control of the Holy Spirit and thus eliminated from the work of God.

Conquest and the Life of Rest

The impulses of the flesh nature were controlling the King of Ai's actions. Reason aside, the king of Ai with his army left the comparative safety of his city to engage the Hebrews, who in turn fled northward. With the enemy in hot pursuit, the Lord directed Joshua to lift his spear to signal the ambushers to come out of hiding, promising to deliver the enemy into Joshua's hands (v. 18). The concealed troops sprang out of their hiding places and entered into unprotected Ai at this time, and perhaps Bethel also. The city was quickly conquered and set on fire (v. 19). With this accomplished, the ambush party left Ai and approached the enemy from the rear (v. 22).

When the army of Ai saw their city on fire, which meant the destruction of their homes and loved ones, they lost all motivation to fight (v. 20). It was at this time that Joshua halted his retreat and turned back to engage the enemy with full veracity (v. 21). The Canaanite army realized too late that the Israelites they fought a few days earlier were not the same people before them now. Before they were self-willed and cocky, but after divine chastening, they came to the battle with pure hearts and clean hands, which meant Jehovah was with them. With the enemy surrounded, the Jewish forces rapidly overwhelmed and slaughtered their opposition and then reentered the city to destroy the remaining inhabitants: no one escaped the onslaught (vv. 22-26). It was a complete victory; the death toll of Ai numbered 12,000 and no Jewish losses were noted (v. 25). Bethel also fell that day, but the details of that victory are not known.

The king of Ai was captured alive and then was hung on a tree. At evening, Joshua commanded that his body be taken down in accordance with Deuteronomy 21:22-23, which did not permit bodies to be hung on a tree past sundown. The king's body was then placed in the entrance to Ai and a pile of stones was heaped upon it (vv. 23, 29). The king's grave would serve as a lasting testimony to the inhabitants of Canaan as to what happens to those who would oppose the Israelites and their God. As permitted, the Jews kept the spoils of Ai and Bethel for themselves; all that remained within the cities was burned (vv. 27-28).

The Israelites enjoyed complete victory because the Lord was with them again. While the accursed thing was among them, Jehovah had promised Joshua, *"I will not be with you anymore"* (7:12). As H. F. Witherby warns, this solemn declaration should be deeply pondered by every true soldier of the cross:

Until the evil God exposes be cast out from the midst of His people, defeat follows their steps. The really effective soldier of Christ is not only a constant and energetic worker for God, he is also a truly humble and dependent man walking with God. Unless the Christian be in a right state before God, the Spirit is grieved, and His fire in the soul is quenched. True power in the believer is not his own might, but God's strength in him; he is but a vessel filled by the Lord. As Jehovah was not with Israel, and as He withdrew from Samson, so does He now leave His people when their ways are evil in His sight. He never leaves nor forsakes in the sense of casting off forever; but in His governmental dealings He does leave unfaithful servants, even as the fondest parent turns his face from his child until the child forsakes his evil way.[1]

With this understanding, it is most encouraging that the Lord used the past failures of His people in such a way to lure the enemy from its safe confines to be defeated in the engagement. If there had not been the previous Jewish failure at Ai, this battle plan would not have been as prosperous. Thankfully, failures are never final unless we make them so – God wants us to succeed. *"For a righteous man may fall seven times and rise again, but the wicked shall fall by calamity"* (Prov. 24:16). It is not falling that makes one a failure, but rather choosing to stay submersed in pity and guilt that renders us unusable. It is a gracious aspect of the Lord's character which permits Him to incorporate our failures into His sovereign plan, such that we can learn from our mistakes and rise in grace to be victorious in Christ again!

Meditation

> The first attempt of David Livingstone to preach ended in failure: "Friends, I have forgotten all I had to say," he gasped, and in shame stepped from the pulpit! At that moment, Robert Moffat who was visiting Edinburgh advised David not to give up. Perhaps he could be a doctor instead of a preacher, he advised. Livingstone decided to be both. When the years of medical study were done, he went to Africa and many years later died there. He walked tens of thousands of miles in the interior of Africa and preached in word and deed the gospel of Jesus Christ wherever he went.[2]

Blessings and Curses
Joshua 8:30-35

From a military standpoint, what Joshua does next seems to be a poor decision; instead of securing the interior of Canaan after decimating its two primary strongholds, he leads the Jewish nation on a spiritual pilgrimage. The Israelites (i.e., all the men, women, children, and strangers among them per Deut. 27:11-14) would trek north up the Jordanian valley, then westward, and finally southwestward to a specific location between the mountains of Ebal and Gerizim, which were near Shechem (vv. 30, 33). This relatively easy traveling route was about thirty miles in length through a sparsely populated region of Canaan, which may explain why no battles with the inhabitants were reported.

Shechem was a fortified city which guarded the entrance to the valley between Ebal and Gerizim. Was it defeated by the Israelites to gain unhindered passage into the valley? Did the city surrender without a fight? Joshua did not record the details of every battle, so we do not know how Shechem was conquered during the conquest of Canaan. However, since Shechem was in the heartland of Canaan and Joshua would again address the nation there at the close of his ministry several years later, we are confident that the fortress did fall (24:1). Another possible explanation for their ease of travel and the lack of a recorded battle at Shechem is suggested by F. C. Cook, who believes this portion of Scripture actually belongs after the conquest of Canaan and before its tribal allotments:

> It is on the whole likely that, for these and other reasons, this passage does not, in our present Bible, stand in its proper context; and it has been conjectured that the place from which these six verses have been transferred is the end of chapter 11. The "then" with which verse 30 opens in our present text may well have served to introduce the account of the solemnity on Gerizim and Ebal at the end of the record of Joshua's victories, to which indeed it forms a suitable climax.[1]

Regardless of the timing of this national event, its grandeur is quite spectacular. Whether Joshua declared a temporary cessation of the invasion to lead the Israelites to Shechem or whether it occurred after the conquest is unknown. What is recognized is that Joshua was obeying the command issued by Moses just before his death: after Joshua arrived in Canaan, he was to lead the nation to Mt. Ebal and there do three things.

First, he was to set up great stones, plaster them together, and then chisel the words of God's Law into the dried plaster (v. 32; Deut. 27:2-4, 8). As there is no frost in that dry air to split or disintegrate the graven lettering, the constructed monument would be a lasting record of the Law which was to govern the land.

Second, Joshua was to erect an altar with stones which had not been modified by human instruments. He was then to sacrifice burnt offerings and peace offerings on this altar on behalf of the nation (v. 31; Deut. 27:5-6). The location was ideal; it was in the center of Canaan and from the twin mountain peaks of Ebal and Gerizim much of the Promised Land could be viewed. Thus, in the heart of Canaan, the valley of Shechem represented the entire land; it was here that God wanted His Law prominently displayed for all to view and to appreciate. F. B. Meyer provides a vivid panoramic view of the location before us:

> The people were assembled in the valley of Shechem, which lies from east to west, sentineled on the north by the sterile slopes of Ebal, rearing itself gaunt and barren against the intense blue of the Eastern sky; and on the south by its twin-giant Gerizim, a majestic mass of limestone, with stately head and precipitous sides, but fruitful and picturesque, girt with foliage and beauty. The valley between these two is one of the most beautiful in Palestine. Jacob's well lies at its mouth; and all its luxuriant extent is covered with verdant beauty of gardens, and orchards, and olive-groves, rolling in waves of billowy beauty up to the walls of Shechem; whilst the murmur of brooks flowing in all directions fills the air. The width of the valley is about a third of a mile; though the summits of the two mountains, in the lap of which it lies, are two miles apart. It is remarkable that where the two mountains face each other and touch most closely, with a green valley of five hundred yards between, each is hollowed out, and the limestone stratum is broken into a succession of ledges, so as to present the appearance of a series of regular benches. Thus, a natural amphitheater is formed, capable of containing a vast audience of people.[2]

The priests took up a position with the Ark of the Covenant in between the two mountains. It is a noble scene: the Lord in the midst of His people and in the land of majestic beauty and profound blessing that He promised to bestow to His people. This would be the location years later in which the Lord Jesus would converse with an immoral Samaritan woman who came to Jacob's well for water. The Samaritans, during the Persian Empire, built a temple on Mt. Gerizim and there they continued to worship God for nearly a millennia while they waited for Messiah's coming. Since that time, Messiah has come; He came preaching peace to those who would obey by faith God's living Word, Himself. Those who would reject His message would remain cursed of God (John 3:16-18). Many Samaritans from the village of Sychar (which is near Shechem) did believe on Him after hearing the conversion testimony of the immoral woman who then brought them to hear Messiah (John 4:1-42). Obedience by faith to God's Word ensures His blessing in any dispensation of His working (Gal. 3:6-9)!

Third, Joshua was to read *"all the words of this Law"* in the hearing of *"all the assembly of Israel"* (v. 35). In accordance with Moses' instructions (Deut. 27:9-27), the larger and more prominent tribes of Simeon, Levi, Judah, Issachar, Joseph (Ephraim and Manasseh), and Benjamin were to be situated on the north side of Mt. Gerizim to acknowledge the blessings God promised to bestow for obedience. The lesser tribes of Reuben, Gad, Asher, Zebulun, Dan, and Naphtali were to take a position on the sterile southern face of Mt. Ebal and acknowledge by an "amen" (literally, "so be it"), each curse pronounced for disobedience. Moses issued no command in Scripture for the tribes on the fruitful slopes of Gerizim to verbally acknowledge specific blessing with an "amen." H. F. Witherby explains why the tribes on Gerizim were not to shout "amen" after each blessing was read:

> The curses were read with a loud voice by the Levites, and, as each curse for disobedience sounded in Israel's ears, the hundreds of thousands, assembled upon Mount Ebal, responded with unanimous Amens. Twelve times said they "Amen" to the twelve-times-uttered curses, and the twelfth – "Cursed be he that confirms not all the words of this law to do them" – included every possible neglect or failure of which they could be capable. Blessings also were read (Josh. 8:33-34); but concerning the Amens, sounding from Mount Gerizim, Scripture is silent. It records not one responsive "So be it" to blessings earned by

the obedience of fallen man (Deut. 27). Man may justly assent to all "the judgments" (Ex. 24:3) of God's law, but they who remain under the law must remain under its curse (Gal. 3:10).[3]

Mankind may well agree to the judgments that accompany disobedience to the Law, but mankind is unable to keep the Law, and therefore has no claim to its blessings.

Joshua did read all of the Law of God that day and the echo of a million people repeatedly shouting "amen" vibrated off the stony-walled amphitheater and rumbled through the valley like thunder. The Law of God was also inscribed in a stone monument on Mt. Ebal for every passerby to see. There would be no excuse for future ignorance; God had posted His Law in the center of Canaan and the Law had been orally declared to all the people, who affirmed its meaning. If the Jews wanted to commune with Jehovah and experience His love and power, they must choose to obey the Law which would govern their relationship with Him.

The irresistible love of God can only be experienced by answering His invitation to know Him through His revealed Word. Our understanding of God's plan and our commitment to live it out will be directly proportional to the extent that we have known and experienced Him. The Lord Jesus said, *"He who has My commandments and keeps them, it is he who loves Me. And he who loves Me will be loved by My Father, and I will love him and manifest Myself to him"* (John 14:21). Continued submission to divine truth is the pathway to intimately experiencing and knowing God in deepening degrees. This is what Jehovah wanted for the Israelites and it is what the Lord Jesus wants for His Church today.

The Lord Jesus promised that if we obey His commandments He will manifest Himself to us in deeper fellowship (John 14:21). In order to walk with the Lord, we must be in agreement with Him on the matter of sin. For, *"can two walk together except they be agreed?"* (Amos 3:3). Surely, light has no communion with darkness; thus, may each of us walk with God according to divine truth and in moral integrity. We read in 1 John 1:5-7 that walking with God requires walking in the light of divine truth. A willingness to walk according to revealed truth brings happy fellowship with God and with other believers. We must have light to walk safely. When we choose to walk in the dark, we are inviting injury – the chastening hand of God.

Conquest and the Life of Rest

Listen to Paul's medley of exhortations concerning the walk of the believer: do not walk as fools (Eph. 5:15), the way you formerly did (Eph. 5:8), or the way the Gentiles walk in the vanity of their minds (Eph. 4:17); walk as children of light (Eph. 5:8). In other words, do not be foolish; walk according to the truth, not in the darkness that you once did. At Shechem, the light shone clearly. Joshua ensured that every Jew knew how he or she should walk: *all* the Law was written in stone, *all* the Law was read, *all* heard it, and *all* consented to it. The variable of ignorance had been thoroughly removed from the daily conduct of every Jew – they knew what God expected of them.

The scene at Shechem as the Israelites were just embarking upon the conquest of Canaan well resembles the events at Marah forty years earlier. Moses had delivered the Israelites from Egypt and was leading them to Mt. Sinai to meet their God, Jehovah. The Lord spoke of His statutes and commandments for the first time after transforming the bitter waters at Marah into satisfying, life-sustaining drink (Ex. 15). The principle Moses conveyed to the people was a simple one: obedience would be rewarded with His blessing, but disobedience would be met with severe judgment, even with plagues like those used to punish Egypt. The precise timing of this revelation, as Arthur Pink explains, is important to understand:

> Nothing had been said to Israel about Jehovah's "statutes and commandments" while they were in Egypt. But now that they were redeemed, now that they had been purchased for Himself, God's governmental claims are pressed upon them. The Lord was dealing with them in wondrous grace. But grace is not lawlessness. Grace only makes us the more indebted to God. Our obligations of obedience can never be liquidated so long as God is God. Grace only establishes on a higher basis what we most emphatically and fully OWE to Him as His redeemed creatures.[4]

The truth presented to the children of Israel was a simple one; it represents the same reality that parents must teach their children early in life: obedience brings blessing, but disobedience results in punishment. Accordingly, our children have a choice as to whether they will receive our warm embrace or the rod of reproof. Every child of God has the same choice: *"Be you therefore followers of God, as dear children"* (Eph. 5:1); *"As obedient children, not fashioning yourselves according to the former lusts in your ignorance"* (1 Pet. 1:14); *"For whom the*

Lord loves He chastens" (Heb. 12:6). On this noble day, all the Law was read, all heard it, and all consented to it, thus, the variable of ignorance was removed from the daily conduct of every Jew. They knew God's will for them; there were no excuses – obedience ensured God's blessing and disobedience His curse.

Meditation

> To walk out of God's will is to walk into nowhere.
>
> — C. S. Lewis

> I find doing the will of God leaves me no time for disputing about His plans.
>
> — George MacDonald

> To know the will of God is the greatest knowledge, to find the will of God is the greatest discovery, and to do the will of God is the greatest achievement.
>
> — George W. Truett

Conquest and the Life of Rest

Gibeonite Trickery
Joshua 9:1-15

The Ai calamity occurred directly after the astounding victory at Jericho and the Jews, having just been spiritually rejuvenated in the valley of Shechem, would face their next crisis in Joshua 9. The Israelites' excursion to Shechem allowed plenty of time for the local inhabitants to investigate the aftermath of the huge billows of smoke rising to their east. What they found was the charred remains of cities which were once thought to be invincible. These Hebrew victories served as a catalyst to unite various people groups throughout Canaan to fight against God's people. Alliances among the inhabitants were formed in three separate regions: the hill country of central Canaan, the lowlands and foothills near the eastern plain, and the coastal plain northward towards Lebanon (vv. 1-2). The remainder of the conquest of Canaan is divided into two summary sections: the southern Campaign (Josh. 10) and the northern Campaign (Josh. 11). In the Lord's wisdom, the deep wedge that Joshua had driven into Canaan prevented all of the inhabitants from unifying against the Hebrews at the same time.

Apparently, the Gibeonites, who lived about twenty miles southwest of the Israelite encampment, did not want to join one of the larger confederations mobilizing to war against the Israelites. They knew the God of Moses had granted the Israelites the land of Canaan and that they were to destroy all the inhabitants (v. 24). The Gibeonites believed this was true and were in fear for their lives. They were in a precarious predicament: they did not want to fight the Hebrews but they did not want to leave their homeland either. This is where their actions contrast with the faith of Rahab who, also fearing for her life, openly declared her faith to the spies and then chose to fully identify with Jehovah and His people; she was therefore brought into the commonwealth of Israel. The Gibeonites only wanted to be spared from death. They had no desire to worship Jehovah, to submit to His will, or to identify with the Israelites and receive Jehovah's blessings promised to them.

The Gibeonites' dilemma was resolved by contriving a cunning plan to trick the Israelites into forging a peace treaty with them. It is noted that Scripture does not speak of any kings of Gibeon or of the other nearby Hivite towns. Apparently, these cities were governed by elders who considered the common safety of the people more important than personal dignity. If this decision had rested in the hands of a king, perhaps this sensible response would not have occurred. A king would not be so eager to forfeit his authority, fame, and wealth by yielding to the Israelites in such a passive manner.

The elders believed that all their lives would be spared if they could enter into a treaty with Jehovah's representatives. The Israelites would be required to honor a covenant established in Jehovah's name, even if fostered in deceit. The plan, from a Gibeonite perspective, was a good one and, in the conclusion of the matter, the elders did well for themselves and their people. The Gibeonite delegation would represent the intentions of all three Hivite towns in the region (v. 17, 10:2). The Hivites were descendants of Canaan, the son of Ham, and had dwelt in the land of Canaan for centuries (Gen. 10:17).

The plan was to portray themselves as a group of ambassadors who had traveled from a faraway country after learning about Jehovah's astonishing feats against Pharaoh and, more recently, the kings of the eastern plateau. After arriving at the Jewish camp, this phony envoy would express their respect for Jehovah and their desire to live in peace with His people (vv. 4, 6, 11). To strengthen the ruse by giving the appearance of having undergone a long journey, the Gibeonites loaded their donkeys with worn-out sacks and patched-up wine skins; they also wore ragged clothes and scruffy shoes. They carried a portion of dried out moldy bread to deceive the Israelites into thinking their supplies were nearly depleted (vv. 4-5, 12-13).

This evil strategy has a classic satanic signature and counter-signature to it. The first indication of this is that the mixing of truth and deception to create a bold solicitation to confuse and to stumble the hearer is a method he has used from the beginning. This same tactic worked on Eve in the Garden of Eden. God forbade the man and woman to eat of a certain tree, saying, *"when you eat you shall surely die"* (Gen. 2:17). Satan told Eve, *"You shall not surely die"* (Gen 3:4): the addition of one three-letter word changed God's intended meaning completely. Satan was referring to physical death while ignoring the subject of spiritual life with God. God warned of immediate spiritual death, though physical death would naturally come to those apart from God. As the Israelites would soon learn, when Satan presents a half-truth, there is only one half that he wants you to consider and act on, and it's the wrong half.

H. F. Witherby suggests a second reason for suspecting the devil was at work through the Gibeonites:

> Satan's ambassadors object to discuss God's victories of today, His work of this hour, the things of all others in which, if His people be walking in the Spirit, they will be most deeply interested. The facts of God's work in bygone days have become, in our own times, history, of which the world is willing to speak; but the effects of God's truth in our own days, its present victories, its demands for present obedience – such home-truths are not to be mentioned. Anyone may speak of victories over pagan Rome, or papal Rome, of centuries ago; but the victories of the gospel in the world of this day and hour, and the Word's authority over the children of God at the present moment, must not be mentioned – as Jericho, Ai, and Ebal were carefully ignored by the Hivites.[1]

We are not told why the Gibeonites mention past Jewish victories, but not recent ones. Perhaps this omission was intentional to further substantiate their ruse (i.e., to convince the Israelites that their long extensive journey had prevented their awareness of new happenings in Canaan). However, given the newly formed alliances among the Canaanites, it seems more likely that their silence about recent events was an attempt to plant doubt in the minds of the Jews, as to whether or not God was still directing the affairs of the Israelites in Canaan. Whether or not this subtle suggestion invoked Joshua's independent response is unknown, but it is a tactic of the enemy that every child of God should be aware of – Do not get lost in minute details and lose the "big picture" perspective of God's sovereign control. Satan caused Eve to forget about all the other permissible trees in the Garden of Eden by calling her attention to the one forbidden tree, thus leading her into sin.

The well-planned previously mentioned deception was put into play after the Gibeonite delegation arrived at Gilgal, but Satan also used a well-ordered presentation to not only deceive, but to play on human emotions. H. L. Rossier describes how the devil stirred up fear, pride, and lusting in the hearts of the Israelite leaders in order to ensure the Gibeonite sales pitch was irresistible:

> Notice how Satan succeeds in making them lose the sense of dependence. He intimidates them by something calculated to strike terror into their hearts; the hatred of the world, a confederation of kings assembled for war (vv. 1, 2). He begins by engaging their attention with this formidable power prepared to crush them, and then, without losing a moment, he offers them *his* resource: the inhabitants of Gibeon come to the camp at Gilgal. Israel was not prepared for this, they had not on the whole armor of God. The leaders of the people failed in detecting what seems to have occurred to the minds of the simple – for a moment, at least; and it is often so; humility and a single eye go together, and are accompanied by true and divine intelligence. "Make ye a league with us," said the Gibeonites. What a good opportunity for Israel! "The enemy is before you," perhaps Satan whispered; "this would be a splendid way of overcoming him."[2]

It is important for believers to remember that God is patient and wants us to understand and to confirm in our minds what is wise before acting in questionable matters (Rom. 14:23). Satan is the high-pressure salesman! If you do not know what to do in a particular situation because Scripture is silent – wait! Study the guidelines, warnings, and lessons-learned recorded in Scripture; pray for divine guidance; and consult wise counselors. God will direct your path if you will patiently wait on Him.

Although the Gibeonite plan and presentation were executed brilliantly, Joshua seemed to know that something was wrong. The sudden appearance of this envoy was suspicious and prompted Joshua to ask a probing question: *"Perhaps you dwell among us; so how can we make a covenant with you?"* (v. 7). However, after listening to their well-orchestrated yarn, he was duped by the imposters' story. Without seeking counsel from the One who knew the full truth about their visitors, the Jews sampled their lousy provisions and convinced themselves that their story was true (v. 14). Joshua and the leaders of the people then swore by Jehovah's name to live peaceably with the very ones He had commanded them to utterly destroy (v. 15). Without any physical conflict, the enemy scored a great victory in Canaan, one that would have been eliminated if Joshua would have asked the Lord just one simple question: "What do You want us to do about these visitors?" Moreover, the urim in the high priest's breastplate could have been used to discern the issue as well.

Conquest and the Life of Rest

Paul reminded the believers at Ephesus that their real battle was not with flesh and blood (i.e., people in the world), but rather *"against principalities, against powers, against the rulers of the darkness of this age, against spiritual hosts of wickedness in the heavenly places"* (Eph. 6:12-13). The leader of the powers of darkness is Satan. Satan consistently opposed the Lord Jesus Christ throughout His ministry on earth, and today he continues to oppose Jesus Christ, His gospel message, and those who would spread it. Satan despises Christ and those who identify with Him and works to manipulate various world systems of thinking to exclude Christ from consideration. Paul identifies Satan as *"the god of this age"* (2 Cor. 4:4), and *"the prince of the power of the air"* (Eph. 2:2). On three occasions the Lord Jesus said that Satan is *"the prince of this world"* (John 12:31, 14:30, 16:11). The world is Satan's delegated domain, but he must function within divine boundaries. God is holy, and He cannot tempt anyone to sin (Jas. 1:13), although Satan is allowed to test man's resolve to obey God. The Gibeonites, Satan's tricksters, were permitted to test the Israelites; unfortunately, they were deceived and in ignorance disobeyed the Lord.

The devil's main ambition is to lead as many of those who bear the image of God away from Him and the salvation He offers. This realization is shown to us in Genesis 14 where the king of Sodom is used as another allegorical depiction of Satan. The king of Sodom ruled over a wicked domain, he had been overthrown, and he cared not for the spoil reclaimed by Abraham, but rather wanted only the souls that Abraham had rescued. As Satan knows his doom is sealed (Rev. 12:12, 20:10), he is determined to lead as many as possible into hell's eternal flames (Rev. 13:15, 19:20-21). The interchange between the king of Sodom and Abraham reminds us that Satan's desire is to keep souls from turning to Christ that they might be saved (John 8:44; 1 Tim. 5:15; 2 Thess. 2:9-10) and that he will let Christians have their "stuff" to accomplish this objective.

The prophet Ezekiel informs us that before his fall, Lucifer (who is now called Satan or "the accuser"), was a beautiful cherub, sheathed with precious stones and inherently equipped with musical ability (Ezek. 28:11-16). He was likely the most powerful created being that God made and, thus, is a cunning and dangerous enemy only God can control. Accordingly, believers are not commanded to confront Satan, but rather to resist him by submitting to God in faith (Jas. 4:7). Believers are to be knowledgeable of his tactics so that he does not gain an advantage over them through ignorance. Paul reminded the Christians at Corinth of this fact, saying, *"we are not ignorant of his devices"* (2 Cor. 2:11). Because Satan repeatedly uses the same strategies to oppose the things of God, believers are able to become more aware of his confrontational tactics by obtaining counsel from God's Word. Joshua did not do so and was deceived; may we learn from his costly mistake.

Meditation

The following story is a modern example of how Satan continues to use deception to trick gullible people from following the truth:

> Dr. Peter A. Angles, a 32-year-old assistant professor at the University of Western Ontario, told a luncheon audience in Toronto that he had incurable cancer and would be dead in three months. Then he encouraged people not to worry about eternal life, but to be engaged in world betterment. He later confessed he did not have cancer. "I wanted to make it powerful," he explained. He had even added that it would be his last public appearance before his death.[3]

The Consequences of Deceit
Joshua 9:16-27

It was three days before the deception was discovered, *"for a lying tongue is but for a moment"* (Prov. 12:19). A Hebrew contingency was sent to the four cities that the Gibeonites represented (vv. 16-17). The people wanted to destroy the Hivites and certainly could have, but were not permitted to do so because of the covenant their leaders had sworn with the Gibeonites in the name of Jehovah (v. 18). The Jewish people were not happy with their leadership and complained against them. The people understood God had commanded them to remove the inhabitants of Canaan from the land and they also had learned from their experience at Jericho that disobedience has an expensive price tag.

Sin has its price and for that reason the Lord did not permit the slaughter of the Gibeonites. The leaders of Israel had created the current problem because they exercised their own discretion without humbling themselves and seeking counsel from the Lord. The Jewish elders were so positive they knew what was best in the matter, but they were very wrong. The evil of their hasty self-sufficiency had been sown and now the entire nation would reap the awful consequences for years to come, for the way was now open for idolatry to take root in the bosom of Israel.

Joshua was the Lord's man and thus represented Jehovah in the affairs of the people. Jehovah is not a lying God and Joshua was thus compelled to honor his agreement with the Hivities, no matter how wrong it was. Matthew Henry explains the seriousness of issuing an oath in Jehovah's name:

> He that ratifies a promise with an oath imprecates the divine vengeance if he willfully breaks his promise, and has reason to expect that divine justice will take him at his word. God is not mocked, and therefore oaths are not to be jested with. The princes would keep their word, though they lost by it.[1]

Accordingly, the Hivites would remain in the land unharmed, but only as slaves (vv. 19-20). This allowance was in direct violation of the commandment Moses issued just before his death: the Jews were to wipe out the inhabitants of Canaan to ensure that they would not later ensnare them into idolatry (Deut. 12:28-30). But Joshua and the elders chose not to right a wrong with another wrong, but to submit themselves to Jehovah and suffer the consequences for one rash mistake, rather than two. It is noted that this was the honorable way forward, for years later King Saul's family would be punished for Saul's attempt to eliminate the Gibeonites (2 Sam. 21).

The leaders of Israel quelled the grumbling of the people by affirming that the Gibeonites would be *"hewers of wood and drawers of water"* for the entire congregation and for the Lord's altar (vv. 20-23, 27). Faced with death or slavery, the Hivites agreed to be perpetual servants of the Israelites. Later, David appointed non-Jewish servants, called the Nethinim, to assist the Levites in temple ministry. It is quite possible that the Nethinim were descendants of these Hivities, who even in Ezra's day (a millennium later) were still serving in the temple (Ezra 8:20). Unfortunately, the Hivite settlements in time became a social barrier between the northern and southern Jewish tribes, which ultimately led to a national split. Thus, it was not through weapons of war that the Israelites were overcome in this trespass, but by the subtlety of a lying tongue.

The strongholds of Jericho and Ai had miraculously fallen by the hands of the Israelites as empowered by their God Jehovah. Obviously, the enemy would not be able to overcome the Jews through direct assault or by hiding within fortifications; a different strategy was necessary. What if the Canaanites could infiltrate the Jewish camp and establish a friendly dialogue leading to a mutual agreement to coexist in peace; would not this thwart God's agenda in Canaan? This was the objective of the Gibeonites and represents the same tactic Satan used against the Israelites forty years earlier after being soundly beaten in Egypt by the plagues of Moses. The Jews left Egypt as a *"mixed multitude"* (Ex. 12:38) and those not of Abraham's lineage continually stirred up the Jews to complain, grumble, and rebel against the Lord.

This tactic of unnatural unions was later used successfully against Jehoshaphat as he partnered himself with evil Ahab (2 Chron. 18). Ahab, the king of Israel, suckered Jehoshaphat, the king of Judah, into forging an alliance with him in order to pool their resources and retake

Ramoth-gilead, a city of refuge thirty miles east of the Jordan River. The Syrians controlled and inhabited this city. Ahab was an evil king and godly Jehoshaphat should have known better than to unite with Ahab, especially in a meaningless religious cause that God had not sanctioned. The result of this union nearly cost Jehoshaphat his life, and it would have if he had not cried out for God to save him (2 Chron. 18). After Jehoshaphat returned to Jerusalem, the prophet Hanani rebuked the king, *"Should you help the wicked, and love them who hate the Lord?"* (2 Chron. 19:2). Though Jehoshaphat had done many good things for the Lord, God would punish him for aligning with wicked Ahab (2 Chron. 19:2-3).

Thankfully, the satanic strategy of unnatural unions would not be successful against the Jews who returned from the Babylonian exile determined to rebuild a temple for Jehovah in Jerusalem (Ezra 4:1-4). Zerubbabel, the governor, and Jeshua, the High Priest, knew that their enemies did not worship Jehovah and, thus, would not allow them to have any part of their work. The Jews alone were God's covenant people and no outsiders would work alongside them to accomplish what they alone had been tasked to do. Satan often uses the device of unnatural unions to cripple or terminate what may start out as a good ministry. The solution to this tactic is to completely avoid any associations with the children of the devil while accomplishing the Lord's business.

Unfortunately, Joshua fell prey to the Gibeonites' trickery: *"we are your servants ... we know your God ... make a peace treaty with us"* (vv. 6-11). He listened to the enemy, did not seek God's counsel on the matter, and paid a high price for submitting to the deception. Paul warned the Corinthians that Satan often transforms himself into an angel of light and his servants into ministers of righteousness because he knows it is easier to deceive God's people than it is to deter them from a purpose (2 Cor. 11:14-15). Hence, Paul's warning to the Corinthians to not be yoked with non-believers is appropriate for God's people in any age, including Joshua and the Israelites:

> *Do not be unequally yoked together with unbelievers. For what fellowship has righteousness with lawlessness? And what communion has light with darkness? And what accord has Christ with Belial? Or what part has a believer with an unbeliever? And what agreement has the temple of God with idols? For you are the temple of the living God* (2 Cor. 6:14-16).

Joshua Devotions

Regrettably, many believers today are reaping God's judgment for ignoring this command and teaming up with the unregenerate in marriage or business partnerships, or to accomplish some religious cause or support some charitable activity. As the Israelites painfully learned, it is possible for the devil to be in the midst of our camp without us recognizing him. One fact is certain: if the children of God and the children of the devil are harmoniously working together, it is not God who is glorified in the endeavor, but the one who has wanted God's glory and station from the beginning (Isa. 14:12-15).

Summary

Three different enemies of the believer have been introduced to us in typological form in the book of Joshua thus far: the world (Jericho), the flesh (Ai), and the devil (Gibeon). Those who have been born again overcome the world by faith as they submit to God's Word: *"For whatever is born of God overcomes the world. And this is the victory that has overcome the world – our faith"* (1 Jn. 5:4). By faith we hold to the truth and reject God-denying secular philosophies and human traditions, rather than be ruined by them (Col. 2:8). A different strategy is needed to overcome the flesh. Victory over the flesh is achieved by identifying with Christ in His death and in His life (Rom. 6:1-10), choosing not to strengthen the flesh nature by engaging in its deeds (Col. 3:5), but rather through the power of the Holy Spirit mortifying desires outside of God's will for us (Rom. 8:13). This strengthens the inner man to resist temptation in the future (Eph. 3:16). The third enemy, the devil, is not to be directly confronted, but resisted by submitting to God in faith (Jas. 4:7). There is no need for believers to fear or flee the devil; if they continue resisting him in truth, he will be the one to depart. Believers are to be knowledgeable of his tactics so that he does not gain an advantage over them through ignorance (2 Cor. 2:11). May God give us grace to *slay* the deeds of the flesh, to *submit* by faith to the truth and not be moved from it, and to *stand* fast in the faith to resist evil!

Meditation

The relationship the Israelites established with the Gibeonites did nothing to move them God-ward; rather, the service rendered promoted their own ease. Comfort and complacency among God's people have always been indications of worldliness. Harry Ironside relates the following story to illustrate how worldliness adversely affects a believer's fervency to live for Christ and long for His coming:

> I remember one night in Stockton, California, ... I was preaching about the coming of Jesus. As I was in prayer I was conscious of a woman getting up and going out, for in those days the skirts would swish whenever a lady walked. It seemed to me that this lady must have gone out in a hurry. When I finished my prayer and went to greet the friends at the door, I found a woman pacing back and forth in the lobby. The moment I came, she said to me, "How would you dare to pray like that – 'Come Lord Jesus?' I don't want him to come. It would break in on all my plans. How dare you!" I said, "My dear young woman, Jesus is coming whether you like it or not." Oh, if you know Him and love Him, surely your heart says, "Come, Lord Jesus!"[2]

The Lord Fought for Israel
Joshua 10:1-14

The situation in central Canaan had become desperate for the inhabitants of Jerusalem. Only a few weeks after arriving in their land, the Israelites had conquered or taken control of all the main cities in route between Jerusalem and Gilgal, the Jewish encampment (v. 1). Their alliance with the stronghold of Gibeon, only five miles north of Jerusalem, was especially unnerving. Gibeon was a principle city in Canaan, and well-known for its many mighty warriors (v. 2). It was also located near the pass of Beth-horn on the main thoroughfare that, passing through Jerusalem, marked the way between the lower Jordan valley and Joppa and thus the Mediterranean Sea. Jerusalem would be an obvious target for the Israelites.

Having been cut off by the Israelites to the north and the west, and there being no help to the east, the king of Jerusalem, Adoni-zedek, turned to the south for assistance. He contacted the kings of the chief cities of southern Canaan: King Hoham of Hebron, King Piram of Jarmuth, King Japhia of Lachish, and King Debir of Eglon (v. 3). The message was an urgent appeal: *"Come up to me and help me, that we may attack Gibeon, for it has made peace with Joshua and with the children of Israel"* (v. 4). Adoni-zedek feared that if the news of Gibeon's peaceful surrender spread throughout southern Canaan, more cities, which were inferior to Gibeon's military strength, would also surrender to the Israelites without a fight.

Adoni-zedek represents the prince of the power of the air, Satan, the god of this world. His name means "lord of righteousness" and he stands in direct contrast to the only other King of Jerusalem known before this, Melchizedek, the priest of the Most High God. Melchizedek, the King of Salem (peace) is a beautiful type of the Lord Jesus Christ. Adoni-zedek brought war, while Melchizedek was the ruler of peace. The former, was the accuser of the brethren, and the latter, the blesser of

Conquest and the Life of Rest

God's people. Satan will always have his counterfeit to confront the goodness of God in Christ.

Adoni-zedek's invitation to the other kings to join forces was accepted. Whatever past differences may have existed between these five cities, they were put aside for this all-important cause. Their united forces marched on Gibeon, encamped outside the city, and initiated an assault on that city (v. 5). It seems as if the Canaanite kings knew they could not beat Joshua and his God in battle, but they felt it was important to punish the Gibeonites for deserting their hopeless cause, thus making them an example to discourage others from doing the same. There had been previous revelation of the one true God in this region centuries earlier, but, as H. F. Witherby explains, these cities had rejected that revelation and sided against God's people:

> The king of Jerusalem, Adoni-zedec (the Lord of Righteousness), bore a similar title to his predecessor, Melchizedek (King of Righteousness), when Jerusalem (peaceful possession, or possession of peace) was called Salem (Peace). How the king of Righteousness, and king of Peace (Heb. 7 and Gen. 14) waited on God's servant, Abraham, with the bread and the wine, we know. In those days the living God was honored in Salem, and through all ages Melchizedek shines brightly as a type of Christ, the Priest and King. Hebron also, one of the earliest seats of civilization in Palestine, had its old associations in connection with the patriarchs. But now to Hebron comes the first call to fight against Israel. In the time, therefore, of the combination of the kings, the fear of the Most High had been shaken off by the nations of Canaan. The sun and the moon, Baal and Ashtaroth (Judg. 2:13), were worshipped, their iniquity was full, their harvest had passed, their summer ended, and the wrath of God was about to fall upon them. No foes are so bitter in their hatred of God as those who once recognized His Name.[1]

Jehovah had revealed Himself to them through the testimony of Abraham, then through the many great works accomplished in Egypt, which they had heard about, and then more recently through the success of His people against the Amorite kings east of the Jordan and against the cities of Jericho, Bethel, and Ai in their own land. The kings of southern Canaan were without excuse; they had rejected God's revelation and instead become idolaters. The harvest in Canaan was fully ripe and God's sickle of wrath was in motion.

Being tremendously outnumbered, the Gibeonites sent a distress call to Gilgal, pleading for help: *"Do not forsake your servants; come up to us quickly, save us and help us, for all the kings of the Amorites who dwell in the mountains have gathered together against us"* (v. 6). At first glance, this message seems like a blessing in disguise. After all, the Israelites had been tricked into a treaty with the Gibeonites; could their error be now corrected by simply abandoning the Gibeonites to their doom at the hand of their own people? However, as H. L. Rossier suggests, that would not be a permissible outcome of the scenario before us:

> The men of Gibeon send to Joshua to Gilgal saying: "Slack not thy hand from thy servants." What is Israel to do? Danger is there, whatever course he pursues. Not to go up, and to allow the Gibeonites to be cut to pieces by others, would deliver them from the consequences of their failure, but where would be the needed humiliation? Would it be upright towards God or man? To go up, on the other hand, would look like a definite allowance of association with the world. Such dilemmas are common with Satan. How many times he placed them in the pathway of the perfect Man! The only way to get out of the difficulty is by simple dependence on God, realized in the school of Gilgal. The lesson of the snare of Gibeon is learnt, and Satan is foiled.[2]

Certainly, the Israelites had learned a lesson in their past dealings with the Gibeonites, and it was one that the Lord did not want them to soon forget. Thus, the humiliating outcome of their error, the existence of the Hivites in Canaan, would be a lasting reminder of how they needlessly fell prey to their chicanery. Beyond this point, there are two other reasons why Joshua decided to answer the Gibeonite call for help. First, he, in Jehovah's name, had entered into a treaty with the Gibeonites, and therefore felt obliged to honor their agreement. Second, the situation provided an outstanding military opportunity to advance the conquest of Canaan. Thus far, the Israelites have had to confront their enemies in fortifications, but now all the forces of southern Canaan were camped out in the open before Gibeon. If he reacted quickly, the Israelites could march through the night, and catch the enemy by surprise around dawn. If successful, this plan would lead to the conquest of all the major forces of southern Canaan in one battle. And so Joshua mobilized all of his troops for battle (v. 7).

The journey to Gibeon could not have been an easy one, for the twenty-five-mile route wound through rugged hill country that ascended some 3500 feet above Gilgal. The Israelites marched all night to reach their objective early in the morning (v. 9). Given the description of the moon in verse twelve (i.e., in the western horizon), the Israelites would have had a half-moon to illuminate their pathway most of the night. No doubt they were exhausted, but Jehovah would have it no other way; He reassured Joshua en route, saying, *"Do not fear them, for I have delivered them into your hand; not a man of them shall stand before you"* (v. 8). Marching uphill all night after being awake all day would deplete the Israelites of all their natural strength for engaging the enemy in the coming day; they would need a new kind of strength which did not come from within, but from above. In a similar situation Paul recorded what God told him:

> *And He said to me, "My grace is sufficient for you, for My strength is made perfect in weakness." Therefore most gladly I will rather boast in my infirmities, that the power of Christ may rest upon me. Therefore I take pleasure in infirmities, in reproaches, in needs, in persecutions, in distresses, for Christ's sake. For when I am weak, then I am strong* (2 Cor. 12:9-10).

The Lord delights to demonstrate His power through the weakness of His people and such is the case before us. The Israelites surprised the southern army of Canaan with an early morning strike (v. 9). The enemy could not withstand the advance of the Hebrews and went into a full retreat. They fled the ten miles up the ascent to the high ridge of Beth Horon the Upper and then down the rugged stone-cut road on the western slope which dropped some seven hundred feet in a two-mile stretch. With breakneck speed these escaping fugitives made for their fortified citadels in the valleys below. But it was not to be, for the Jews charged vigorously after them. They too, having witnessed the power of God, could shout the battle cry of David centuries later: *"Jehovah, mighty in battle"* (Ps. 24:8).

Joshua clearly accredited Jehovah for every aspect of the onslaught; the record states: *"So the Lord routed them before Israel, killed them with a great slaughter at Gibeon, chased them along the road that goes to Beth Horon, and struck them down as far as Azekah and Makkedah* (v. 10); *"The Lord cast down great stones from heaven"* (v. 11); *"The Lord fought for Israel"* (v. 14). Joshua reported that the Lord struck down more enemy soldiers with great hailstones than the Israelites slew with the sword (v. 11). This demonstrates not only the value of strategic air-strike, but that when the Lord fights our battles the outcome is much more prosperous than when we "go it alone"!

The confrontation was going wonderfully for Israel: the enemy was fleeing to the southwest down the Aijalon valley and was being smitten as they fled. There was only one problem – the children of Israel needed more daylight hours in order to fully take advantage of the situation before them and decimate the entire southern army of Canaan. Joshua, having full confidence in the greatness of His God, looks toward heaven and in the hearing of his people utters a brief, but spectacular prayer: *"Sun, stand still over Gibeon; and Moon, in the Valley of Aijalon"* (v. 12). God *"heeded the voice of man"* (v. 14) and immediately responded to Joshua's prayer of faith; *"So the sun stood still, and the moon stopped, till the people had revenge"* (v. 13). As a result of God's response, the Israelites, in the strength of the Lord, battled their enemies for the space of a full day, because God supernaturally provided them with light after affixing the sun overhead and moon in the western sky (v. 13).

There have been countless attempts to undermine the clear meaning of the text. Some have suggested that Joshua was merely using a poetic expression to convey the thought that it was a long day of fighting – one that seemed to never end. Others have suggested that through the fraction of special cloud layers the Lord provided more daylight even though the motions of the sun and moon were not augmented. However, Joshua stated, *"the sun did not hasten to go down for about a whole day. And there has been no day like that, before it or after it"* (vv. 13-14). This statement clearly indicates that something happened and it was so radical it only happened this one time. This supernatural feat is also referred to in *The Book of Jasher* which is a collection of ancient Hebrew poetry honoring the accomplishments of Israel's leaders (v. 13). Besides the book of *Joshua, The Book of Jasher* also documents that the miraculous events in this chapter actually occurred.

The smiting hailstones, which selectively hit only the Canaanites, had already made it clear that God was at work in the situation and it was for this reason that Joshua could utter such a profound prayer regarding the celestial bodies. J. G. Bellett explains:

> He [Joshua] knew that judgment was God's work and he would put it into His hands. He knew that God fought for Israel, and he would put

the battle upon Him. This tone of decision, because of distinctness in the light and knowledge of the mind of Christ, is something very fine.[3]

Indeed, fanatical prayers of faith made in the will of God accomplish the fantastic or, as the world would put it, "the unbelievable." Joshua seems to have captured the holy fervor that the Lord Jesus exhorted His disciples to have when they would encounter what seemed to be insurmountable problems: *"I say to you, if you have faith as a mustard seed, you will say to this mountain, 'Move from here to there,' and it will move; and nothing will be impossible for you"* (Matt. 17:20). Same God, same power, same faith, same result – the problem with no solution is answered from heaven. H. L. Rossier reminds us that believers today have much in common with Joshua in the way we choose to resolve our difficulties:

> However feeble we may be, we can go to God by the Spirit of Christ, and present to Him the highest requests. Nothing was too great for Joshua to ask; he knew Jehovah's heart, and he knew the place His people occupied in it; he could ask that the heavens, the sun, and the moon might be at the service of His beloved people! From this time nothing arrests Israel's victorious progress (v. 19); they must smite the enemies till none remain.[4]

Joshua was determined not to allow the Canaanite soldiers an opportunity to escape back to their walled cities and continued to pursue them for a full day down through the Aijalon Valley. The entire battle, the judgment of the five kings who opposed Joshua at Gibeon, and the destruction of the city of Makkedah all occurred before the sun set that day (vv. 26-27). Given the context of the narrative, the outcome of the battle, and the distance traveled during the confrontation, a literal interpretation of the text is warranted. It is suggested that the Lord slowed the rotation of the earth to allow one revolution on its axis in lieu of two for the same forty-eight-hour period.

Though the deist would deny such a feat, our God, who spoke all creation into existence, would be certainly able to counter the cataclysmic effects on earth this miracle would have otherwise caused. Whether it be opening dry walking corridors through seas or rivers, or daily airlifting 4,500 tons of manna to His people in a wilderness for forty years, or instantaneously calming the wind and waves of a sea during a raging storm, or keeping a man alive for three days in the belly of a great fish, or etc. – our God is able! May we, like Joshua, be people of faith who ponder what could be, instead of being defeated by our circumstances. There is no problem that catches God by surprise and none too hard for Him to handle.

Meditation

> This is a wise, sane Christian faith: that a man commit himself, his life, and his hopes to God; that God undertakes the special protection of that man; that therefore that man ought not to be afraid of anything.
>
> — George MacDonald

Step on Their Necks
Joshua 10:15-28

The Israelites had soundly defeated the armies of the five southern Canaanite kings. The five kings themselves fled the battle to hide in a cave at Makkedah, some thirty miles southwest of Gibeon (v. 16). Joshua was informed of the situation and instructed his officers to seal and guard the cave until the battle was over and he could arrive (vv. 18-19). Until then, every available Jewish man was needed to slay the fleeing soldiers before they could gain the safety of their fortified cities, which apparently some did reach (v. 20).

After the fighting ceased, all the Jews returned peacefully to their temporary camp at Makkedah. It is noted that the references to the Jews returning to Gilgal in verse 15 and to the Lord fighting for Israel in verse 14 are summary statements that have the general conflict in view; they are repeated at the end of the chapter after the specifics of the entire southern campaign are revealed in verses 16-41. It is suggested that the Jewish forces did not return to Gilgal until after the confrontation throughout southern Canaan had concluded.

As previously stated, Joshua, "Jehovah's salvation," is a strong Old Testament type of Christ; this will again become apparent to us in this narrative. When Joshua arrived at the cave, he commanded the five kings to be brought out. He then addressed his captains:

> *So it was, when they brought out those kings to Joshua, that Joshua called for all the men of Israel, and said to the captains of the men of war who went with him, "Come near, put your feet on the necks of these kings." And they drew near and put their feet on their necks. Then Joshua said to them, "Do not be afraid, nor be dismayed; be strong and of good courage, for thus the Lord will do to all your enemies against whom you fight"* (Josh. 10:24-25).

After Joshua's captains stepped on the necks of the kings, Joshua slew all five kings himself and had their bodies hung on five trees as a public testimony of their defeat. In accordance with the Law, the kings' bodies were removed from the trees before sundown and then placed in the very cave in which they had previously sought refuge (vv. 26-27). Stones were then piled up to block the entrance; this heap, like those at Jericho and Ai, would provide a lasting testimony of the Israelite victory.

What is the significance of pressing one's foot on the neck of an enemy? In the first place, this was an eastern custom to demonstrate complete victory. Moreover, the situation conveys an important spiritual lesson: God allows His children to share in the victory that is only possible through Him. It was not the captains who ultimately defeated the enemy, but Joshua, representing Christ. Accordingly, it was appropriate for Joshua alone to slay the kings with a sword. It was not the first time victory was shown to come at his hand. Forty years earlier, although many Israelites fought the Amalekites, Scripture records that *"Joshua defeated Amalek and his people with the edge of the sword"* (Ex. 17:13). Whether it was over the Canaanites or the Amalekites, victory came through Joshua, and victory over our enemies only comes through the Lord Jesus.

The overall picture before us has its prophetic origin in Genesis 3:15, which foretold Christ would bruise the serpent's head, and was fulfilled at Calvary: *"'Now is the judgment of this world; now the ruler of this world will be cast out. And I, if I am lifted up from the earth, will draw all peoples to Myself.' This He said, signifying by what death He would die* [speaking of crucifixion]*"* (John 12:31-33). In Genesis, God had said to the serpent (Satan), *"And I will put enmity between you and the woman, and between your seed and her Seed* [Christ]*; He shall bruise your head, and you shall bruise His heel"* (Gen. 3:15). At Calvary Satan was defeated by the seed of the woman. Yet, Paul uses the same analogy to encourage believers to stand strong in the Lord against evil and false teachers:

> *For your obedience has become known to all. Therefore I am glad on your behalf; but I want you to be wise in what is good, and simple concerning evil. And the God of peace will crush Satan under your feet shortly* (Rom. 16:19-20).

Paul may be referring to Christ's Second Advent, when He will return to the earth to judge wickedness and put Satan in the bottomless pit

(Rev. 19:17-20:3) or he may be speaking of the victory that a believer can have over evil today in Christ. The child of God is to constantly discern between what is holy and what is evil, between what is wise and what is foolish. That which is holy and wise should be obeyed, and that which is evil and foolish should be shunned. As a believer relies on God's grace to accomplish holy living, the victory is won through Christ, and the devices of Satan are spoiled. This ongoing spiritual victory is pictured by the captains, at Joshua's command, stepping on the necks of their conquered enemies, but then Joshua finishes them off. It is Joshua holding the sword, but the captains who relish in the victory.

The head of Satan was crushed at Calvary by the foot of the Lord Jesus. Consequently, the believer (being in Christ) has ultimate victory over Satan, the world, and the flesh. We are therefore able to proclaim this victory in the present life as we rely on Christ's grace and His word and loathe evil in thought and deed. It is His life within us that is pleasing to God, and if we choose to yield to Him, then He will accomplish something by us that counts for eternity: *"I have been crucified with Christ; it is no longer I who live, but Christ lives in me; and the life which I now live in the flesh I live by faith in the Son of God, who loved me and gave Himself for* [or "as"] *me"* (Gal. 2:20). If allowed, Satan may kill the body (Matt. 10:28), but that is the worst he can do, for the spirit, soul, and body of the believer belong to Christ (1 Thess. 5:23). As the bodies we presently have are not fit for heaven anyway, why then should we fear to lose what we must ultimately leave behind?

The Israelites were laying hold of their possession in Canaan by faith. Likewise, believers today only have the earthly benefits of their God-given possessions when they are empowered by God through active faith. Believers must co-labor with the Lord to be victorious in spiritual conflict – we war in response to His wherewithal. Paul acknowledges this same truth to the believers at Ephesus:

> *Finally, my brethren, be strong in the Lord and in the power of His might. Put on the whole armor of God, that you may be able to stand against the wiles of the devil. For we do not wrestle against flesh and blood, but against principalities, against powers, against the rulers of the darkness of this age, against spiritual hosts of wickedness in the heavenly places. Therefore take up the whole armor of God, that you may be able to withstand in the evil day, and having done all, to stand. Stand therefore, having girded your waist with truth, having put on the*

breastplate of righteousness, and having shod your feet with the preparation of the gospel of peace; above all, taking the shield of faith with which you will be able to quench all the fiery darts of the wicked one. And take the helmet of salvation, and the sword of the Spirit, which is the word of God; praying always with all prayer and supplication in the Spirit, being watchful to this end with all perseverance and supplication for all the saints (Eph. 6:10-18).

The Lord has made available spiritual armor for the believer to wear, but he or she must utilize it to be effective against the enemy. As a believer matures in Christ, endures trials, and continues probing God's Word ever more deeply, he or she becomes aware of other kinds of spiritual weaponry at his or her disposal. Using spiritual armor and weapons properly requires maturity and training: this requires active duty and full reliance on God.

An astounding victory was achieved over the southern Canaanite army and the city of Makkedah (v. 28) because the Israelites fought with full confidence that their God was able to defeat their enemy. F. B. Meyer reminds us that great difficulties are permitted to elicit the greatness of God's grace:

All through the conflict, Joshua's heart was in perpetual fellowship with the mighty Captain of the Lord's host, who rode beside him all the day. So amid all our conflicts, our hearts and minds should thither ascend, and there dwell where Christ is seated, drawing from Him grace upon grace, as we need; like the diver on the ocean floor, who inhales the free breeze of the upper air. At these times it is very necessary not merely to ask God to help us, because the word help may mean that there is a great deal of reliance on self and whatever there is of ourselves is almost certain to give way in the strain of battle. The divine part of our deliverance will be nullified by the alloy of our own energy, strength, or resolution. Let us substitute the word keep for the word help. Let us put the whole matter into the hands of God; asking Him to go before us, to fight for us, to deliver us, as He did for His people on this eventful day.[1]

Practically speaking, what commander would lead his troops on an all-night twenty-five-mile march uphill and then engage an enormous army without resting first? Yet, that is what Joshua did, and he did so without one murmur from his soldiers (v. 21). They marched all night without sleeping beforehand, then fought in hand-to-hand combat for another full day after arriving at Gibeon; in their weakness they learned of God's surpassing strength. As Paul explains, this is categorically the means in which God accomplishes His doings, for the purpose of securing His glory among men:

For you see your calling, brethren, that not many wise according to the flesh, not many mighty, not many noble, are called. But God has chosen the foolish things of the world to put to shame the wise, and God has chosen the weak things of the world to put to shame the things which are mighty; and the base things of the world and the things which are despised God has chosen, and the things which are not, to bring to nothing the things that are, that no flesh should glory in His presence (1 Cor. 1:26-29).

As in the second battle of Ai, the Lord used the previous failure of His people (i.e., the treaty with the Gibeonites) within His sovereign plan to ensure that a superior blessing was still achievable, if the Israelites would explicitly trust Him. The outcome was beyond anything they could have imagined – the strength of southern Canaan was brought to nothing in one day! Man fails, but God is able to pick up the pieces of each disaster and fashion a spectacular outcome; in so doing, every onlooker is prompted to extol Him with glory and honor.

Meditation

He who glories, let him glory in the Lord (1 Cor. 1:31).

"But let him who glories glory in this, that he understands and knows Me, that I am the Lord, exercising lovingkindness, judgment, and righteousness in the earth. For in these I delight," says the Lord (Jer. 9:24).

The Southern Campaign Continues
Joshua 10:29-43

With the main army of southern Canaan destroyed, Joshua quickly reassembled his troops for a series of swift raids against strategic cities. Moving southward in a zigzag pattern the Israelites conquered: Makkedah (v. 28), Libnah (v. 29), Lachish (v. 31), Eglon (v. 34), Hebron (v. 36), Debir (v. 38). Apparently, Makkedah fell on the same long day that the Israelites defended the Gibeonites. Most of the remaining cities were conquered soon thereafter and usually on the initial day of engagement, although the defeat of Lachish required two days of fighting (v. 28). Archeological evidence has confirmed that Lachish was a large city, second only to Hazor; this is probably why a second day was required to secure the city.[1] Most of these cities guarded thoroughfares into the southern highlands. Centuries later both the Assyrians under Sennacherib and then the Babylonians led by Nebuchadnezzar followed the same attack strategy on Judah.[2]

After securing the main military outposts in the region, the Israelites concentrated on the Shephelah, a region between the the central highlands and the Plain of Philistia, and the Neveh, a wilderness region in the far south of Canaan (v. 40). Verse 40 vividly describes what the Israelites did to the inhabitants of southern Canaan: *"they left none remaining, but utterly destroyed all."* This action was in obedience to Jehovah's command issued to them through Moses just before entering Canaan:

> *When you have crossed the Jordan into the land of Canaan, then you shall drive out all the inhabitants of the land from before you, destroy all their engraved stones, destroy all their molded images, and demolish all their high places; you shall dispossess the inhabitants of the land and dwell in it, for I have given you the land to possess* (Num. 33:51-53).

Conquest and the Life of Rest

The inhabitants of Canaan had the option of leaving, but instead the general population remained to withstand the Israelites. Rahab's testimony in Joshua 2 affirmed that the Canaanites knew about Jehovah and His past accomplishments both in Egypt and east of the Jordan, but despite this information they rebelled against the God of the Jews and suffered the harsh consequence – destruction. Of primary interest to Jehovah was that the land be a clean inheritance for His people (i.e., be swept clean of idolaters and idols). This the Jews labored to do, and God blessed their efforts. The entire region was quickly brought under Hebrew control: from Gaza in the west, to Kadesh-barnea in the south, to Gibeon in the north, and presumably to the Dead Sea in the east (v. 41).

While the armies of Jerusalem, Hebron, Jarmuth, Lachish, and Eglon were decimated in the initial battle for Gibeon, the fortified cities home to these armies still had to be conquered, and indeed they were. One city mentioned, Hebron, was particularly obstinate. The citizens of Hebron quickly appointed a new king to lead them into battle against Joshua, who had slain their previous king at Makkedah (vv. 26, 36-37). H. F. Witherby suggests that an instructive lesson concerning spiritual warfare may be gleaned from the second victory over Hebron:

> The king of Hebron was one of the five who had been slain at Makkedah, but a fresh king had been set up in the city. This center of government, with "all the cities thereof" and "all the souls therein," was now overthrown. In their rapid conquest, Israel had not had time to search out all the hiding-places of the fugitives, who therefore returned, and re-peopled and refortified old Hebron; hence it had to be reconquered. And in Christian warfare victory must be thorough. It is not enough to disperse and to scatter foes: the stronghold must be utterly destroyed. Spiritual foes, if baffled or even defeated, are not easily annihilated. Their lurking-places must be sought out, else the enemy recovers his strength and returns to the war with revived activity. No sitting still nor rest is lawful in this strife; spiritual energy and watchfulness need to be incessant, otherwise the wars will have to be fought over and over again.[3]

It is our nature to relax after realizing a goal or accomplishment, but spiritually speaking, there can be no final victory over the forces of evil until we are with the Lord. Thus, all of our present achievements are merely part of a continuing saga; we are at war, and no matter what the enemy might do to convince us otherwise, that fact will not change.

Until the Lord Jesus arrests the forces of evil, may we guard ourselves against capitulation and compromise, lest we too have to battle again to retake our Hebron.

The above victories in southern Canaan were secured so proficiently and abruptly that it seemed as if Joshua had vanquished the region all *"at one time"* (v. 42). With this said, Joshua was careful to record the reason for the achievement: *"the Lord God of Israel fought for Israel"* (v. 42). Israel had driven a wedge into the middle of Canaan and now the southern portion lay at their feet. The "divide and conquer" strategy employed by Joshua had been most effective, but only because the Lord had fought for His people.

With the lower half of Canaan now conquered, the Israelites came back to Gilgal before turning their attention northward. The fighting had been intense; a stay at their home encampment was needed to provide Joshua's weary troops with some much-needed rest and to permit him to prepare for the northern campaign. Fathers and sons were again joined with their families and expressions of joy and thanksgiving no doubt filled the camp.

Meditation

Onward, Christian soldiers, marching as to war,
With the cross of Jesus going on before.
Christ, the royal Master, leads against the foe;
Forward into battle see His banners go!

Crowns and thrones may perish, kingdoms rise and wane,
But the church of Jesus constant will remain.
Gates of hell can never against that church prevail;
We have Christ's own promise, and that cannot fail.

— Sabine Baring-Gould

The Northern Campaign
Joshua 11

The Canaanites in the North soon learned of the utter devastation the Israelites had inflicted in the South. In an act of sheer desperation, Jabin, the king of Hazor, summoned the inhabitants of northern Canaan to put aside their differences and to come together for the purpose of crushing the Israelites once and for all. The Amorites, the Hittites, the Jebusites of the mountains, the Perizzites, and the Hivites of Mizpah all responded. The combined forces and resources of all these people-groups are astounding: the gathering included *"as many people as the sand that is on the seashore in multitude, with very many horses and chariots"* (Josh. 11:4).

The first-century Jewish historian Josephus estimated the strength of this northern confederacy to be 300,000 armed foot soldiers, 10,000 cavalry, and 20,000 chariots (Antiq. 5.1.18). If this estimate is correct, the Israelite army was significantly outnumbered, aside from having neither cavalry nor chariots. As previously mentioned, Joshua probably commanded an army between 175,000 to 200,000 troops. Given their advanced weaponry, the northern confederacy would, statistically speaking, have about a 2 to 1 advantage over the Israelite force.

Apparently, the northern army was going to assemble themselves at the waters of Merom (Merom being about ten miles southwest of Hazor), and then march southward to attack the Hebrews in their encampment at Gilgal (v. 5). However, after learning of this coalition, Joshua assembled his troops and marched northward. Merom was ninety miles to the north – a five-day trek. As Joshua and the Israelites neared Merom, the Lord spoke again to Joshua: *"Do not be afraid because of them, for tomorrow about this time I will deliver all of them slain before Israel. You shall hamstring their horses and burn their chariots with fire"* (v. 6). The next day the Israelites descended on the northern army in a surprise attack which split their forces (v. 7). The Israelites continued driving their enemy westward to the seacoast and eastward to the Valley of Mizpah, slaughtering them as they went (v. 8).

Although the horses and chariots captured could have given the Israelites a strategic advantage in future battles, they obeyed the Lord's command and lamed the horses and burned the chariots (v. 9). There are at least two reasons for this. First, the Canaanites used horses in some of their pagan rituals and Jehovah did not want the resources available for the Jews to adopt similar practices. Unfortunately, centuries later, apostate Judah would ignore this historical lesson and employ both chariots and horses in ceremonies where the sun was worshiped (2 Kg. 23:11). The second reason for laming the horses and burning the chariots is best explained by King David:

> Now I know that the Lord saves His anointed; He will answer him from His holy heaven with the saving strength of His right hand. Some trust in chariots, and some in horses; but we will remember the name of the Lord our God. They have bowed down and fallen but we have risen and stand upright (Ps. 20:6-8).

The Lord did not want His people trusting in the devices of men or the strength of horses, but exclusively in Him for protection and victory. With good success on both battlefronts, Joshua turned his attention to conquering the cities which took part in the attack. Especially noted is the attack on the fortress of Hazor, the city responsible for organizing the northern confederacy. Archeological evidence suggests that Hazor was the largest city of ancient Palestine, with an estimated population of 40,000:

> Known as *Tell el-Qedah* in Arabic, Hazor is the largest biblical era site in Israel ...which is located about 10 miles north of the Sea of Galilee. The site consists of a mound, or tell of about 30 acres, the area of the acropolis or compound of administrative palaces, and to the north the lower city measuring some 175 acres. Covering roughly 200 acres, Hazor is four times the size of Lachish, Israel's second largest site.[1]

These findings would then suggest that Hazor was over twenty times larger than Jericho. Its prominent size explains why Joshua utterly destroyed the city and then burned it with fire (vv. 10-11); if the magnificent stronghold of Hazor was completely decimated by the Israelites, what city could possibly withstand them? With this example made of

Hazor, the spirit of resistance was broken in northern Canaan. Joshua did conquer the other cities engaged in the conflict and left no survivors (vv. 12, 14). These cities were spoiled, but would remain intact for Jewish occupation later. Only the city of Hazor was burned and made unfit for resettlement (v. 13).

J. N. Darby suggests an important spiritual principle conveyed to us in the destruction of Hazor: "Hazor was the capital; and it is the only city that Joshua burns during the northern campaign. That which is the seat of strength and energy according to the world cannot become the center of power according to the Spirit."[2] Just as the Lord did not want the Israelites to rely on Canaanite horses and chariots for wherewithal in future conflict, He did not want them to rely on earthly fortifications for protection either. He alone was to be their strength and solace; beloved, He alone is to be ours as well.

Meditation

> My hope is built on nothing less
> Than Jesus' blood and righteousness.
> I dare not trust the sweetest frame,
> But wholly trust in Jesus' Name.
>
> When darkness seems to hide His face,
> I rest on His unchanging grace.
> In every high and stormy gale,
> My anchor holds within the veil.
>
> — Edward Mote

The Rest of Conquest
Joshua 11:16-12:24

Reading the biblical narrative up through Joshua 10, one might get the impression that there were two swooping battles, one in the south and the other in the north, and that the Israelites conquered all of Canaan quite expediently. However, that was not the case; Joshua did not record the details of every battle and in fact notes that he *"made war a long time with all those kings"* (11:18). How long is a *"long time"*? Caleb's dialogue with Joshua in chapter 14 reveals the conquest of Canaan required seven years. This means that what was described to us previously were merely the initial battles in Canaan and the two greatest encounters of the entire campaign.

In reality, there were many conflicts, some of which Joshua specifically mentions in chapters 11 and 12. The entire region was in turmoil for seven years, so obviously there were many battles that occurred without an explicit biblical reference. Joshua did identify the extent of their military engagements: eastward to Arabah, a valley area north and south of the Dead Sea; southward to Mt. Halck and the Negev wilderness region; northward to the Valley of Lebanon and Baal Gad; and westward to the Mediterranean Sea (11:16-17).

The text highlights another accomplishment of the conquest: the Anakim, the giants who terrified most of the spies Moses sent into Canaan some forty-five years earlier had been vanquished (11:21-22). The spies who acted in fear instead of in faith planted doubt in the minds of the Israelites with their report and conclusion: *"Who can stand before the descendants of Anak?"* (Deut. 9:2). The Israelites now knew the answer: "We can, when Jehovah fights for us!" H. F. Witherby exhorts Christians to maintain the same attitude in Christian warfare:

"At that time came Joshua, and cut off the Anakim from the mountains." It will be remembered how the terror of the giants stood in the way of Israel gaining their possession when at Eshcol. Now these terrible foes were cut off from fastness and from city, and with their strongholds were utterly destroyed. When God's soldiers apprehend His strength, the giants fall before them. It is well always to be in our own eyes as grasshoppers, yes, to be less than the least, to be nothing, for when we are weak then are we strong; but it is well always to measure the enemy's might against the Almighty, and to go to war not only for the Lord, but entirely in His strength, and, when this is so, "at that time" the giants will fall.[1]

The Jews had discovered that without the Lord they were helpless, but with the Lord even the giants could not stand against them. Paul applies this principle to the ministry of believers in the Church Age: *"So then neither he who plants is anything, nor he who waters, but God who gives the increase"* (1 Cor. 3:7). It is natural for us to boast of our temporal accomplishments, but this is not profitable for eternity. May we remember the lesson that the Israelites came to appreciate: if the Lord is not in the work – we are wasting our time and resources! Conversely, when we are in the will and strength of God, we "can do all things through Christ" (Phil. 4:13).

While the Anakim were defeated, Joshua notes that some of the giants escaped to Gaza, Gath, and Ashdod. Centuries later this outcome proved to be regrettable, for Goliath, the giant from Gath, withstood the army of Israel and Jehovah (1 Sam. 17). How was the problem resolved? David, a lad zealous for the Lord, took down Goliath with a stone from his sling. A few years later his mighty men would also finish off Goliath's four oversized brothers in battle. Their testimony proves that when God's people become desperate for Him and are willing to fully trust Him, mountains are moved and giants are toppled (Matt. 17:20). Unfortunately, there was not an abundance of that type of faith in Israel after the land was possessed and divided.

Scripture records that the only people-group to seek peace with Israel was the Gibeonites; consequently, they alone survived the slaughter (v. 19). Why did not others capitulate? The Canaanites did not surrender despite their inability to retard the Jewish advance because God hardened their hearts. He caused them to unsuccessfully battle the Israelites until they were extinct (v. 20). Apparently, there had been a day of grace shown to the inhabitants of the land (which Rahab, her family, and the Gibeonites received), but in time this offer of mercy expired. Their choice was made and God then hardened their hearts in order to ensure His sovereign plan for His people was accomplished.

Jehovah dealt in a similar way with Pharaoh in the days of Moses. Though at times God hardened Pharaoh's heart to accomplish a particular purpose in time in accordance with His will, Pharaoh's heart was not entirely hardened by God, for he hardened it himself afterwards. Pharaoh maintained free choice in his overall decision-making. James states, *"Let no one say when he is tempted, 'I am tempted by God;' for God cannot be tempted by evil, nor does He Himself tempt anyone. But each one is tempted when he is drawn away by his own desires and enticed"* (Jas. 1:13-14). James confirms that it would have been impossible for God to cause Pharaoh to sin, for a holy God does not tempt anyone to sin; such behavior would be an affront to His righteous character.

Like the Canaanites, Pharaoh had free choice in whom he would choose to revere. God did not force Pharaoh to worship Egyptian gods, for a Holy God does not tempt humanity with evil or force anyone to do evil. Between Exodus 4 and 14, Pharaoh's heart is mentioned 20 times: on ten occasions it is the king's stubbornness at work (Ex. 7:13 {twice}, 13, 22, 8:11, 15, 28, 9:7, 34, 35, 13:5) and ten times it is God who hardens his heart to accomplish His will (Ex. 4:21, 7:3, 9:12, 10:1, 10, 27, 11:10, 14:4, 8, 17).

God would have been perfectly just to destroy a pagan like Pharaoh, but instead He designed ten specific plagues to prove to Pharaoh that He was superior to specific Egyptian gods. Pharaoh rejected this revelation and hardened his own heart against the Lord – he prepared himself to be a vessel of wrath fit for destruction (Rom. 9:17-22). God brought glory to His name by honoring Pharaoh's decision, one that God already foreknew. Jehovah's dealings with Pharaoh and the Canaanites show how human responsibility and sovereign design ensure that God will receive all the glory in every situation.

Similarly, the Canaanites had rejected the revelation God had shown them through creation (Rom. 1:19-23), their conscience (Rom. 2:15), and through a variety of spectacular miracles and wonders which were widely attested. God would have been just to speak the Canaanites out of existence, but rather He provided a window of opportunity for them to be spared. Rahab took advantage of that day of grace, humbled herself, and pleaded for mercy – she and those who would believe her testimony were saved from destruction.

Joshua 12 includes two lists of Israelite victories, the first under Moses' leadership and the second under Joshua's command. Moses had conquered the territories ruled by Sihon and Og which extended approximately 150 miles north to south on the eastern side of the Jordan River. This land would be settled by the tribes of Rueben and Gad, along with half the tribe of Manasseh. The second list contains a roster of sixteen kings of cities in southern Canaan and fifteen kings of cities in northern Canaan who would not yield to Jehovah and His people. Rather, these resisted and rebelled against the plan of God and were accordingly wiped out, along with all they represented. God is a longsuffering God, but there is a limit to His patience. His election (i.e., His purposes in time) for Israel must stand despite what man would do, or would not do.

A summary of all that had occurred thus far in time as well as a glimpse into what happened shortly thereafter is provided at the end of Joshua 11: *"So Joshua took the whole land, according to all that the Lord had said to Moses; and Joshua gave it as an inheritance to Israel according to their divisions by their tribes. Then the land rested from war."* This generalization seems to contradict what the Lord said to Joshua at the onset of chapter 13: *"there remains very much land yet to be possessed"* (13:1). Joshua did destroy the cities and all who were in them, however, many Canaanites chose to hide in rocky formations, caverns, and caves in the vicinity and then return to their homes after the Israelites had passed. Though conquered, the inhabitants were not completely removed. This fulfilled the prophecy of Moses who predicted the Lord would remove the inhabitants of Canaan *"little by little"* (Deut. 7:22). This would prevent wild beasts from multiplying in the area and keep the farmland from falling into disarray during the years of conquest.

So, while it was true that there were pockets of resistance remaining in Canaan (13:2-5), the Lord decreed that the land had been sufficiently conquered to be divided among His people as an inheritance. If the Jews remained faithful to the cause, Jehovah promised to continue to help each tribe or clan drive out the remaining inhabitants from their possession (13:6).

As previously mentioned, the Hebrew words *nuwach* and *shaqat* are translated "rest" six times in the book to express the Israelite's overall existence of tranquility, despite the necessity of further personal conflict in the land. This restful quality of life was enjoyed by the two and a half tribes who settled in the Eastern Plateau after Moses vanquished the warrior inhabitants (1:13, 15). Now, rest was apprehended by the nation in general, for the whole of Canaan had been conquered under Joshua's leadership (14:15, 21:44, 22:4, 23:1). The inward spiritual tranquility associated with this rest was only realized because the Israelites exercised faith in Jehovah through active conquest. By faith and obedience they had entered the land (their inheritance) and engaged in conquest to possess the land. That accomplishment now permitted them to rest within the land.

"The land rested from war," but a resting heart does not mean it has rest from difficulties, but rather we choose to tranquilly abide with the Lord through them. It is at such times that we learn more of Christ (His mind, His will, His character, etc.). Though believers are first possessed by Christ through grace, it is also by grace that we possess more of Him. Therefore, as F. B. Meyer explains, there is much to be gained during this resting process:

> Our best work for God cannot be done unless we have learned to be quiet; still, that God may mold us; tranquil, that the tremor of our nerves may not interfere with the thrill of his energy ... The restful heart lives above the storm and strife, with Christ, sensitive to human sorrow and to its own, but able to discern the purposes of divine wisdom to await the unfolding of the divine plan; and to trust the love of the divine heart.[2]

How does one gain a restful heart? The writer of Hebrews answers this question; we must *"be diligent to enter that rest"* (Heb. 4:11). In the same verse the writer informs us why the Israelites were not able to secure God's rest in the land, *"lest anyone fall according to the same example of disobedience."* The Greek noun *katapausis* is rendered "rest" in this passage and means "peace, repose, and tranquility." It implies a thoroughly settled disposition despite circumstances. It is by faith and obedience that we practically gain our inheritance in Christ. Once a particular portion is possessed, we must continue to exercise faith and obedience to retain that resource, else we will lose its benefit in time.

Reason thus dictates that faith is not a substitute for effort, nor is effort a substitute for faith. Neither can courage replace obedience, nor obedience, courage. The life of possession and rest is dynamic. Joshua learned in chapter 1 that such a life presses ever forward in faith, in obedience, and in courage. The child of God will be thankful for what has been gained, but will never be satisfied with his or her spiritual condition or wherewithal to serve God – for the glory of God there is a compelling urge to apprehend more of Christ and Christ-likeness. On this point, W. Graham Scroggie asserts:

> The truth about practical holiness has suffered at times, because it has been represented as something that needs not the effort of man for its realization. This, however, is not true. Just because we are rational and moral beings, we have some responsibility for our own sanctification. We are to consider, then, a quality of life which involves a forsaking and following, and which is entered into and maintained by faith which is trust in God, and by continuous energetic effort to translate belief into practice, to demonstrate in terms of character and conduct the truthfulness and power of one's creed.[3]

Collectively, the Jewish nation had prevailed against all the main outposts of opposition; now, it would be up to individual clans and tribes to rid the land of the remaining pagans. It is good for us to remember that on this side of heaven, God's people will never have an existence without opposition, but by resting in the Lord and working with Him we can be overcomers instead of overcome.

Meditation

> Sovereign Ruler of the skies, ever gracious, ever wise;
> All my times are in Thy hand, all events at Thy command.
> Plagues and deaths around me fly; till He bids I cannot die;
> Not a single shaft can hit, till the God of love sees fit.
>
> — Ryland

Land for Some and the Lord for Others
Joshua 13

The second and last main section of the book (Joshua 13-24) commences with a warning from the Lord: *"There remains very much land yet to be possessed"* (v. 1). As a result of seven years of faithful conquest, the Jews now possessed the land (i.e., all the main armies, military garrisons, and fortified cities had been defeated). Unfortunately, God's people became complacent after the land was divided and were not able to retain God's rest in the land. The corporate conquest of the first half of Joshua transitions to the confrontational efforts of the individual tribes in the latter portion of the book. In general, the Israelites did not continue in faith and obedience to conquer the remaining pockets of resistance. Their failure is a reminder to us that as long as an enemy is present (e.g., sin and the devil), conflict will be necessary and that such conflict can only conclude in two ways – in victory or in defeat.

Consequently, the astounding victories in the first section of Joshua are supplanted by the general weakness and inertness of God's people in the latter portion. With that said, there are portions of this narrative which gleam with grace. Caleb, for example, demonstrated that when individuals rise above the complacency of their nation, they are enabled by the Lord to do the seemingly impossible. Hence, there are practical lessons to be gleaned from this latter portion and the reader is therefore urged not to become discontented with a less than dynamic narrative.

In the concluding portion of the book, Canaan rests from warfare, the land is divided among the tribes, Shiloh becomes the location where Jehovah is worshipped, and six Cities of Refuge are established to uphold His righteous Law. The Israelites are given responsibility to maintain that which has been gained and to acquire what has not yet been subdued. The nation's history since that time indicates they did not follow either mandate well.

Conquest and the Life of Rest

Although generally speaking the Israelites had conquered the whole land (11:23), there was still a lot of land to yet possess (13:1), meaning there were several pockets of resistance remaining in Canaan. These are listed in verses 2 through 5. Yet, the Lord deemed the land sufficiently conquered to be divided among the nine and a half tribes for an inheritance; He would assist them in driving out the remaining inhabitants (v. 6-7). General Joshua, *"old and advanced in years"* (v. 1), was prompted by the Lord to become executor of the estate and oversee the land allotment process in the region before he died. He was approximately one hundred years of age at this time.

The land the Jews would settle can be divided into four parallel stripes running north and south: the coastal plain to the west, the central hill country, the Jordan River valley, and the eastern plateau (Transjordan). Accordingly, the main travel routes in Canaan ran in a north-south direction, except in the region of Galilee where five successive east-west valleys cut through the central Galilean mountain range. The vast and fertile Jezreel Valley marked the southern border of Galilee. As these valleys were easily traveled, people, communication, and invading forces often moved through them in an east-to-west fashion or vice versa.

The remainder of the chapter details the boundaries of the eastern plateau that would become the home of the two and a half tribes (vv. 8:13), and what portions of this region were allotted to each: Reuben (vv. 15-23), Gad (vv. 24-27), and Manasseh (vv. 29-32). Joshua again acknowledged Moses had given these two and a half tribes permission to settle on the eastern side of the Jordan River, rather than within the land of Canaan. This agreement required them to assist in the military campaign in Canaan. Having fulfilled their commitment, the fighting men from the tribes of Rueben and Gad and a half tribe of Manasseh were ready to cross the Jordan and return to their families. Joshua noted not all the inhabitants had been expelled from Transjordan; some giants still resided at Edrei (v. 12), and the Maacathites and Geshurites remained in the land and, unfortunately, were permitted to stay (v. 13).

As the various tribal allotments were about to commence, Joshua reminded the Levites they would not be given any particular territory, for the Lord Himself was their inheritance and their priestly service on behalf of the nation their great privilege (v. 14). H. F. Witherby speaks as to the prestigious ministry the Levites were given and how Christians today can likewise enjoy the Lord as their portion:

Levi was "scattered in Israel," according to the prophecy of Jacob; but Levi's portion was the most sacred and the most precious of all. Wherever the other tribes dwelt, there was Levi; wherever the devout spirits in Israel worshipped the Lord, there Levi had his inheritance. The Lord – not a position – was Levi's lot: "The Lord God of Israel is their inheritance." And so it is that the happiest and wealthiest Christians are they who find in the Lord Himself their portion.[1]

The Levites would be provided with forty-eight cities to live in, with a perimeter of pasture land around each city (14:4, 21:41). Their disseminated presence throughout the Promised Land meant that God's Word and those who understood it would be readily available to all the people. Anyone desiring to know God's Law would only need to travel a few miles to consult a Levite. This explains why the Levites were exempt from military service and were not permitted to settle in one region. Jehovah was to be the Lord of the entire land, not just one portion of it. By having Levites present at all times throughout Israel, there would be no excuses for ignorance or neglect – God's Law would be known and He would be revered by all His people.

Why were the Levites singled out for this great honor? We find the answer to this question in the book of Exodus. After leading the Israelites out of Egypt to the base of Mount Sinai, Jehovah summoned Moses to ascend the mountain. After spending forty days there, Moses descended to the Israelite camp carrying the Law of God written in two stone tables. Moses was angered to find the Israelites worshipping a golden calf and committing lascivious acts. The Law in his hands had already been violated and he was prompted to sternly rebuke the people. The golden calf was a direct challenge to the supremacy of Jehovah; thus, a call of separation was given: *"Whoever is on the Lord's side – come to me!"* (Ex. 32:26). Moses, fresh from God's presence, was altogether on the Lord's side in this controversy, but only the sons of Levi responded to the invitation (v. 27). After the opportunity of separation had passed, Moses pronounced judgment upon the unrepentant rebels. The Levites then were commanded to slay the idolaters and three thousand souls perished that day. Apparently, for their zeal, the Levites would be consecrated to full-time service at the tabernacle and, therefore, be exempt from going to war.

The firstborn males among the Hebrews had been spared death in Egypt by the substitutional death of a lamb. Redeemed by blood, these preserved souls were now the Lord's and represented the entire nation to God. In the wilderness, a transaction occurred to exchange all the firstborn of Israel for the tribe of Levi (i.e., soul for soul). Additional substitutional sacrifices and redemption money were required to account for the 273 more firstborn males in the nation than the total number of men in the tribe of Levi (Num. 3:39-51). As a result of this exchange, the entire tribe of Levi would be consecrated to serve the Lord and to affect worship in the tabernacle/temple on behalf of the nation. The other tribes would be responsible for supporting them and their ministry at the tabernacle and later in the temple.

Returning to the narrative, Joshua defined the land to be given to the two and half tribes settling east of the Jordan River. The Reubenites would settle in the land previously occupied by the Moabites east of the Dead Sea. The tribe of Gad would inherit the land directly north of them in the region of Gilead. The half tribe of Manasseh was granted the region of Bashan, which was directly east of the Sea of Galilee (referred to today as the Golan Heights).

Ironically, these two and a half tribes were the first to obtain their inheritance and also the first tribes to be completely dispossessed of it (1 Chron. 5:6). Why? This group of Israelites would be the first to embrace idolatry and, consequently, be divinely punished. Pul or Tiglath-Pileser III, the king of Assyria, deported Jews from the Eastern Plateau in 734-732 BC. Yet, the two and a half tribes had already lost some of their inheritance prior to this event. The Reubenites, for example, settled in the cities of Nebo and Kiriathaim (v. 19; Num. 32:37-38). These cities and others in the region were later captured by the Moabites. Heshbon had been the capital of Sihon, king of the Amorites, until the Israelites conquered it prior to entering Canaan (Num. 21:25-29). The tribe of Reuben rebuilt the city (Num. 32:37), but years later Moab recaptured it from Reuben.

It was not Jehovah's intention for the two and a half tribes to settle on the eastern side of the Jordan when the Hebrew nation first entered into Canaan, but He permitted it in response to their request. They had surmised that what God had for them in Canaan could not be better than the rich pasturelands they already knew existed on the eastern plateau. It would seem that their lusting for what was outside the will of God eventually led to idolatry, which then resulted in loss of their inheritance. May God's people today learn from this important lesson: continued lusting for what is beyond the will of God invariably leads to sin, the loss of God's blessings and fellowship, and finally destruction (Jas. 1:14-15).

Meditation

> The dearest idol I have known, whatever that idol be,
> Help me to tear it from Thy throne and worship only Thee.
>
> — Willam Cowper

Give Me This Mountain
Joshua 14

Having designated the land allotments east of the Jordan to the two and a half tribes, Joshua turned his attention to dividing and proportioning the land within Canaan to the remaining tribes. Joshua and the High Priest Eleazar would oversee the land disbursements as determined by the drawing of lots (vv. 1-2). This method of distribution had been previously commanded by Moses (Num. 26:55). Jewish tradition states the name of a tribe was drawn from one urn while the associated land allotment was drawn simultaneously from another urn.[1] It was understood that Jehovah was guiding the process, and the proceedings left nothing to chance (Prov. 16:33). This mindset would alleviate any assertion of unfairness or favoritism.

Does this mean that Christians should cast lots today to determine the will of God in a particular matter? The answer to this question is "no." The casting of lots was a God-sanctioned practice for the Jews to determine His mind on a particular issue. Scripture does not record the casting of lots as being a practice of the early Church to obtain divine insight. W. Graham Scroggie suggests that this Jewish practice has been replaced by several more intimate means of distinguishing God's will:

> In our time, in place of the "lot" are the Holy Spirit, the Word of God, the Throne of Grace, and the open or closed door, that is, circumstances. By these means we may discover what God's will for us is, and if we are subject to them, these means will never fail us.[2]

"The will of God," or the related phrases "the Lord's will," "the Lord will," or "Thy will" occur thirty-four times in the New Testament. Nineteen times the sovereign plan of God to accomplish a distinct purpose is in view. There are four references to the will of God being done or that it shall be done, and seven references to believers doing God's will. Scripture further declares that the expressed will of God should be understood, and three times it is specifically declared for all believers to know.

The term relates to a sovereign God accomplishing His purposes in time, whether it be through a specific event, or in conforming the behavior and attitudes of believers to be like that of His Son's. Several times in Scripture "The will of God" refers to the overall holy behavior that all believers should exhibit. For those aspects of God's will which are not fully revealed, the believer learns to trust God's guiding hand. In this way, God works on our attitudes, motives, and refines the quality of our faith. As an example, God is *"long-suffering towards us, not willing that any should perish"* (2 Pet. 3:9). How can God desire something, but yet not force it to happen? It is a mysterious unfolding of His foreknowledge and predestined blessings in Christ which are guaranteed to benefit those who in time repent and receive His Word. Thankfully, we don't have to completely understand the mind of God to obtain His blessing; God simply wants us to trust Him for what cannot be fully understood and obey what He has revealed to us. For those aspects of God's will which are clearly revealed, the believer learns to yield to the Lord – our conduct is brought into alignment with His will. This pleases God and promotes Christ-likeness, the ultimate goal of our salvation (Rom. 8:29).

Paul instructs believers to *"be not unwise, but understanding what the will of the Lord is"* (Eph. 5:17) in order to *"prove what is that good, and acceptable, and perfect, will of God"* (Rom. 12:2). Consequently, Paul exhorted the believers at Colosse, *"stand perfect and complete in all the will of God"* (Col. 4:12). Knowing, yielding to, and demonstrating the will of God is the goal of the Christian life. We are *to learn* the revealed will of God (Ps. 143:10) and *to delight* in doing it (Ps. 40:8). This was the example of the Lord Jesus Christ: *"Then said I, Lo, I come (in the volume of the book it is written of Me,) to do Thy will, O God"* (Heb. 10:7-9).

Following the Lord's example of doing God's will is not easy, in fact, it is impossible without relying on God's grace. Doing the will of God does not come naturally to us; in fact, our nature opposes God's will (Gal. 5:17). Any selfish motive or action to abide in the will of God will fail miserably. The only way to remain in fellowship with the Lord is to yield to His will – to do that which delights Him.

As pertaining to the revealed will of God, what does God expect of all true Christians? The following behaviors are the expressed will of

God for all believers. Before reviewing the list ask yourself, "Do I want to do the will of God?" If the answer is "yes," then read on. If the answer is "no," ponder the words of the Lord Jesus: *"Why call Me, Lord, Lord, and do not the things which I say"* (Luke 6:46). In other words, "Don't call Me Lord if you are not going to do what I say!" Though the whole of Scripture declares the will of God, the following are specific statements pertaining to the Lord's will for all Christians:

1. Serve and please the Lord instead of men (Eph. 6:6).
2. Do not be conformed to the world (Rom. 12:2).
3. By well-doing put to silence the ignorance of foolish men (1 Pet. 2:15).
4. Abstain from fornication (1 Thess. 4:3).
5. In everything give thanks (1 Thess. 5:18).
6. Suffer for well doing, rather than for evil doing (1 Pet. 3:17).
7. Do not be controlled by the lusts of the flesh (1 Pet. 4:2).

A true believer will long to know the will of God and then to do the will of God. Love for the Lord Jesus Christ prompts obedience: *"If you love Me keep My commandments"* (John 14:15). The believer is challenged to live for and invest into eternity. John wrote, *"And the world passes away, and the lust thereof: but he that doeth the will of God abides forever"* (1 Jn. 2:17). All that is of this world is going to vanish someday – only what is done for Christ has lasting value. May each of us know and yield to the revealed will of God and trust God's leading hand for that part of His will which has not been revealed to us. Let us obey what is known and trust the Lord to lead through the unknown.

The Jews in Joshua's day did not have the fuller revelation that we enjoy today, but they would soon learn that the lot was not per chance, but rather by divine providence. By lot, each tribe received the very portion that had been promised to them by prophetic utterance centuries earlier. This confirmed that a sovereign God was in full control of the distribution process. Likewise, in the Church Age, we learn that our possession of our inheritance in Christ is not only gained through conflict, but according to providence. As equipped by Christ, believers are enabled to fulfill their calling within the body of Christ (Eph. 4:11-12; 1 Tim. 4:14), and do the works for which God predetermined them to accomplish (Eph. 2:10). Accordingly, we too can be encouraged that nothing in our Christian experience is left to chance, for *"we know that all things work together for good to those who love God, to those who are the called according to His purpose"* (Rom. 8:28).

Before the allotment activity began and to eliminate any confusion among the tribes, Joshua explained again that the two and a half tribes mentioned in Joshua 13 already had their inheritance east of the Jordan and that the Levites were to dwell in cities. Therefore these tribes would not be taking part in the present lot-casting exercise (vv. 3-4).

Prior to the first lot being cast, the veteran Caleb stepped forward to assert his claim. Until now he had been quietly waiting because Joshua had been attending to the distribution in the Transjordan region first. Caleb's interruption was warranted and he reminded his lifelong friend, Joshua, of what Moses had promised him forty-five years earlier: *"Caleb the son of Jephunneh; he shall see it [the Promised Land], and to him and his children I am giving the land on which he walked, because he wholly followed the Lord"* (Deut. 1:36). The fortification of Hebron was to be the city of his possession, which still required the expulsion of the powerful Anakim (giants, see Deut. 9:2) who resided there.

Caleb, a Kenizzite, would not have received a land allotment with the tribes of Israel; thus, he presents a short autobiography as a prelude to his appeal (v. 6). Moses had promised him Hebron as an inheritance when the years of wandering had concluded and the nation entered into Canaan and conquered it. Moses rewarded Caleb for being a faithful scout in Canaan and for withstanding the rebel spies at Kadesh Barnea; Caleb was forty at the time (vv. 7-8). What was Caleb's motivation for standing with Moses at that turbulent junction? Caleb declares the answer in Joshua 14: *"I wholly followed the Lord my God"* (v. 8). Forty-five years later Caleb was still devoted to the Lord. He was faithful among a faithless nation, for he is one of the few who refused to establish an alliance with the Canaanites. He stood faithful with Joshua as a spy in the land and now he stood faithful among his people in the land.

The thirty-eight years of wandering and the seven years of warring in Canaan had passed since that tragic day of disbelief at Kadesh Barnea. Despite years of blistering desert heat and numerous military engagements, the Lord had wonderfully preserved Caleb; he was now eighty-five years of age (vv. 9-10). Despite his age, he remained strong in the Lord:

> *Yet I am as strong this day as on the day that Moses sent me; just as my strength was then, so now is my strength for war, both for going out and for coming in. Now therefore, give me this mountain of which the Lord spoke in that day; for you heard in that day how the Anakim were there, and that the cities were great and fortified. It may be that the Lord will be with me, and I shall be able to drive them out as the Lord said* (vv. 11-12).

The King James Version of the Bible translates verse 12: *"If so be the Lord will be with me."* However, there was no question of Caleb mistrusting the Lord; rather, he mistrusted himself. As H. L. Rossier explains, Caleb understood that if there were any obstacle to the Lord's being with him, it originated with himself:

> *We realize strength in proportion as we mistrust self,* and these two things surely go together. It is thus that we go from strength to strength. Isaiah 40:28-31 beautifully expresses the same truth: *"Even the youths shall faint and be weary, and the young men shall utterly fail."* This is the end of man's best strength, but *"the everlasting God, the Lord... faints not, neither is weary."* Our confidence is in Him, and more: *"He gives power to the faint; and to them that have no might He increases strength."* He communicates His strength to the feeble; it is made perfect in weakness. Then he adds: *"But they that wait upon the Lord shall renew their strength; they shall mount up with wings as eagles; they shall run, and not be weary; and they shall walk, and not faint."* Such was the case with Caleb. He walked in the consciousness that his strength was in and with God.[3]

Caleb is a great example to us in our present day of weakness and complacency. His character upholds the finest virtues to be found in soldiers of the cross today: one who is sold out for the Lord and yet mistrusts oneself. He exhibited unabated divine strength because he lacked self-confidence. His humility and continued dependence on God were unrelenting. H. F. Witherby suggests that Caleb's testimony should inspire every true believer to rise above the doldrums of earthly existence to experience real spiritual vitality:

> *"If so be the Lord will be with me, then I shall be able to drive them out, as the Lord said."* How this noble possessor shames the feeble, nerveless soul! To have lived for thirty-eight years in a very chorus of murmurings and yet still to sing "the Lord is my strength and my

song," is a miracle indeed, and a miracle it was, as Caleb owned, *"And now, behold, the Lord hath kept me alive, as He said." "As He said"*; three great words, greater than the accumulated murmurings of all Israel for eight and thirty years; *"As He said,"* for Caleb had not dropped down like other men of war and died. Few soldiers of Christ can so speak. Too many an aged Christian soldier seems to regard his long term of service as a plea for immunity from that hourly dependence on God, which at the first won him his victories; and "if the Lord be with us" becomes exchanged for the vainglorious and the degenerate, *"I will go out as at other times before, and shake myself"* (Judg. 16:20).[4]

Caleb understood that his dependence on the Lord infused him with divine power; thus, it did not matter to him that his possession was a fortification occupied by giants. Hebron, which the Anakim called Kiriath-arba, was his inheritance and he wanted to bravely claim it for God (v. 15). This city had special significance for the Jewish nation as Abraham and Sarah were buried there (Gen. 23:19, 25:10). Even though he was eighty-five years of age, he knew the Lord was with him and therefore he had confidence that he would drive the Anakim from his inheritance.

Joshua was moved by his friend's address and responded by blessing him and granting his request. Hebron was Caleb's possession (vv. 13-14), and in the power of the Lord he subdued the giants and restored to the city its proper name – Hebron (15:13-14). Caleb's fortitude demonstrates how God's people in any dispensation are able to overcome their adversaries and adversities: *"Not by might nor by power, but by My Spirit, says the Lord of Hosts"* (Zech. 4:6). May we, like Caleb, experience ongoing personal revival by wholly following and depending on the Lord God. Then, we too will be strong in the Lord and live in the enjoyment of heavenly things as we patiently engage in earthly conflict. Certainly, the abundant blessing of our True Joshua resides on every Caleb-like Christian.

Meditation

> Revival is a renewed conviction of sin and repentance, followed by an intense desire to live in obedience to God. It is giving up one's will to God in deep humility.
>
> — Charles Finney

Conquest and the Life of Rest

We cannot train ourselves to be Christians; we cannot discipline ourselves to be saints; we cannot bend ourselves to the will of God: we have to be broken to the will of God.

— Oswald Chambers

A Portion for Judah
Joshua 15

Having blessed Caleb and confirmed his inheritance, Joshua initiated the allotment process for the nine and a half tribes determined to settle in Canaan. The lots were cast and the tribe of Judah was chosen first. Joshua 15 describes the land endowed to Judah. Ephraim was the second tribe selected and Joshua 16 documents the land granted to them. Manasseh was the third tribe to receive its inheritance, the details of which are in Joshua 17. After battling the inhabitants in every nook and cranny of Canaan for seven years, the Jews had obtained a good geographical understanding of the Promised Land. Accordingly, the portions for each tribe are described in vivid detail to minimize any confusion later as to what land God's people would call home.

Judah was the largest tribe and would therefore receive a greater portion of land. Judah's southern boundary stretched from the bottom end of the Dead Sea westward to the River of Egypt (some 120 miles east of the Nile River). The Great Sea (the Mediterranean Sea) then formed the western boundary and the Dead Sea the eastward boundary. The northern boundary extended from the northern tip of the Dead Sea westward to the Mediterranean Sea (vv. 5-12). Although composing some fertile sections, especially in the western coastal plain, much of the region was rough and barren hill county.

Hebron was located within Judah's portion and Caleb not only took the city from the Anakim, but with the help of his courageous nephew Othniel, he captured Debir also (vv. 14-15). Caleb had promised that whoever was victorious at Debir would have his daughter Achsah's hand in marriage, so Othniel (who would later become a judge in Israel; Judg. 3:8-11) became Caleb's son-in-law (vv. 16-17). Caleb bestowed Achsah and Othniel with an arid region of land south of Hebron for their own inheritance, but after their marriage, Achsah asked her father Caleb for the springs near this land also, which Caleb granted her (vv. 18-19). W. Graham Scroggie suggests that this narrative portrays an important application for all believers to consider in obtaining their portion from the Lord:

> Achsah was not satisfied with this, and during the marriage celebrations she approached her father Caleb who asked her, "What do you want?" and this was her reply: "Give me a blessing; for you have given me a south land, give me also springs of water." "And he gave her the upper spring and the nether springs." For our present purpose the important words in this passage are: "You have given me," "give me also," and "he gave her."
>
> These words we may take over into the New Testament, and apply them to Christ and ourselves. Every believer can say to Him, "Thou hast given me," and we may well contemplate what He has given us; but could we know all that we have received from Him, we may still say, "give me also." Having any portion in Christ should lead us to long for more. So far as possession of our inheritance is concerned, no true Christian can ever feel satisfied, but will ever be yearning for and reaching forth towards something more, a richer portion, a completer blessing. If we will but say to Him: "Thou hast given me: give me also," how swift He will be to bestow blessings more and richer. He will give us the "upper and nether springs," so that we shall be like a well-watered garden.[1]

While the heritance of all believers is in Christ in heavenly places, we have previously seen that each believer must labor to possess what divine providence agrees to confer. In this chapter, we learn that the Lord desires us to ask Him for our portion that we might obtain abundant grace. Hence, we read of the Lord Jesus exhorting His disciples to petition His Father in His name for that which is lacking or needful:

> *Ask, and it will be given to you; seek, and you will find; knock, and it will be opened to you. For everyone who asks receives, and he who seeks finds, and to him who knocks it will be opened* (Matt. 7:7-9).
>
> *Therefore I say to you, whatever things you ask when you pray, believe that you receive them, and you will have them* (Mark 11:24).
>
> *Most assuredly, I say to you, whatever you ask the Father in My name He will give you. Until now you have asked nothing in My name. Ask, and you will receive, that your joy may be full* (John 16:23-24).

Years later, James informed carnal believers that they lacked essential spiritual resources because they failed to pray: *"Yet you do not have because you do not ask"* (Jas. 4:2). The Lord's liberality eagerly anticipates our righteous prayers! If we thirst for the abundant springs of heavenly life, we shall find them inexhaustible where we sojourn now, for *"He satisfies the longing soul"* (Ps. 107:9). Achsah had been bestowed a superb gift of land as a wedding present, but the significance of that possession was increased because she gained the nearby springs also. She received more inheritance because she requested it of her father Caleb. Likewise, our heavenly Father is aware of our needs and is able to grant to us all that we lack and all that would enhance our service for Him. Accordingly, may we not forget to respectfully and earnestly plead with Him, "You have given me" ... "give me also."

It is worthy to note that because Caleb trusted his God and engaged the enemy in His strength, he was victorious and, as a result, increased his inheritance. The land allotments were to pass down from generation to generation within the same tribe. In other words, an individual or clan could not increase their inheritance by buying or stealing from their brethren, but only by engaging and defeating the enemy. The prayer of Jabez illustrates this truth:

And Jabez called on the God of Israel saying, "Oh, that You would bless me indeed, and enlarge my territory, that Your hand would be with me, and that You would keep me from evil, that I may not cause pain!" So God granted him what he requested (1 Chron. 4:10).

While the Law prohibited Jabez from gaining land through financial acquisition, he could enlarge his territory through legal conquest (i.e., seizing land from those whom God said should be removed from the Promised Land). To further advance the Kingdom of God today, believers must do more than entertain each other in conquered territories (i.e., their homes and church buildings). They must be willing to venture out beyond these safe havens and storm the gates of Hell with the gospel message of Jesus Christ. The Lord is building His Church through the earnest efforts of His people to evangelize the lost. Let us never be satisfied with the status quo – may the Lord enlarge our capacity to serve Him as He enlarges His Church.

Because Caleb conquered in the name of Jehovah, he obtained more, which enabled him to bless others with more. Besides blessing his daughter and son-in-law with a gift of land which included springs of water, Hebron, the city he captured from the Anakim, became one of the forty-eight priestly cities and one of the six Cities of Refuge. Caleb did not object to sharing with others that which God had empowered him to possess. He was glad to bless others with what he had acquired in the Lord; this is a great example to follow.

Consequently, Paul reminded the believers at Corinth they should not be puffed up in themselves over their possessions: *"For who makes you differ from another? And what do you have that you did not receive? Now if you did indeed receive it, why do you boast as if you had not received it?"* (1 Cor. 4:7). Whatever we have comes from God; there is no room for pride. Paul further exhorted the Ephesians that, rather than stealing from others as they may have done before they were saved, they instead ought to work hard to supply their own necessities and then to assist those in need (Eph. 4:28). With this in mind, may we, like Caleb, not think so highly of ourselves and our possessions that we are not willing to assist others with what God has graciously placed in our stewardship. Caleb's example shows us the more we trust in the Lord for what we need, the more we will have to share with others and the greater our own blessing will be.

To prevent future confusion as to what cities, towns, and villages fell within Judah's portion, a lengthy list is provided in the remainder of the chapter. The tribe was to have twenty-nine towns plus their associated villages in the southern portion of Canaan known as the Negev (vv. 21-32); it is noted that thirty-six towns are listed, but seven of these were later assigned to the tribe of Simeon (19:1-7). More towns, in association with their villages, were allotted to Judah and are listed by region: forty-two in the Shephelah to the west (vv. 33-47), thirty-eight in the central highlands (vv. 48-60), and lastly, six in the wilderness area just west of the Dead Sea (vv. 61-62).

Many years prior to the events of the book of Joshua, the patriarch Jacob was nearing the end of his life and gathered together his twelve sons to bless them. His benediction, made while the nation was sojourning in Egypt, had many prophetic features. We see the direct fulfillment of several of these aspects in the portion of land Judah received in the Promised Land. Jacob had stated Judah would be surrounded by enemies (Gen. 49:8-9) and would inherit a land ideal for growing grapes (Gen. 49:11-12). Both aspects had come true. The spies Moses sent into Canaan had cut down a huge cluster of grapes from a vineyard in the valley of Eshcol, which was in Judah's territory (Num. 13:24). Judah was arguably the strongest tribe; Jacob foretold they would become as formidable as a lion (Gen. 49:9). It is no accident, then, that their land allotment positioned them as a lion to guard the southern entrance to the nation. They would, in fact, be surrounded by enemies: the Moabites on the eastern side of the Dead Sea, the Amalekites situated in the desert southwest of Judah, and the Philistines to the west. The Philistines would become a notable menace to the Jews for centuries to come.

In the far northeast section of Judah's inheritance, Joshua noted the presence of the Jebusites, who lived in Jerusalem, which was then called the "city of the Jebusites" (v. 8). Jerusalem would become the future location of the temple, God's dwelling place among His people. It was fitting for this center of worship (and future capital of the kingdom) to be located within the boundaries of this tribe, as in his prophecy Jacob also stated it would be through Judah that kings would rule over Israel. One day the scepter *"would come to the one it belongs"* (the literal meaning of *"until Shiloh come"*; Gen. 49:10), and it would never depart. This clearly speaks of the kingdom of the Lord Jesus, which will endure forever once He receives it. Jacob then described the manifold abundance of this kingdom in Genesis 49:11-12.

A wondrous scene will grace heaven's throne room just prior to the Tribulation Period, according to Revelation 5:5: *"Behold, the Lion of the tribe of Judah, the Root of David, hath prevailed to open the [scroll]."* In Revelation 5:6, the Lion of the tribe of Judah is identified as a Lamb standing amidst the throngs of heaven appearing as though it had been slain (indicating that the Lord Jesus will bear the marks of Calvary forever). The Lord Jesus, the sacrificial Lamb who took away the sins of the world, was now a Lion ready to unleash His fury and wrath upon those on earth in rebellion against Him. The Tribulation Period begins in Revelation 6:1 when He opens the first seal of the scroll and allows the Antichrist a short dominion over the world. What emotions will engulf us as we gaze upon the thorn-marked brow and the nail-torn hands of the blessed Savior for the first time? Will we weep or perhaps be speechless in the presence of the Lion of the Tribe of Judah?

Isaiah and Zechariah inform us that when Messiah returns to the earth to establish His kingdom, He will rule from Jerusalem (Isa. 66:10-21; Zech. 14:8-21). Although much prophetic excitement centers in the city of Jerusalem, the tribe of Judah chose to dwell peaceably with the Jebusites rather than to drive them out of that city (v. 63, Judg. 1:21). It was not until David captured the city from the Jebusites some five centuries later that it became the City of David (2 Sam. 5:6-8). In time, Jerusalem would expand north and west from the original City of David, and God's temple would be constructed just north of the Hill of Ophel on Mount Moriah (Neh. 3:26). In a coming day, a descendant of David, the Lord Jesus Christ, will return to Jerusalem, and when He does, He will rule all men forevermore (2 Sam. 7:16-17; Ps. 89:34-36).

Meditation

> All praise to Him who reigns above in majesty supreme,
> Who gave His Son for man to die that He might man redeem.
> His name above all names shall stand exalted more and more,
> At God the Father's own right hand where angel hosts adore.
> His name shall be the Counselor the mighty Prince of Peace;
> Of all earth's kingdoms Conqueror whose reign shall never cease.
>
> — W. H. Clark

Two Portions for Joseph
Joshua 16-17

Reuben, the firstborn of Jacob, should have been the leading tribe and the recipient of the double blessing bestowed by Hebrew custom as the birthright of the eldest son. However, Reuben committed adultery with Bilhah his father's wife; this led to the loss of his position (Gen. 35:22). In his final prophetic statement, Jacob likened Reuben's lusts and impulses to turbulent boiling water, saying these would result in his failure as a leader (Gen. 49:4). Indeed, by the time of the Judges, the tribe of Reuben was characterized by indecision and a lack of resolve to go on with the Lord (Judg. 5:15-16).

Because Joseph had preserved the young Hebrew nation from starvation during an intense famine and was the firstborn of Rachel, he was the one who received a double portion of the Promised Land. Ephraim and Manasseh were the two sons of Joseph (16:4) and each, because of Jacob's blessing, became tribal heads along with their eleven uncles. Ephraim at the time of the conquest was the third smallest tribe in Israel, numbering only 32,500 men (Num. 26:35-37) as compared to Judah's adult male population of 76,500 (Num. 26:19-22). However, adding to Ephraim's number were the 52,700 adult men from the tribe of Manasseh; this meant Joseph had more descendants in the Jewish nation than any other of Jacob's sons. In addition to the prominence of their sheer numbers, they would also inherit what was, in many respects, the most lush and fertile portion of the Promised Land.

Jacob not only blessed Joseph with the double portion, but the narrative of Genesis 48 contains several other prophetic statements pertaining to the tribe of Ephraim. After Joseph, the second highest ruler of Egypt, learned that his father Jacob was sick and bedridden, he wasted no time in ushering his two sons, Ephraim and Manasseh, into Jacob's presence for a final blessing. Jacob told Joseph that his two sons would be a part of a future Hebrew nation and, therefore, he desired to bless them. Joseph drew out his young sons from between his knees and carefully placed Manasseh on his left and Ephraim, his younger son, on his right. This positioning was to ensure Jacob's right hand would be upon Manasseh's head, so that he should receive the blessing of the firstborn.

However, Jacob crossed his arms and placed his right hand upon Ephraim's head and his left upon Manasseh's to announce the blessing. This matter displeased Joseph. Yet, Jacob refused to switch his hands. Jacob declared that Manasseh's younger brother would be greater than he and that Ephraim's seed would become a multitude of nations. Jacob called upon the One *"who redeemed him from all evil [to] bless the lads"* (Gen. 48:16). Although he had been slow to trust God in his younger years, Jacob now did so fully and verbally declared his faith in whatever way God deems best as he said to Joseph, *"I know it my son, I know it"* (Gen. 48:19). He understood Joseph's quandary over God's plan, but he had learned just to trust, because God's way always works out to be the best! God had already shown Jacob that He normally works by unconventional means to accomplish His will; in this way there is no question of His presence, and in the end, He achieves the greatest glory. Isaiah put the matter this way, *"For as the heavens are higher than the earth, so are My ways higher than your ways, and My thoughts than your thoughts"* (Isa. 55:9). Like Jacob, we too must remember this.

Jacob concluded his conversation with Joseph by informing him that he was near death and that he was bestowing Joseph with an extra portion of blessing above his brothers. This was the right of the oldest son and Jacob viewed his beloved son Joseph, the firstborn of Rachel, as the one who deserved it. Jacob had previously taken the hill country of the Amorites through conquest and was now giving it to Joseph. Interestingly, the Hebrew word for "portion" is *sekem*. This is apparently a word play on the town of "Shechem," which was that magnificent fortified city in the valley between Ebal and Gerizim. Jacob gave this specific area to Joseph. Later, Joseph would be buried at "Shechem" (Josh. 24:32) in order to be with his descendants when the resurrection occurred.

Joseph received the double blessing. Both Ephraim and Manasseh became the heads of their respective tribes; thus, each received a portion in Canaan and the Transjordan when it was divided. Although the division of the land was decided by lot, Ephraim and Manasseh received the very land that Jacob had specified to Joseph – the foothills and plain of Samaria (Josh. 16-17). Shechem was directly in the middle of this region. Years later, Ephraim would become the leading tribe of the Northern Kingdom and hold a position of superiority over Manasseh. Was Jacob just babbling vain prophecies? Apparently not. Everything he spoke to Joseph concerning his boys came true. Furthermore, the allotment prevented the tribe of Manasseh from being split apart; half of the tribe already had their portion on the eastern side of the Jordan River, and now the other half was to settle in the adjacent territory to the west of the river. God is in control! Let us not forget God is in control of every aspect of our lives.

Ephraim's Portion (Josh. 16)

The tribe of Ephraim would inherit an expanse of land stretching from near the Mediterranean Sea (Gath-rimmon) in the west to Jericho in the east (i.e., just shy of the Jordan River). Their southern boundary would run from Jericho, to Bethel, to Beth-horon, to Gezer and then northwestward to Gath-rimmon and would border Dan's and Benjamin's allotments (vv. 2-5). The northern margin ran along the Kanah River westward to Tappuah, as well as northeastward to Shechem, then southeastward through Ataroth back to Jericho (vv. 6-8). Manasseh lay beyond this northern line; however, to promote unity among the tribes of Joseph, Ephraim had a few towns within Manasseh's inheritance (v. 9).

One significant city within Ephraim's borders was Shiloh, which would be the home of the tabernacle for nearly four centuries until the Ark of the Covenant was captured by the Philistines (18:1). After its return to the Jews, the Ark was eventually moved to Jerusalem by David where it remained until the Babylonian invasion four centuries later. Consequently, Shiloh was the religious center of the nation during the time of the Judges, and it was the location where Samuel was raised by Eli and then called by God to be a prophet.

Unfortunately, like the tribe of Judah in the previous chapter, the Ephraimites did not drive out the Canaanites from their possession. Instead, they sought to profit from their presence by enslaving them (the inhabitants of Gezer are specifically mentioned in verse 10). This, however, proved to be a costly mistake; during the times of the Judges, these roles reversed and the Canaanites enslaved the Ephraimites (Judg. 1:29, 4:2). How often this same tragedy occurs today; the sin that Christians choose to tolerate and manage instead of mortifying grows stronger and,

Conquest and the Life of Rest

in time, ultimately become the master. Surely, if the Ephraimites knew their children would one day be slaves to the Gezerites, they would have obeyed the Lord and removed them from their land. May we count the cost now: a ruined life and testimony is just too high a price tag for a few moments of fleeting pleasure.

Manasseh's Portion (Josh. 17)

Joshua noted the descendants of Makir, Manasseh's firstborn son, settled on the eastern side of the Jordan River; the remainder of the tribe received a possession in Canaan (vv. 1-2, 7-10). Their southern boundary was described above, as it bordered the tribe of Ephraim. Manasseh extended northward with the sea coast to the west and the Jordan River to the east. The northern boundary crossed from the Mediterranean Sea at Dor, and ran through Megiddo, Jezreel, and over to Beth Shean near the Jordan (vv. 11-16). Issachar and Asher would be the tribes adjacent to Manasseh to the north; in fact, Manasseh was given several cities which were within Issachar's and Asher's domains (vv. 11-13).

A special mention is made of the five daughters of Zelophehad, a descendant of Manasseh who had no sons to whom to pass on what was to be his inheritance in Canaan. The women asked Eleazar, the High Priest, to make good on the previous ruling concerning their inheritance. Their case had been heard by Moses before he died and settled by the Lord Himself – these women were to receive a tribal allotment, and so they did (Num. 27:1-11).

The Complaint

Some within the tribes of Ephraim and Manasseh complained to Joshua that the land was not sufficient for them: *"Why have you given us only one lot and one share to inherit, since we are a great people"* (v. 14). They reasoned that because they were *"a great people"* and had only received one portion for Ephraim and the half tribe of Manasseh, they deserved more land. F. C. Cook explains why their argument was foolish on several points:

> The assertion can hardly have been warranted by facts, for at the census (Num. 26) the two tribes of Manasseh and Ephraim together were not greatly more numerous than the single tribe of Judah; and now that half the Manassites were provided for on the eastern side of the Jordan, the remaining children of Joseph could hardly be stronger than

the Danites or the Issacharites. The children of Joseph seem therefore to exhibit here that arrogant and jealous spirit which elsewhere characterizes their conduct (Judg. 8:1, 12:1). A glance at the map shows that their complaint was in itself unreasonable. Their territory, which measured about 55 miles by 70, was at least as large in proportion to their numbers as that of any other tribe, and moreover comprehended some of the most fertile of the whole promised land.[1]

In summary, their allotment was large and fairly portioned with their population: there had been no injustice committed in the process. Joshua was from the tribe of Ephraim; perhaps the tribal leaders thought they would receive preferential treatment in the resolution of their complaint. However, the matter had been decided by the casting of lots, and the outcome was clearly controlled by the Lord. Joshua was not a respecter of persons, but merely sided with the Lord on the matter (Jas. 2:9).

Instead of granting them more land, Joshua turned their statement around and admonishes them. Because they were a powerful tribe, they should be able to drive out the Canaanites and clear the woodlands – then they would gain more land in which to settle (v. 15). The children of Joseph countered this charge by reminding Joshua that the Canaanites who remained in the land had iron chariots, and that much of the hill country was forested and untillable (v. 16). Joshua upheld his decision, telling Ephraim and Manasseh something to the effect of: you will not be receiving any more by lot; there is plenty of land for you to possess, but you will have to work to obtain it (vv. 17-18).

It is our nature to want "freebies," but the spiritual believer will better appreciate what is accomplished though perseverance than what is gained without it. Co-laboring with God in His program and with His power is a great privilege and produces lasting results for which we can glorify Him. On this point, F. B. Meyer suggests the claims of the children of Joseph are not much different than Christians today who desire the thrills of Christian service only if it is what they want to do and if it can be easily accomplished:

> Like so many more they were content to live on the strength of past tradition, upon their numbers and prestige; and to base upon these considerations, claims which they were too indolent to make good by deeds. How often we ask God for wider spheres of usefulness, whilst we fail to utilize those which lie within our reach. "Cut down wood," is an injunction which might very fairly apply to us all. Do not sigh for

> missionary service till you have covered the whole acreage within your reach – in the home circle, or amongst the children of some poor district. The wood may be thick, but the ax of persevering faith will make a clearing there... some Christians *exist*, others *live*; others again *reign in life* .... Some have life; others have it "more abundantly."[2]

Unfortunately, instead of the swinging the ax and wielding the sword to appropriate their possession, those in Ephraim and Manasseh thought it better to tolerate and profit by the Canaanites who resided within their territories, ignoring the clear command to drive them out of the land. What often seems to be the path of least resistance at first becomes the hard and arduous way later; their decision to disobey Joshua's exhortation would prove to have painful consequences in future years. May each of us do our best, showing diligence with present duties and opportunities, for the glory of God that by the grace of God we may be spared agonizing disappoints and repercussions later!

Meditation

> Dr. Ironside, when a boy, helped his widowed mother by working during vacations, Saturdays, and when out of school for a Scottish shoe-worker who was a Christian. He posted Bible verses all over the shop so that everywhere one looked, he would see the Word of God. No package went out to a customer without a tract or a word of testimony, and many came back for salvation. Dr. Ironside's job was to pound leather for shoe soles. A piece of cowhide was cut to size, soaked in water, and pounded until it was hard and dry. After endless poundings, he was weary. One day, he noticed that another godless cobbler was not pounding, but was nailing the soles while still wet. "So they come back quicker," was the reply. The Christian owner explained to Ironside: "I do not cobble just for 50¢ or 75¢ from customers. I do it for the glory of God. In heaven, I expect every shoe returned to me in a pile, and I do not want the Lord to say, "Dan, that was a poor job. You did not do your best."[3]

Seven Portions for Seven Brothers
Joshua 18:1-19:48

The Jewish encampment moved twenty miles northwest from Gilgal to Shiloh, within Ephraim's new borders. Shiloh was a city built on a hill about nine miles north of Bethel. The tabernacle was erected there as a reminder to the people that they must continue to depend on Jehovah to ensure their prosperity in the land (v. 1). With their enemies subdued, this city would be a centralized location in Canaan for all the tribes to offer sacrifices and to keep the feasts. Shiloh would continue to be the religious center of the nation until the days of David.

For over forty years the Jews had been a nomadic people. Perhaps Joshua sensed some hesitancy among the remaining tribes to disseminate and establish homesteads. We are not told what prompted Joshua to exhort the people to take action; perhaps the Jews were just weary and fatigued after a long military campaign (18:2-3). Joshua, wanting to move the allotment process forward, requested three skilled representatives from each tribe work together to survey all the land that remained to be divided and to create a detailed geographical map of it (18:4-9). The survey may have been partly in response to some within Ephraim and Manasseh's ranks who complained about their portion being inadequate. Joshua may have also sought to involve more of the people in the process in order to re-excite them about securing their inheritance. With all the facts at hand, the allotment could continue in a manner that was satisfactory and would hopefully quell further grumbling.

After the map (a scroll) was created, Joshua cast lots for the remaining seven tribes and the land provided was then proportioned according to the tribe's size (18:10). As reviewed in the previous chapter, Jacob gave the birthright blessing and double portion to Joseph's two sons (Gen. 48), and when Joshua cast the lots, Jacob's prophetical predictions for those two tribes were upheld. As recorded in Genesis 49, Jacob gathered and blessed his other eleven sons also. As with Joseph's sons, these blessings were prophetic in nature and were confirmed, at least in part, by the casting of lots by Joshua at Shiloh. For some of these tribes, their destinies in Canaan reflected the moral inclinations and characteristics of their tribal heads long ago.

Seven Portions

Simeon and **Levi** were men of violence, referring to the time they slaughtered the Shechemites (Gen. 34:25-29) to avenge their sister Dinah's defilement. Because of their cruelty, Jacob had said they would be divided and scattered in Israel (Gen. 49:5-7). By the time of the second census of the children of Israel, the tribes of Simeon and Levi are recorded as the smallest two (Num. 26:12-14, 62); accordingly, Simeon now received a smaller portion of land for an inheritance. The Levites, as discussed in Joshua 21, would live in forty-eight cities; the Lord and not land was to be their inheritance (18:7).

As Judah had a vast region of territory, which was more than they needed to settle their tribe, Simeon was given seventeen of their towns with the associated villages for a possession (19:1-9). This tribe would later be mostly absorbed into Judah and lose their distinction. In fact, some from Simeon would later migrate northward and re-settle in Ephraim and Manasseh after the kingdom split following Solomon's death (2 Chron. 15:9, 34:6). Thus, the Southern Kingdom was essentially composed of the tribe of Judah alone, as the tribe of Benjamin had been nearly eliminated by civil war.

Jacob further prophesied that **Zebulun** would be enriched by sea trade (Gen. 49:13) and that **Issachar** would be compelled to work for others and dwell in the Plain of Esdraelon (Gen. 49:14-15). Again the lots cast by Joshua and Eleazer confirm Jacob's prophecy. Both tribes would dwell by the sea, but because of the flatness of the terrain, they often fell prey to invading armies and were compelled to labor for others. Zebulun was given a portion of lower Galilee which likely contained a strip of land through Issachar's possession that gave them access to the sea (vv. 19:10-16). Issachar was given the fertile Jezreel valley south of the Sea of Galilee and a region that wrapped around Zebulun to span the coastal plain (19:17-23). The Jezreel/Megiddo valley has a vast history of warfare with thirty-four historical battles known to have been fought there. It will be the sight of the future battle of Armegeddon during the Tribulation Period (Rev. 16:16, 19:17-21).

Jacob had seen that **Dan**, whose name means "judge," was going to be as treacherous as a snake by the roadside instead of being righteous and providing justice to Israel. The least desirable portion fell to Dan (19:40-48). Their tribal margins are not described because they were bounded by the already-detailed borders of Ephraim and Manasseh to the north, Benjamin to the east, and Judah to the south. Later, after losing part of their territory to the Amorites, many from this tribe abandoned their God-given inheritance and moved north of Naphtali. They conquered and burned the city of Leshem (Laish), settled in that region, and rebuilt the city, calling it "Dan" (Judg. 18:27-29). They would also be the first tribe in Canaan proper to engage in flagrant idolatry (Judg. 18:30).

Asher inherited the coastal plain from Mount Carmel north to Sidon and Tyre (19:24-31). The tribes of Naphtali and Zebulan lay on Asher's eastern border. Apparently, Asher was to guard the Israelites from sea invasions, the Phoenicians being of primary concern. Although this tribe would become insignificant in size and status, they did not lose their distinction as some other tribes did. Anna, who uttered a jubilant prophetic blessing at the sight of the infant Jesus, was from Asher (Luke 2:36-38). On that occasion she demonstrated the meaning of Asher's name, "happy."

According to Jacob, **Naphtali** would enjoy the peace of the high hill country in Israel and when the lots were cast, Naphtali indeed received the north-central highlands for an inheritance (19:32-39). The Sea of Galilee and the Jordan River marked the tribe's eastern boundaries. The Litani River, as it is called today, runs out of the Valley of Lebanon and was their northern border. The land of Asher lay to the west and Zebulun and Issachar lay to the south.

Benjamin was described by Jacob as a tribe that would be as violent in spirit as a ravenous wolf devouring its prey. This prophecy was clearly seen in the wickedness of the tribe of Benjamin in Judges 19 and 20, and in their refusal to repent but rather to war with all the other tribes of Israel. This error nearly resulted in their eradication from the commonwealth of Israel. Their portion of land spread only twenty-five miles east to west, and only between seven and fifteen miles north to south; it was located between the two strongest tribes: Ephraim to the north and Judah to the south (18:11-28). The cities of Jericho, Bethel, Gibeon, Ramah, Mizpah, and Jerusalem fell within their tribal borders.

Every lot fell according to the providence of God. This was demonstrated by the direct fulfillment of Jacob's prophetic statements uttered centuries earlier (Gen. 49). Witnessing the allotment process had to be an exhilarating experience for the various tribes; God had a specific blessing in mind for each of them. Yet, each possession to be distributed also had a unique commission associated with it; this would serve as a test. Joshua would no longer be leading the nation into battle. To enter into and retain God's rest was now the responsibility of every tribal and clan leader. Would these men follow the faithful examples of Joshua and Caleb, or would they become comfortable, complacent, and compromising? The former behavior would secure God's rest in the land, but the latter would diminish the benefit of the possession they fought so hard to obtain.

Meditation

> Until self-effacing men return again to spiritual leadership, we may expect a progressive deterioration in the quality of popular Christianity year after year till we reach the point where the grieved Holy Spirit withdraws – like the Shekinah from the Temple.
>
> — A. W. Tozer

Joshua's Portion
Joshua 19:49-51

Only after Joshua had finished dividing the entire region among the tribes did he request and receive his inheritance. His spirit of humility contrasts with the "me-first" mentality that many church leaders regrettably exhibit today. Caleb (Josh. 14) and now Joshua were specifically rewarded for their past faithfulness at Kadesh-barnea. Joshua did not ask his brethren for a prime piece of real estate, nor did they offer one to him; rather, he requested Timnath-serah for his possession (19:50-51). Timnath-serah was a city situated in the rugged and barren hill country of northern Ephraim about eleven miles southwest of Shiloh. This proposal was readily agreed to by the entire nation (19:49).

We have learned that our possession is obtained by *conquest*, in accordance with *providence*, and is bestowed in grace as *requested*. Each of these aspects may be observed in the receipt of Joshua's inheritance. He labored with his fellow countrymen to drive out the inhabitants from his possession (11:18, 23). His portion, the city of Timnath-serah, was through providence: *"according to the word of the Lord"* and he received the very inheritance that he had asked for (v. 50). A fourth consideration pertaining to the receipt of our inheritance in Christ now is here exemplified. Joshua received his possession in accordance to his *capacity* to retain it and use it to bless others.

Like Joshua's forefather Abraham when he parted from Lot, he was pleased to inherit the lesser position and the greater work associated with it, in order to gain an even better inheritance in God's kingdom (Gen. 13:9-18). Hence, Joshua endeavored to build up the city and live among his tribal brethren until the end of his days. Joshua had no thoughts of retiring, though he certainly deserved a break after years of faithful and arduous service. Instead of relaxing, he chose to improve the quality of life for others in his autumn years. Whether as general or administrator, his tenacious yet unpretentious character in serving others and the Lord is to be admired. His years of moral and spiritual grooming increased his capacity to receive and retain a greater portion from the Lord and for the Lord. Accordingly, Joshua was able to use what he had received to bless others and be a splendid testimony of God's grace to all that would look upon his accomplishments.

To possess our inheritance in Christ now requires active faith and obedience on our part; God's grace in accordance with His foreknowledge accomplishes all the rest. Moses said that it was God's plan for the Israelites to toil in Canaan that He might drive out the inhabitants of the land *"little by little"* (Ex. 23:30). Canaan was only a small section of their overall heritance, but it was the portion to be secured first and it would not happen overnight (Gen. 15:18-21; Josh. 1:4). They were in their infancy as a nation and fresh out of the wilderness; there must be spiritual growth to adequately retain their inheritance and benefit from God's rest in the future.

By God's grace they did conquer Canaan after seven years of conquest. Canaan was the stated objective even before Moses confronted Pharaoh; thus Canaan was the hope of every Jew departing Egypt and years of slavery (Ex. 3:17). While it is true that the descendants of Abraham through Jacob held the title deed to the Transjordan region, it was not in God's purposes for the Jews to settle there at this time. Spiritual maturity must be developed and Jehovah had to teach His people many lessons in Canaan before they would have the capacity to receive and preserve more possession. However, the Eastern Plateau was granted to the two and a half tribes for a possession prior to the nation's entrance into Canaan because they asked for it. It was not God's best, but it was permitted nonetheless because they had requested it. Our heavenly Father longs to grant the requests of His children, and is able to train and develop them through any corridor of time or permutation of circumstances.

The situation with the two and a half tribes and the distribution of land to the tribes in Canaan illustrates another important aspect of our receiving our divine inheritance; it is conferred in measure according to our capacity to benefit from it at the time. For example, the two and a half tribes, because they had much cattle requested of Moses: *"Let this land be given." "Bring us not over the Jordan"* (Num. 32:5). They asked for what had not been appropriated for them, but God permitted it for much the same reason He permitted Israel to anoint a king – to teach His people through difficult circumstances to trust in His rule for them (1 Sam. 8:5-9).

While it is true that God is faithful to work with His children in either case, the best pursuit in life is to affirm that an all-wise God knows what our portion in Christ should be at any particular juncture in time. The Lord knows our spiritual maturity and what we are able to receive in grace, retain by faith, and selflessly exercise for His glory. If He bestowed more blessing to us than what we could spiritually manage, we, in time, would most likely lose the benefit of what we had received previously in grace. The two and a half tribes ultimately lost what they had requested and received because it was outside of God's best timing for them to have it. We learn from their situation that our inheritance in Christ (speaking of the here and now) is not only appropriated by conquest, providence, and request, but it is also possessed according to our capacity to receive and retain it. This principle is not only witnessed in the receipt of Joshua's inheritance, but also in the responses of some of the tribes to their allotted possessions. Three particular examples are noted.

First, after the children of Joseph received their allotment of land, they proclaimed that it was *"not enough"* (17:16). Joshua informed them that it was, and that because they were a strong tribe they must labor to cut down the forest land and to remove the Perizzites dwelling in their portion (17:15). God had provisioned them exactly what they needed in accordance with their capacity to seize it in faith – they were to stop complaining and get to work! This illustrates that in some situations God has provided all that we need to be conquerors, but either fear or complacency rob us of the blessing. At such times we, like the children of Joseph, are to *"get up"* and *"cut down."*

Second, Judah received a portion of land that was *"too much for them"* (19:9). However, in God's plan He would bestow the weaker tribe of Simeon an inheritance within Judah's territory. Without Simeon's presence and assistance, the region would have been too vast for Judah to settle, maintain, and protect. However, the cooperative spirit that developed among these two tribes in driving out and conquering the remaining inhabitants is one of the encouraging highlights of the book of Judges (Judg. 1:3, 17). In some instances, God grants us a greater portion than what we are capable of inheriting alone, that we might learn to grow in grace by working with others for the cause of Christ.

Third, the tribe of Dan determined that their portion was *"too little for them"* (19:47). Initially, it was not so, but in time the Amorites took over much of their position. While the best response would have been to drive out the inhabitants within their designated possession, as God had commanded them to do, they did move north to conquer Leshem and claimed it as their new possession. Like the Transjordan (the home of the two and a half tribes), Leshem was within the vast region of land promised to Abraham centuries earlier. God's permissive will ensures that His grace is available to us, even when we willfully stray from His best plan for our lives. God permits us to choose what we do, but He chooses the consequences of what we do.

There are consequences of choosing the *permissible* instead of the *good*, or choosing the *good* rather than the *best*, but our heavenly Father is capable of bestowing blessing as He chastens, corrects, and redirects. As the writer of Hebrews affirms, this parental discipline is an affirmation of God's love for us (Heb. 12:6). The Lord may bestow to us what we request to teach us a valuable lesson as He did with the nation of Israel after they demanded a king. It was not what He wanted for His people, but His people needed to learn this fact through experiencing the consequences of lusting for what was outside the will of God.

Jehovah's division of Canaan to the various tribes confirms an important principle concerning the believer's capacity to possess and retain his or her inheritance in Christ: Our possession received is related to how we have personally and previously experienced Christ. Because each of us had a unique upbringing, has different emotional, moral, and mental constitutions, has various needs, and has suffered a variety of difficulties, the Lord means something a bit different to each of us. In short, we each have the same blessed Savior, but know Him differently.

In heaven, each of us will appreciate the Lord Jesus to the extent we have practically experienced Him in this life (2 Cor. 4:17). This may explain why each saint in glory will receive a white stone with a special name (presumably of the Lord Jesus) written on it; a name that no one else is aware of (Rev. 2:17). Among the throngs of heaven each person is guaranteed a special intimacy with the Lord Jesus, in which no one else can enjoy. Our lives are diverse, which means the Lord means something different to each of us. To the widow He is "the Faithful Husband." To the orphan He is "the Caring Father." To the abused He is "the Comforter of Sorrows." Etc.

In the Christian experience, the inheritance we each possess presently relates directly to how each believer has experienced the Lord's gracious and holy character. The Lord does not bestow such things as power and authority lightly; these are received in measure and in accordance to our capacity to retain each gift of grace in faith, love, and humility. To apprehend that which cannot be managed in wisdom would surely result in a worse outcome than not having a possession at all. Believers have different spiritual gifts, callings of ministry, talents to serve, and developed maturity in Christ. This means that each of us has different and varying capacities to receive and retain resurrection power as a spiritual possession. Paul puts the matter this way:

> *That I may know Him and* **the power of His resurrection**, *and the fellowship of His sufferings, being conformed to His death, if, by any means, I may attain to the resurrection from the dead.* **Not that I have already attained**, *or am already perfected; but* **I press on, that I may lay hold** *of that for which Christ Jesus has also laid hold of me. Brethren, I do not count myself to have apprehended; but one thing I do, forgetting those things which are behind and* **reaching forward** *to those things which are ahead,* **I press toward** *the goal for the prize of the upward call of God in Christ Jesus. Therefore let us, as many as are mature, have this mind; and if in anything you think otherwise, God will reveal even this to you. Nevertheless, to the degree that we have already attained, let us walk by the same rule, let us be of the same mind* (Phil. 3:10-16).

Paul affirms His desire to know Christ more and further experience His resurrection power in his own life. Paul was not perfect. He had not apprehended all that was available to him, but was determined to press forward to obtain all that could be possessed. He informs those lacking in maturity that they may not understand this principle presently, but just to press forward in faith and obedience in what they knew to be true – spiritual maturity and blessing would come. The same is true for us there is much more inheritance to possess, but God is wise to grant only that portion for which we can both receive and retain. We are to thank God for what has been received, while at the same time continuing in conquest and requesting from Him a greater portion of His riches in Christ. May each believer learn from Joshua's humble and faithful example; he blessed others with his received possession while at the same time preserving God's rest and increasing his capacity for more inheritance.

Meditation

Humility is perfect quietness of heart. It is to expect nothing, to wonder at nothing that is done to me, to feel nothing done against me. It is to be at rest when nobody praises me, and when I am blamed or despised. It is to have a blessed home in the Lord, where I can go in and shut the door, and kneel to my Father in secret, and am at peace as in a deep sea of calmness, when all around and above is trouble.

—Andrew Murray

Map of the Tribal Allotments in Joshua[1]

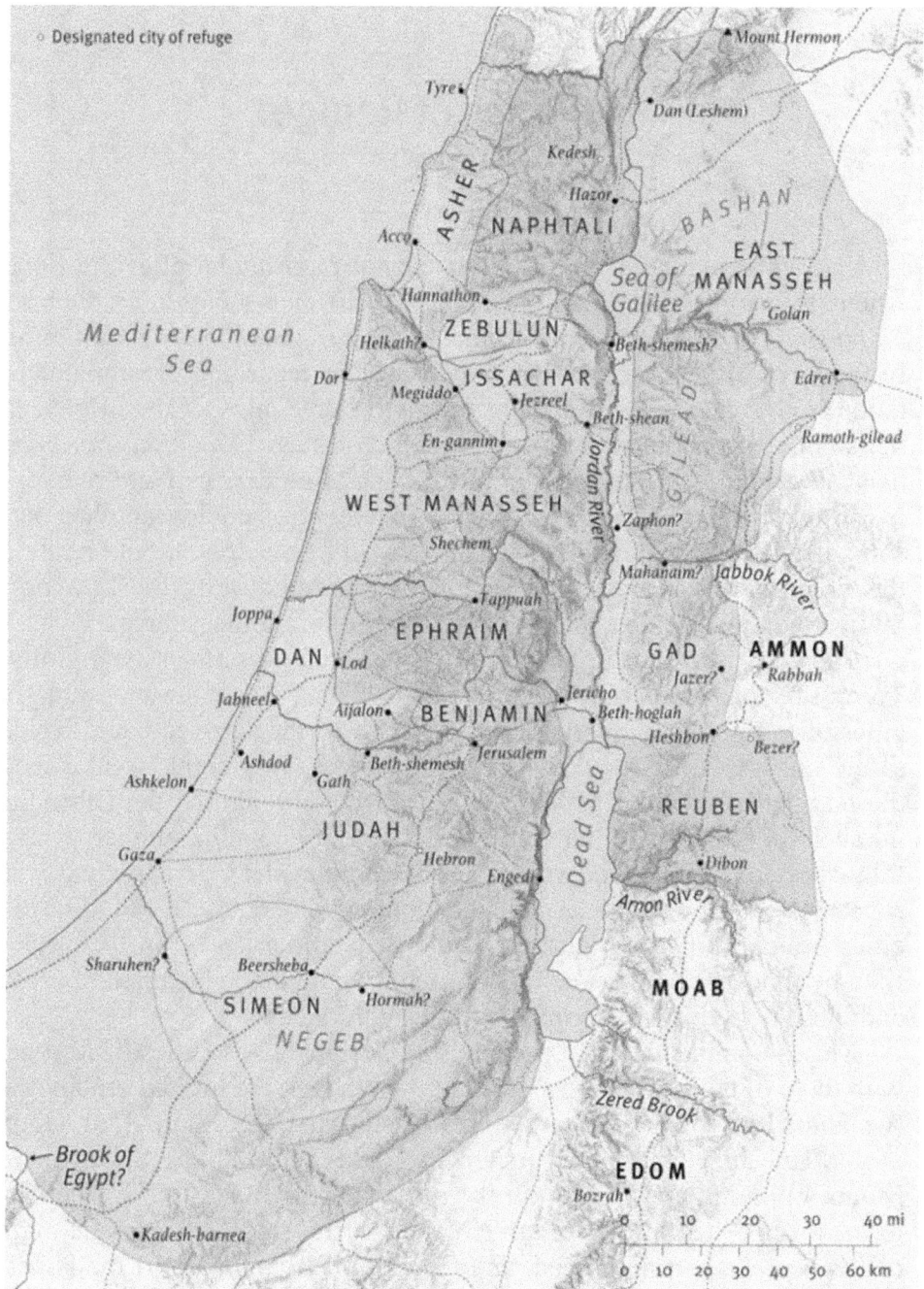

Six Cities of Refuge
Joshua 20

God gave mankind the basis for capital punishment after the flood when He commanded Noah, *"Whoever sheds man's blood, by man his blood shall be shed; for in the image of God He made man"* (Gen. 9:6). In the Law, Moses later provided the specifics regarding the implementation of this decree, as well as affirming the solemnity of the offense in the sixth commandment of the Law, which states: *"You shall not murder"* (Ex. 20:13). Although some translations render the Hebrew word *rasah* as "kill," "murder" (the premeditated act of ending another person's life) is a better translation. One may kill a sheep without breaking this commandment, but sheep cannot be murdered; thus, the Law prohibited the unwarranted ending of human life by another human.

The Law also protected the life of the accused until proven guilty. To ensure this protocol was adhered to, Joshua would now assign six cities of refuge as temporary sanctuaries where the accused could reside safely until his or her case was formally tried. One might wonder why the number of cities of refuge was set at six. Throughout the Bible the number six is tied with human imperfection; it is man's number, which falls short of seven, God's number of completeness. If someone was suspected of falling short of the sixth commandment, there would be six cities to uphold God's righteousness and keep the land from being defiled by innocent blood (i.e., the murderer would be condemned to death and those not guilty of a crime would be pardoned).

Moses commanded that six cities be designated as Cities of Refuge, with three of the six being in Canaan; the others were located among the two and a half tribes who settled in Transjordan (v. 2; Num. 35:6; Deut. 19:2). The three in Canaan included: Kadesh in Galilee, Shechem in Mount Ephraim, and Hebron in the mountains of Judah (v. 7). The Cities of Refuge east of the Jordan River are also listed: Bezer in the plain of Reuben, Ramoth in Gilead, and Golan in Bashan (v. 8). If the Israelites remained faithful and obedient, Jehovah promised to enlarge their borders; for this outcome the Jews were to add three more cities of refuge for a total of nine (Deut. 19:8-10). The name of each city has a meaning which relates to is designated functional as a City of Refuge:

- Kedesh – Holiness or Sanctuary
- Shechem – Shoulder or Strength
- Hebron – Joining or Fellowship
- Bezer – Safety or Defense
- Ramoth – Heights or Uplifting
- Gad – Great Exodus or Happiness

All six cities were evenly spread from north to south on both sides of the Jordan River. However, it is noteworthy that in the land of promise the Cities of Refuge were all located on the tops of mountains; this is not stated for those in flat grasslands of the eastern plateau. Though all six cities were to uphold the righteousness of God in the land, the three cities in Canaan would be easier to see from afar. In the land where God chose to reside with His people, the path of justice would be more easily seen, and thus less difficult to find. It is the same for believers today: the closer our communion with the Lord, the easier it is to sense the way He would have us walk. In any case, the gates to the Cities of Refuge were always to be open, so that every manslayer might find a shelter of protection until justice could be determined (v. 9; Deut. 19:3). F. B. Meyer further notes the Jewish provisions to assist a fleeing fugitive:

> The manslayer who had killed any person unwittingly and unawares might flee from the pursuit of the next of kin. The roads were kept in good repair; clearly written directions at the cross-ways indicated the route; and, according to Jewish tradition, runners learned in the Law, were stationed at various stages to direct and help the fugitive.[1]

When someone sought refuge in a City of Refuge, no retaliation by the relatives of the deceased was permitted (v. 3). Appointed judges would then hear the case in the public place of decision – the gate of the city (v. 4). All the inhabitants of the city were to uphold the ruling of the judges (v. 6). If the accused was found innocent of intentional manslaughter, he or she could dwell within the confines of that city without the threat of familial revenge. Upon the death of the high priest, all who

Conquest and the Life of Rest

had been found innocent of murder were allowed to return to their inheritance without any further threat of retaliation.

If the slayer was found guilty of premeditated murder, he or she was put to death; a lesser penalty was required for accidental deaths or those caused by a non-premeditated act of violence. Under the Law, certain types of crimes carried the death penalty:

1. Premeditated murder (Ex. 21:12).
2. Murdering one's parents (Ex. 21:15).
3. Kidnapping (Ex. 21:16).
4. Cursing or rebelling against one's father or mother (Ex. 21:17).
5. Injuring a pregnant woman and causing her unborn child to die (Ex. 21:21-22).
6. Allowing a bull, known for "pushing," to kill someone (both the bull and the master were to die; Ex. 21:29).
7. Adultery (Deut. 22:22-25)
8. Intrusion into the priestly office (Num. 18:7).

That the offense of killing an unborn child invoked the death penalty clearly shows God considers the life of the fetus to be of equal value to that of an adult. Although offenders could be spared the death penalty if they slew without premeditation, there was no mercy given to one who caused the death of an unborn child, even if it were not premeditated. This law specifically highlights the great concern God has for protecting unborn children, and also His anger against those who destroy what He has wondrously created. David reminds us in the Psalms that each one's life has been planned out by the Lord and his or her name has been recorded in God's *Book of the Living* before birth:

> *I will praise You, for I am fearfully and wonderfully made; marvelous are Your works, and that my soul knows very well. My frame was not hidden from You, when I was made in secret, and skillfully wrought in the lowest parts of the earth. Your eyes saw my substance, being yet unformed. And in Your book they all were written, the days fashioned for me, when as yet there were none of them* (Ps. 139:14-16). Note: The *Book of the Living* is also spoken of in Psalm 69:28 and Exodus 32:31-33.

Enthusiasm and felicity in life are the believer's when he or she understands God has foreordained wonderful plans for his or her life: *"For we are His workmanship, created in Christ Jesus for good works, which God prepared beforehand that we should walk in them"* (Eph. 2:10). Before creation, God previewed the corridors of time, considered all the possible permutations of natural cause and effect as well as the future choices of cognitive beings, and made sovereign choices to bless humanity, glorify His name throughout time and eternity, and use each one of us in the elaborate process. As only a triune God existed when the plan of redemption was devised, the plan is solely His – it originated in His mind and He deserves all the glory for it. God's choices ensure that humanity will receive the greatest possible blessing and that He will obtain the most glory as a result. Why we are the recipients of such extraordinary grace is a question that will require all of eternity to ponder (Eph. 2:7).

For now, believers can rejoice to be at peace with God (Rom. 5:1) and to know the rest of His salvation as we labor in our Canaan in His resurrection power. As mentioned earlier, the writer of Hebrews reminds us that Canaan was not the final rest for the believer; there was something more extraordinary to follow:

For if Joshua had given them rest, then He would not afterward have spoken of another day. There remains therefore a rest for the people of God. For he who has entered His rest has himself also ceased from his works as God did from His (Heb. 4:8-10).

God labored for six days in creation and rested on the seventh day; as mentioned previously, seven is the number associated with perfection. Man must follow this pattern to enter into God's perfect rest in salvation: those who have ceased from working to earn salvation have entered into this rest through the finished work of Christ (i.e., their spirit and soul are saved). Because believers are united with Him, the writer of Hebrews explains that they are eternally secure in Him:

Thus God, determining to show more abundantly to the heirs of promise the immutability of His counsel, confirmed it by an oath, that by two immutable things, in which it is impossible for God to lie, we might have strong consolation, who have fled for refuge to lay hold of the hope set before us (Heb. 6:17-18).

While we wait to enter into our heavenly abode with Him, the Lord Jesus Christ is our Refuge. At His coming our earthly sojourn will conclude and our bodies will experience glorification – the finale of our salvation. In this spiritual sense, believers, who are also spiritual priests, are safe in their City of Refuge until they can come into their final rest (2 Cor. 5:8; 1 Pet. 2:5, 9). The six Cities of Refuge also have a typological meaning for the nation of Israel, which H. L. Rossier explains:

> The involuntary murderer prefigures Israel, murderers of Christ *"through ignorance."* It was of them that the Lord Jesus said on the cross: "Father, forgive them, for *they know not* what they do." They had not known the day of their visitation. … But in another sense both the leaders of the Jews and the people were murderers *willfully,* yea, deliberately and knowingly rejecters of God and of His Christ. "This is the heir," said they, "come, let us kill him, and let us seize on his inheritance," (Matt. 21:38). "We will not have this man to reign over us" (Luke 19:14). Moreover, it is said that the voluntary murderer must be put to death, and with several other prophecies relating to the Jews, this judgment has been partially fulfilled in the fall of Jerusalem (Matt. 22:7).
>
> But this judgment of the willful murderer, unduly hidden in the city of refuge (Deut. 19:11, 12), is in reality yet to come. The Jews, since the rejection of the Messiah, are kept, as at the present time, under the providential care of God, out of their inheritance … will be brought forth to fall into the hands of the avenger. Allied with Antichrist, they will become the miserable objects of divine judgment. As for those who killed unawares, they may recover their lot and inheritance at the time of the change in the priestly office (Josh. 20:6) that is to say, [when the Jews acknowledge the Aaronic priest has been replaced by a Priest after the eternal order of Melchizedek – Christ]. … The Israelite, a slayer by ignorance, type of the nation at the present moment, flies to the city of refuge with the very uncertain hope of escaping the avenger of blood, and of entering one day into possession of his inheritance from which he is kept out until the death of the high priest, typically the end of the Aaronic priesthood of Christ.[2]

Two thousand years ago the Jewish manslayer lifted up his hand and shed innocent blood and since that time the land of Canaan has been defiled by the blood of Jesus. The Jewish manslayer has lost his inheritance, he has fled from his own abode and lives a banished existence in another land (i.e., scattered among the nations). Though many Jews have recently returned to the land, they still do not have an unthreatened possession. Such will be the case until the Time of the Gentiles (i.e., the Church Age) is complete (Dan. 9:26-27; Rom. 11:25).

Presently, Israel remains in spiritual blindness and under the providential care of God in a world which, for the most part, despises them. Today, Jehovah has provided a refuge for His covenant people in the land of Israel, from which they will enter into the Day of Lord. During the Tribulation Period, the judgment on the Jewish nation for being a willful slayer (i.e., for crucifying Christ) will be complete; then, as a refined remnant (i.e., as the unintentional slayer), the nation will inherit their full and eternal possession promised by God to Abraham and secured by Christ.

Today, the Cities of Refuge represent the gracious ongoing work of God to bring condemned sinners into a safe and secure resting place to escape judgment. Those who openly admit their guilt before a Holy God can flee to a refuge far safer than any available from the avenger of blood – Christ Himself. The Lord Jesus Christ has already suffered for the condemned and in Him alone do we find divine forgiveness and peace with God.

Meditation

> Justice Gray of the U.S. Supreme Court once said to a man who had appeared before him in one of the lower courts and had escaped conviction by some technicality: "I know that you are guilty and you know it, and I wish you to remember that one day you will stand before a better and wiser Judge, and that there you will be dealt with according to Justice and not according to law."[3]

Forty-Eight Levitical Cities
Joshua 21:1-42

The only Israelites yet to receive their possession in the Promised Land were the Levites. The leaders of the various clans of this tribe stepped forward and requested that Joshua and Eleazar assign them the forty-eight cities and their adjoining pasture lands which Moses promised to provide for them (Num. 35:5). Six of the forty-eight cities were to be designated as Cities of Refuge (Num. 35:6). Each city included an amount of outlying pasture land, as measured 1500 feet from the city wall in each direction (Num. 35:2-5). The majority of this chapter deals with the distribution of these cities to the Levites.

Levi had three sons: Kohath, Gershon, and Merari (vv. 4-7). Each son originated a sect of ministers with specific tabernacle ministries. The Kohathites bore the covered things of the tabernacle when it was time to relocate the tent of meeting; Moses and the priests (who were descendants of Aaron) came from Kohath. The Gershonites carried the tabernacle coverings and curtains, while the Merarites were in charge of transporting the boards, bars, sockets, and pillars. After the tent of meeting was settled at Shiloh, the priests went to Shiloh in turns to offer worship to God on behalf of all Israel, and then returned to their homes in the cities designated for them.

Thirteen southern cities, nine in Judah and Simeon and four in Benjamin, were delegated to the priests (vv. 8-19). Ten more cities in Ephraim, Dan and Manasseh were designated for the remaining Kohathites (20-26). Hebron, the city Caleb seized from the Anakim, would also be a City of Refuge, though Caleb would keep the surrounding villages and land (vv. 12-13). As mentioned earlier, this is a precious lesson for believers: the spiritual blessings we possess by faith provide us with the opportunity to bless others for the glory of God. Hebron would be the abode both of those dedicated to worshipping God and teaching His Word and also the panic-stricken manslayer fleeing from his home and loved ones in order to preserve his life. Caleb was not a Jew by nature, but a Kenizzite; yet, he had repeatedly experienced the power of God in his life. Can there be any doubt that a man so blessed by God would be anything but pleased to see what he had labored for with God now used to bless others?

The Gershonites were the next Levitical clan to receive their inheritance: thirteen cities within the tribal lands of Manasseh, Issachar, Asher, and Naphtali (vv. 27-33). Two of these cities, Golan in Bashan (on the eastern side of the Jordan) and Kedesh in northern Galilee were selected to be Cities of Refuge.

Lastly, the Merarites received twelve cities in the territories of Zebulun, Reuben, and Gad (vv. 34-40). Bezer in the eastern pasture lands of Reuben would also be a City of Refuge (v. 36). In Gad, Ramoth-Gilead was to be a City of Refuge (v. 38). In all, there would be ten of the forty-eight Levitical cities in Transjordan, three of which were Cities of Refuge. Unfortunately, some of these cities were still under Canaanite control, and the Levites, not being warriors themselves, and apparently not receiving much assistance from the other tribes, did not do well in driving the pagans from their possessions (vv. 41-42). In time, some of these priestly cities were lost and the Levites were forced to relocate (1 Chron. 6:54-81). But at the present, Joshua was implementing God's design and that was for the Levites to be evenly dispersed among His people.

While it is true that the Levites were responsible for all the service of the tabernacle (and later the temple), they were also keepers and teachers of the Law in Israel (Deut. 33:10). The Levites, such as Ezra, who specialized in the meticulous work of copying sacred scrolls to preserve God's written Word were called scribes. Their familiarity with Scripture enhanced their effectiveness as teachers. With Levites strategically positioned throughout Canaan, there would be no excuse for spiritual ignorance among the Jews. The Levites were divinely called to expose their brethren to the mind of God.

Although as a nation, God's covenant people would repeatedly stray from God's Law, the prophet Ezekiel informs us that during the Millennial Kingdom of Christ this will not be the case. In fact, it will be the Levites who once more teach their brethren God's Word and, through the power of the Holy Spirit, they will never abandon it again (Ezek. 44:23-24). This reminds us of the statement: *"For the gifts and the calling of God are irrevocable"* (Rom. 11:29); His calling for the Levites to establish His Word in the land of Israel will ultimately be fulfilled.

Conquest and the Life of Rest

Why did Moses choose the number forty-eight as the priestly allotment of cities among the Jews? We are not told, but Bible numerology suggests a possible reason. The number twelve is used to symbolize "governmental perfection" throughout Scripture. This number indicates completeness of a government or administration, usually a divinely appointed one. In the Old Testament the number twelve is often used as the signature of the nation of Israel (which was composed of 12 tribes). In the New Testament twelve is used to show the complete administration of the Church (the doctrinal foundation was laid by 12 apostles). The number four, on the other hand, is used to speak of God's created order in the earth. We read of four winds, four directions, four phases of the moon, four seasons, and four places creatures dwell (upon, above, and beneath the earth, and in the sea).

The combination of the two numbers, then, suggests that, from God's perspective, His disbursement of the Levites throughout Israel's inheritance was a complete administration of His Word to those on the earth who were to relate to it. The structure and content were in place to ensure His covenant people remained in communion with Him. The Levites were to teach the people and parents were in turn to teach their children (Deut. 6:6-9). Unfortunately, it did not take long for the Jewish nation to neglect this perfect administration of His Word; in fact, it only took one generation:

> *Now Joshua the son of Nun, the servant of the Lord, died when he was one hundred and ten years old. ... When all that generation had been gathered to their fathers, another generation arose after them who did not know the Lord nor the work which He had done for Israel. Then the children of Israel did evil in the sight of the Lord, and served the Baals; and they forsook the Lord God of their fathers, who had brought them out of the land of Egypt; and they followed other gods from among the gods of the people who were all around them, and they bowed down to them; and they provoked the Lord to anger* (Judg. 2:8-12).

After Joshua died, the Levites quit instructing the people and parents became apathetic in teaching God's Law to their children. As a result, the next generation forsook the Lord and embraced false gods. The aftermath of Joshua's death illustrates the fallacy of depending upon any spiritual influence outside the family to maintain your family's spiritual welfare. How did God respond to His people's departure from Him?

Now these are the nations which the Lord left, to prove Israel by them, even as many of Israel as had not known all the wars of Canaan; only that the generations of the children of Israel might know, to teach them war, at the least such as before knew nothing thereof (Judg. 3:1-2).

God seized the role of the parent in order to teach the new generation about Himself. He loves His people too much to leave them void of truth and the knowledge of His presence. What was God's instrument for making His presence known? The disciplinary rod of military invasion and conquest. Israel did not remember God's awesome means of delivering them from slavery and from Egypt, so God used death, invasion, and servitude to awaken them again to His presence. All this occurred because the Levites and the parents failed to instruct the children of Israel in the ways of the Lord.

What is the history lesson for us? Christians are not to neglect the assembling of themselves in the local church; this is where the Word of God is to be administered (1 Cor. 14:22-31; Heb. 10:25). The Lord Jesus Christ has provided the Church with teachers and the indwelling Holy Spirit to guide believers into a deeper understanding of divine truth. Christian parents must know the Lord and His Word to properly teach their children to know and love Him too. If we neglect this duty, the Lord will impose harsher methods to ensure that He is known by our children! Children must be trained up for the Lord. Thus, the Bible should never be neglected, but rather should be the rulebook for all family matters.

A Christian family is not a household of Christians, but a Christian household. It is more than Christ dwelling within the hearts of family members; it is a family that is pursuing the heart of God. If the Bible is not at the center of family life and all home affairs, that home cannot be called a true Christian home.

Untrained children, not surprisingly, remain foolish (Prov. 22:15) and predictably absorb from outside influences what seems appropriate to fill their void of understanding. Children are natural sponges: they are compelled to learn and to develop an understanding of the world in which they live. The next generation in Israel did not know God, so they embraced false gods, and God had to judge His covenant people – a bitter chastening resulted because the parents neglected to raise spiritual children.

The same travesty is occurring today. *What* our children are being taught will directly affect their understanding of God and, consequently, the course of this nation, and even more importantly, how God regards our country. *Who* is training our children directly impacts *what* they are being taught. God's choice instruments to train children are their parents (Prov. 22:6; Eph. 6:1-4). Our children must know God. The Jews painfully learned that the Lord was faithful to demonstrate His presence to their children despite their parental negligence.

Meditation

> When the archaeologists were digging in the ruins of Nineveh, they came upon a library of plaques containing the laws of the realm. One of the laws read, in effect, that anyone guilty of neglect would be held responsible for the result of his neglect.... If you fail to teach your child to obey, if you fail to teach him to respect the property rights of others, you, and not he, are responsible for the result of your neglect.[1]

The Lord's Faithfulness
Joshua 21:43-45

The lengthy narrative detailing the division of the land draws to a close with this short summary of all that has transpired previously. Joshua, the earthly commander of the Jewish forces and the able historian, now peers back to the beginning of the conquest and supplies a panoramic acknowledgment of God's faithfulness. Jehovah had given His people the land that He had promised to their forefathers as a possession (v. 43). Jehovah had delivered the enemies of His people into their hands and provided them rest in the land (v. 44). In fact, Joshua proclaims, *"Not a word failed of any good thing which the Lord had spoken to the house of Israel. All came to pass"* (v. 45). Were there botched affairs and disappointments in Canaan? Definitely. But Joshua's point is this: if there is an apparent failure in the work of the Lord, it is not God's fault; look inwardly for the cause and to the Lord for the answer.

Nowhere in Scripture do we find the faithlessness of man thwarting the faithfulness of God. When man doubts, disobeys, or delays doing God's Word, the Lord merely incorporates these failures into His sovereign purposes. His final objective is to bring all the redeemed into the full blessing of His presence and goodness (Rom. 8:15-17, 28-30). Paul expresses this wonderful mystery this way: *"For what if some did not believe? Will their unbelief make the faithfulness of God without effect? Certainly not! Indeed, let God be true but every man a liar"* (Rom. 3:3-4); *"If we are faithless, He remains faithful; He cannot deny Himself"* (2 Tim. 2:13). Some, like the objector in Romans 3, may assert *"that the word of God has taken no effect"* because of Israel's past failures. However, Paul explains that God already foreknew these and predetermined to incorporate all human rebellions and fiascoes into His overall plan which would extend the most blessing possible to others (e.g., salvation to the Gentiles) and magnify Himself before mankind in the process (Rom. 9:6-7; 23).

Conquest and the Life of Rest

The Jews were living in the land God promised them, but clearly there were still Canaanites who dwelled there also (13:1-6). In God's purposes, He did not intend to bestow all the land promised to Abraham to his descendants all at once (1:4; Gen. 15:18-21). Nor did He want all of the inhabitants of the land to be driven out all at once. The plan, as revealed to Moses, was for the Jews to first secure Canaan (Num. 34:1-12). After conquering all the major strongholds and armies in Canaan, the land was to be divided among the tribes as an inheritance and the various clans were then to rely on the Lord to drive out the remaining habitants (13:6). This plan preserved the agricultural integrity of the land and provided an opportunity for the Jews to rely on Jehovah for victory in day-to-day life.

With the dividing of the land now complete, the testing of God's people would be brought to a personal level, for Joshua would no longer be looking over their actions. As demonstrated in Caleb's life, personal faith and obedience would be divinely rewarded. God would fulfill His promise to Abraham by giving his descendants all the land in stages, as determined by their faithfulness and willingness to conquer and possess it in the years that followed (Deut. 19:8). Jehovah would deliver to His people what they were willing to seize in conquest! God fulfills all His promises, so we know that in a day which has yet to come, the Jewish nation will possess all that was promised to Abraham forever (Gen. 17:8; Amos 9:14-15).

It is with this understanding that we must comprehend the concept of "rest" referred to in verse 44. As stated previously, Canaan represents the benefit of *"heavenly places"* in the earthly realm. Intermingled with the joy and blessings of knowing God's power and presence, there are also warring, testing, disappointments, failures, and pain in Canaan. Our earthly turmoil cannot suppress heavenly peace; this rest is divine peace which is beyond human comprehension, but not our appreciation. H. F. Witherby concisely summarizes the faithfulness of Jehovah up to this point in order to bring His people into this privileged position of "rest":

> Jehovah had been unwearied in bringing Israel into the possession of the land promised to the fathers. He had now fulfilled His own sure word. He had come down into Egypt, the land of Israel's bonds; He had been afflicted there in their afflictions; He had ransomed them from captivity, and, having given them the spirit of pilgrims, had guided them as a flock through the wilderness, where He fed them daily,

went before them, and was their reward; He had healed their wilderness backslidings, and forgiven their unbelief in His grace; He had brought them through the river into the promised land, fought for them, given them victory over all their enemies, and had made the promised inheritance their possession. All that Jehovah had given them to anticipate was fulfilled. Israel was at rest – rest in the midst of fulfilled promises, in the midst of possessed blessings.[1]

The Israelites had been delivered from bondage, Pharaoh's army, and Egypt itself to enter into and possess a land full of milk and honey. Promises merely dreamed about for years had now been realized. In the general sense, considering all that transpired during the seven years of faithful conflict in Canaan, it could be stated that *"the land rested"* (11:23). Through intense spiritual conquest God's rest came to the land, but it could only be sustained by unremitting watchfulness and unwavering resolve to exterminate the enemy that remained in the land. Therefore, the rest in the land was not absolute; it was contingent on the Jews pressing forward in their calling. Whether an Israelite of yesteryear or a believer in the Church Age, Paul's aspiration rings true:

> *Brethren, I do not count myself to have apprehended; but one thing I do, forgetting those things which are behind and reaching forward to those things which are ahead, I press toward the goal for the prize of the upward call of God in Christ Jesus* (Phil. 3:13-14).

Rest in the land is enjoyed as the believer continues to strive to lay hold of his or her spiritual possessions in heavenly places. However, the peace God grants His people, despite turmoil in the land, is complete and absolute, for it is secured in His faithfulness. In fact, the tranquility of God's peace surpasses human comprehension – it is enjoyed by faith, not reasoning (Phil. 4:7). As Israel would learn, peace in the land was conditional, but the peace from above was infinitely dependable.

Consequently, Christians should long for heaven, our final resting place, but also understand that the measure of rest secured and available today is quite extensive. H. F. Witherby explains:

> The Christian, as the result of Christ's victory, enjoys through faith present rest over sin, the world, and Satan, even while warring with these foes. It is his portion, by faith, to know full deliverance from the judgment of the world through the precious blood of Christ, his Passo-

ver; to know that Christ, being risen from among the dead, has broken the power of death and Satan; from both of which He has delivered His redeemed people. The Christian knows, too, that Christ is in the heavenly places, and that he is seated in Him there; that he is God's freed man, and in the power of this liberty and rest, and, in his Lord's might, he fights against spiritual wickedness in heavenly places. The Christian enjoys the peace of his Shiloh, worships the Father in spirit and in truth in the true tabernacle, where the glory-cloud ever abides. But while all these blessings are his to enjoy and to dwell in, yet there is a rest which he is anticipating, a rest which he has not at present entered, even the rest of God. ...[Thus,] hope and possession are woven together in his soul.[2]

The rest God provided for His people in Canaan had reached its desired zenith. The remainder of the book is a series of warnings, for though the Lord's rest was available to the Jews, they fell short of retaining it (Joshua 22). The exhortations of Joshua 23 and 24 relate to those individuals who had experienced God's rest, to continue to abide in the power of it. F. B. Meyer comments on this point:

There was a very distinct measure of rest. The land rested (Josh. 21:23), and the people also. But it is equally clear that Canaan did not exhaust God's ideal. Fair as it was, its benediction did not go beyond the narrow circle of mere worldly prosperity and material interests. And these were manifestly inadequate. How impossible it is for the soul to take its ease, just because of some large increase in worldly prosperity! As well expect it to grow fat on husks! It was equally impossible that the mere possession of the Land of Promise could give rest to hearts with infinite capacity for love, or to minds with an insatiable appetite for truth. The rest of Canaan, like so much else in the book, could at the best be only a type and shadow of the spiritual repose, that holy tranquility, that unspeakable peace, which fill the souls of men with the rest of God Himself.[3]

Joshua's final exhortations are good for us to consider today: with our final rest still before us, let us take full advantage of the divine rest available today. In so doing, you can rest assured that *"the peace of God, which surpasses all understanding, will guard your hearts and minds through Christ Jesus"* (Phil. 4:7).

In the Millennial Kingdom, Israel's ultimate rest will be realized: all their foes will be defeated, they will be esteemed by their enemies, and dwell in the presence of the Lord in complete peace (Zech. 8:20-23). Meanwhile, Christians are to eagerly long for all that was accomplished at Calvary to come to fruition in God's timing. The Lord Jesus Himself waits with blissful anticipation of being with His glorious bride and establishing His eternal kingdom (Isa. 53:11; Eph. 1:22-23). Until summoned home by the call of the archangel and the trump of God may each believer count on the faithfulness of God to enter into His rest (1 Thess. 4:16). This serenity of mind and soul is only enjoyed through ongoing dependence and ceaseless vigilance, for the adversary remains active.

When at last the Bright and Morning Star standing alone in the dreary predawn hue becomes the rising sun in its full glory, then all of our earthly school days will be done. On that day, while basking in the inconceivable bliss of God's glory, we too will proclaim: *"Not a word failed of any good thing which the Lord had spoken ... all came to pass"* (v. 45).

Meditation

> Cast not away your confidence because God defers his performances. That which does not come in your time, will be hastened in His time, which is always the more convenient season. God will work when He pleases, how He pleases, and by what means He pleases. He is not bound to keep our time, but He will perform his Word, honor our faith, and reward them that diligently seek Him.
>
> — Matthew Henry

When you have no helpers, see your helpers in God. When you have many helpers, see God in all your helpers. When you have nothing but God, see all in God. When you have everything, see God in everything. Under all conditions, stay thy heart only on the Lord.

— Charles Spurgeon

The Altar of Misunderstanding
Joshua 22

Having faithfully fulfilled their commitment to secure Canaan for their brethren, it was now time for the two and a half tribes to return to their homes on the eastern side of the Jordan (vv. 1-3). Joshua reminded them that they had requested this region as a possession, and Moses had honored their request (v. 4). He also exhorted them to obey the Law if they wanted to keep their inheritance (v. 5). Afterwards, Joshua blessed them, released them from active military duty, and sent them home.

As they traveled eastward from Shiloh and approached the fords of the Jordan a sudden anxiety of future isolation and abandonment from the commonwealth of Israel overcame them. They thought in years to come the Jordan River might become a barrier to national fellowship. Their solution was to construct an altar which would stand as a lasting testimony of their commitment to follow the Lord and obey His Law (v. 28). It was not a monument of a few stones either, but *"a great, impressive altar"* (v. 10). Verse 10 indicates this altar was erected in Canaan, and verse 11 suggests it was on the very edge of Canaan's frontier (likely a high place next to the Jordan and thus visible from both sides of the river).

The altar was to be a lasting memorial. It was not intended for sacrifices, which the Law strictly prohibited (vv. 26-27). The two and a half tribes called the altar, "Witness:" *"...for it is a witness between us that the Lord is God"* (v. 34). Note that although the King James Version of the Bible refers to the altar by the proper name "Ed," the corresponding Hebrew word is not to be found in most manuscripts, nor in the Septuagint.

While the motives of these Israelites were likely genuine, the erection of the altar, as F. B. Meyer explains, was a phenomenal blunder:

> It was a great altar to see to, not intended for burnt-offering or meal-offering, or for religious rites; but as a perpetual witness that its

builders were real-hearted Israelites. But it was a great mistake. No pattern for its shape had been received from God, nor any direction as to its construction, whilst if they had obeyed the divine instructions, that three times in the year all their males should appear before God in Shiloh, there would have been no need for this clumsy contrivance. In their view the unity of the people could not be preserved by merely spiritual bond, but by an outward and mechanical one. The common ties of the altar at Shiloh were insufficient; there must be in addition the great altar of Ed.[1]

Unfortunately, as the altar was not directed by God, the nine and a half tribes west of the Jordan immediately misunderstood its purpose and assumed the worst – their brethren had become apostates (vv. 10-11). These tribes assembled at Shiloh with every intention of correcting the matter, even if it meant civil war (v. 12). Thankfully, cooler heads prevailed and a delegation that included Phinehas the son of the high priest Eleazar and ten representatives (men of renown from each tribe west of the Jordan) was sent to investigate the matter (vv. 13-15).

As is often the case today, investigation is nothing more than a polite term for accusation; the delegation commenced their discussion with the leaders of the two and a half tribes by denouncing them for rebellion against the Lord (v. 17). The blood of the western tribes was running hot: verses 17-20 provide some explanation for this:

> *Is the iniquity of Peor not enough for us, from which we are not cleansed till this day, although there was a plague* **in the congregation** *of the Lord, but that you must turn away this day from following the Lord? And it shall be, if you rebel today against the Lord, that tomorrow He will be angry* **with the whole congregation** *of Israel. Nevertheless, if the land of your possession is unclean, then cross over to the land of the possession of the Lord, where the Lord's tabernacle stands, and take possession* **among us**; *but do not rebel against the Lord,* **nor rebel against us**, *by building yourselves an altar besides the altar of the Lord our God. Did not Achan the son of Zerah commit a trespass in the accursed thing, and wrath fell on* **all the congregation** *of Israel? And that man did not perish alone in his iniquity* (emphasis added).

The delegation recounted two recent experiences in which the entire nation had been punished for the sins of the guilty within their company. The first historical example referenced by the delegation to provide credence to their appeal happened just before the nation entered Canaan. At Baal-Peor, the conniving doctrines of Balaam led some Jewish men to ignore the law of separation and embrace Midianite women and their gods (Num. 25:1-2). God was angry with *"the whole congregation"* and smote the nation with a judicial plague (Num. 25:3). Moses commanded the leaders of the offenders to be hanged for endorsing such a hideous sin through complacency. All those who had joined themselves with Baal were to be executed (Num. 25:4-5).

This particular situation would have been especially on the mind of Phinehas. It was his zeal for the Lord, demonstrated by spearing a fornicating Midianite woman and a Jewish man with a javelin, which satisfied the Lord's anger and stayed the plague (Num. 25:6-8). The delegation pointed out that in this instance the sin of a few resulted in the deaths of many who did not actually engage in the sin; in fact, twenty-four thousand Israelites died in that plague (Num. 25:9). Phinehas then pleaded with the Transjordanian tribes to repent lest *"God be angry with the whole congregation"* (v. 18). The western tribes had no desire to be punished with their supposedly rebellious brethren in the east.

To press their point, the delegation cited the example of Achan; one man sinned but *"wrath fell on all the congregation"* (v. 20). The Jews understood that God viewed them collectively as His people and held them responsible to keep each other accountable in matters of the Law. Accordingly, if the Transjordanian tribes rebelled against the Lord, they were rebelling against the remaining tribes also (v. 19).

The western tribes were so fearful of God's wrath for the perceived disobedience of their brethren that they were willing to share their land to resettle the Transjordanian tribes in Canaan (v. 19). This principle has at least two scriptural corollaries. First, it is better to part with temporal things to regain the fellowship of a brother or sister (1 Cor. 6:6-8). Paul states that he was quite willing to suffer loss to gain the weak. *"To the weak I became as weak, that I might win the weak. I have become all things to all men, that I might by all means save some"* (1 Cor. 9:22). Second, the work of restoring a fallen believer must be done with a spirit of humility: *"Brethren, if a man is overtaken in any trespass, you who are spiritual restore such a one in a spirit of gentleness, considering yourself lest you also be tempted"* (Gal. 6:1). Thankfully, the nine and a half tribes west of the Jordan dispatched a humble delegation to plead with their erring brethren, instead of an army to exact justice based on

Joshua Devotions

the mere appearance of evil. May the Lord extend us grace and wisdom to rightly put all these principles into practice!

Finally, the Transjordanian tribes were permitted to clarify their actions. They denied transgressing against the Lord, saying they had no plan to offer sacrifices upon this altar or to turn away from Him (vv. 21-29). They called on Jehovah as their witness, for certainly He would know their true intentions (v. 22). Their only motive in building the Altar of Witness was to encourage a sense of oneness among the tribes through a visible and lasting reminder (vv. 27-28). This humanized creed, their "confession of faith" so to speak, was the source of the entire misunderstanding. Their sincere and humble response pleased the delegation and those they represented and, mercifully, a bloody civil war was averted (vv. 30-33).

Instead of jumping to the wrong conclusion, one wonders why the delegation did not consult the Lord before pursuing the matter. Surely the Lord would have not wanted His people to go to war over a false impression and would have provided counsel, if asked. Regardless, the narrative serves as a good reminder not to jump to conclusions or think negatively about others until we have the facts in hand. Much damage has been done within the Body of Christ through both the spreading of and the listening to rumors and hearsay. Proverbs provides wise counsel concerning how to avoid this damaging conduct.

> *In the multitude of words sin is not lacking, but he who restrains his lips is wise* (Prov. 10:19).

> *The words of a talebearer are like tasty trifles, and they go down into the inmost body* (Prov. 18:8).

> *Where there is no wood, the fire goes out; and where there is no talebearer, strife ceases* (Prov. 26:20).

Yes, building the altar was a mistake, but we should not be too critical of the two and a half tribes for doing so; for Christians are continually erecting similar altars in the same attempt to procure visible uniformity. However, as the Transjordanian tribes soon learned, promoting spiritual unity among God's people through a humanized means results in division. The building of an unscriptural altar gave every appearance of denying unity, not fostering it. This resulted in new complications and misunderstandings. It is therefore a flawed notion to think that besides the Church which God has formed, some tangible body of believers can be successfully formulated through common creeds, human declarations, and Church traditions. In the end, these have the opposite effect and draw away Christians from the true gravitation point in the Church – Christ. The unity of the Church is preserved by the power of the Holy Spirit as Christians pursue a better understanding of Scripture; it is not upheld by fabricated "altars of witness" (Eph. 4:3, 13-15). H. L. Rossier remarks on the Church's historical tendency to erect "altars of witness" for the sake of creating unity, but ultimately the outcome is more destructive than good:

> Dear readers, this is but the history of Christendom from the first, only it has sunk much lower than the two and a half tribes. It has collected for itself a vast number of confessions of faith more or less correct, but which are not Christ; and then awaking to the fact, that the unity is well-nigh disappearing, these confessions are made more and more elastic, until in place of the sought-for unity, open infidelity itself is introduced into the midst of the profession of Christianity.[2]

Unity is spiritual and reflects the glory of God (John 17:21-23), but *uniformity* is carnal and ultimately divides the Church (1 Cor. 3:1-4). This is clearly seen in the text before us. Jealousy and fear were the immediate reactions of the western tribes to the construction of the altar. What was perceived as a barrier (i.e., the Jordan) was no barrier at all; instead, the solution forged of human device proved divisive among God's people. Christ desires that there be no divisions in the Church, but rather that all believers enjoy fellowship to the fullest degree possible in reference to their common foundation of scriptural truth. It is only on this foundation that true unity among believers can occur.

The teaching and understanding of truth is vital to the building up of the Church: *"He who prophesies* (i.e., declares divine truth) *speaks edification and exhortation and comfort to men"* (1 Cor. 14:3). We also recognize that Scripture is the tool God uses to remove from us what is not sound in life and doctrine and to establish that which pleases Him (2 Tim. 2:15). Yet, doctrine alone is insufficient to guide believers in proper conduct; we need a work of grace in our hearts also: *"Knowledge puffs up, but love edifies"* (1 Cor. 8:1). Love and grace must temper our actions to ensure the edification of others (1 Cor. 8:1; Eph. 4:15-16).

Separation among believers will occur when divine truth is embraced and false doctrine is shunned (2 Thess. 3:6). Yet, not all division is profitable. If love does not guide one's activities, isolation of the members within the body of Christ will occur over minute points of disagreement; the result of which will hinder the Church's working and growth.

Just as grace and truth are inseparable aspects of God's character (John 1:14), the believer should not invoke one quality without the other. On this point, Paul commands, *"But, speaking the truth in love, may grow up in all things into Him who is the head – Christ"* (Eph. 4:15). The challenge, then, is to have fellowship with all believers to the degree that doctrine allows. I can walk farther in harmony with some Christians than with others, but I can go some distance with all Christians (e.g., there is at least agreement in the gospel message). Those within our own local churches and our homes will likely share a high degree of commonality.

The love of Christ promotes fellowship in truth; unbiblical religious traditions prompt confusion and division. The Church cannot thrive if it forsakes biblical order and sound doctrine to create a friendly atmosphere in which even the pagan and the apostate feel at home. If division is necessary, let it be for upholding the truth in love and not the result of stumbling over some contrived religious mandate, such as the Altar of Witness. May the Lord save us from both spiritual confusion and moral compromise.

Meditation

> We are not diplomats but prophets, and our message is not a compromise but an ultimatum.
>
> — A. W. Tozer

Joshua's Final Charge
Joshua 23

The events of this chapter likely occurred several years, perhaps even a decade, after the division of the land. The narrative states that Joshua is nearing the end of his earthly sojourn (v. 1), and he has a pressing message to deliver to the nation before he dies; accordingly, he summoned Israel's leaders to appear before him (v. 2). Whether the proceedings in Joshua 23 and Joshua 24 transpired at the same meeting or at two distinct meetings separated by a brief interval of time cannot be categorically stated. Location is not addressed in chapter 23; however, it could be understood to take place at Shiloh. Since the tabernacle resided in that city, it was the designated gathering place of the people unless otherwise stated in the narrative (e.g., 24:1). The narrative seems to indicate two separate meetings, with the leaders of the nation (and perhaps all the people with them) gathered at Shiloh in Joshua 23, and with the entire nation before Joshua at Shechem in Joshua 24. Perhaps the latter gathering occurred on the anniversary of the former.

The interim between the division of the land and Joshua's muster of the people in this chapter had been characterized by rest. There were certainly regions in the land that remained unconquered, but apparently these Canaanites had no stomach for waging war with the Israelites. Their resolve to fight, at least for the present time, had waned. Jehovah had defeated the main forces of the Canaanites (vv. 3-4), but had allowed pockets of resistance to remain in the land to test His people. If the Jews would be faithful to confront them, the Lord would prove Himself a noble ally by driving their enemies from the land (v. 5). If, however, His people settled into a peaceful co-existence with their pagan neighbors, there would be drastic consequences ahead.

There are two recurring themes of Joshua's message: God has been faithful to you (vv. 3, 9, 14) and you had better be faithful to Him (vv. 6-8, 11, 15-16). God is faithful both to bless the obedient and to punish the rebel. Joshua's speech is reminiscent of Moses' final charge to the nation just prior to his death (Deut. 29-30). J. G. Bellett observes this type of concern for the Lord's people is a sign of spiritual vibrancy:

> It is blessed to mark all this – the fervency of spirit, with which this aged servant of God and this full-hearted friend of Israel, thus closes his ministry. It may remind us of Moses speaking to Israel on the edge of the wilderness, in the words of the book of Deuteronomy – or of David counseling his son, his nobles, and his people, as he was about to leave them, in 1 Chronicles – or of Paul exhorting and warning the elders of Ephesus, when seeing them, and as it were, his ministry, for the last time in Acts 20. True affection, the love that makes the interest of others our own, dictated all these occasions, the Spirit of God using them, whether in Moses, in Joshua, in David, or in Paul. In distant, separated parts of the Word are these occasions found, but how does one Spirit fill His vessels with like treasure, and quicken them, and the same gracious, serving affections![1]

Joshua reminded the Jews that Jehovah had been faithful to expel the nations from their land (v. 3), that He had enabled them to triumph in battle (v. 9), and that He had, in fact, fulfilled every promise to bless them (v. 4). Joshua superbly declares the goodness of God to His people: *"And you know in all your hearts and in all your souls that not one thing has failed of all the good things which the Lord your God spoke concerning you. All have come to pass for you; not one word of them has failed"* (v. 14). Speaking of the Lord, the Psalmist declares, *"You are good, and do good"* (Ps. 119:68). In the New Testament, Paul likewise declares the faithfulness of God: *"And we know that all things work together for good to those who love God, to those who are the called according to His purpose"* (Rom. 8:28). Every lover of Christ can thus agree with David's exclamation: *"O taste and see that the Lord is good: blessed is the man that trusts in Him"* (Ps. 34:8). Truly, God had proven Himself faithful in Canaan and He deserved the affection and devotion of His people.

Joshua admonished his brethren to continue walking the pathway of separation with the Lord in order to remain in joyful fellowship with Him and receive His blessing. Therefore, dispersed among the reminders of God's faithfulness are three exhortations to the people: obey the Law (v. 6); do not intermingle with the nations (vv. 7-8, 12-13); love the Lord (vv. 9-13). On the night before His crucifixion, the Lord Jesus addressed the same three concerns with His disciples:

Conquest and the Life of Rest

> *If you love Me, keep My commandments* (John 14:15).
>
> *If the world hates you, you know that it hated Me before it hated you. If you were of the world, the world would love its own. Yet because you are not of the world, but I chose you out of the world, therefore the world hates you* (John 15:18-19).
>
> *If anyone loves Me, he will keep My word; and My Father will love him, and We will come to him and make Our home with him* (John 14:23).

The Lord knew misplaced affection among His disciples would lead to their disobedience and worldliness. Joshua was likewise concerned the Jews would settle in among the remaining Canaanites. While he did not use the Lord's term of "world," Joshua does mention the influence of "the nations" among the Jews seven specific times in his short address. He knew that the continuing presence of the Canaanites was a "worldly" threat to the spiritual vitality and overall well-being of his people. Accordingly, Joshua's closing statement included a volley of forceful warnings to his countrymen (vv. 14-16): incomplete obedience has consequences; God has been completely faithful, but you have not been; disobedience will be punished.

These same truths are still valid today and believers will do well to heed them. Paul, at death's doorstep, also encouraged his spiritual son Timothy to actively resist the pull of the world in day-to-day life: *"No one engaged in warfare entangles himself with the affairs of this life, that he may please him who enlisted him as a soldier"* (2 Tim. 2:4). A good soldier of the cross endures hardship; he is single-minded, has rigorous discipline, and submits to the commander – Christ. The soldier is on active duty, and therefore does not get entangled with the cares of this world. The soldier strives to master himself and wars lawfully. The Greek word translated "entangles" is *empleko* which means "to entwine" or, figuratively, "to be involved with." The tense is present (indicating an ongoing activity), the voice is passive (meaning the affairs of life are acting upon the soldier), and the mood is indicative (it is a statement of fact). Paul wanted Timothy to understand that even after he made a decision not to engage in worldliness, the world would still be pursuing hard after him. Thus, a good soldier does not allow the affairs of life to control him – he or she must continually beat them back as one trying to escape the tentacles of a gigantic octopus.

Meditation

> To entangle oneself in the business of life means really to give up separation from the world by taking one's part in the outward affairs as a bona fide partner in it.
>
> — William Kelly

The true man of God is heartsick, grieved at the worldliness of the Church, grieved at the toleration of sin in the Church, grieved at the prayerlessness in the Church. He is disturbed that the corporate prayer of the Church no longer pulls down the strongholds of the devil.

— Leonard Ravenhill

Choose You This Day
Joshua 24

Joshua commenced his final address to the nation by informing them of something they already knew, that Abraham and his family were previously pagans in Mesopotamia (v. 2). For this reason, Moses described Abraham as *"a Syrian ready to perish"* (Deut. 26:5). Though an idol-worshipper on the road to condemnation, Stephen declares that the *"God of Glory"* appeared to Abraham in Ur and called him to a land he had never heard of before that time (Acts 7). Why did God pick a man tainted by idol worship for His covenant? God had to choose somebody – He chose Abraham (formerly called Abram) who responded in faith (Isa. 51:1-2). God rules over His creation in whatever way He deems to be the best. God made a sovereign choice to establish Abraham's descendants as a privileged nation, from whom the Messiah would eventually come.

Joshua continued on from Abraham through the course of Israel's history to show all God's dealings with Israel were forged in His grace (vv. 3-13). Joshua, speaking for the Lord, declares His many acts of kindness to His covenant people; note how the dialogue is punctuated with the following statements: *"I took," "I gave," "I sent," "I plagued," "I did," "I brought," "I destroyed,"* and *"I delivered."* There is no mention of human strength or wisdom in the process of developing and placing the nation in the Promised Land; even Joshua and Israel's mighty men of valor are absent from the narrative. God planned how to bless the Jews and had accomplished that end regardless of the obedience or disobedience of His people, and the abrasive opposition or subtle deceit of their enemies.

After noting their origin in faithful Abraham, and that they had been recipients of God's abundant grace, Joshua charged the people to follow Abraham's example and obey the Lord. Joshua's initial remarks concerning Abraham would undergird his entire message. It is suggested that there are three reasons for this.

In the first place, Abraham maintained the proper disposition concerning the land promised to, but not yet possessed by, him. He continued to trust God with the "big picture" and the "timetable" while he waited for God's promise to be realized. During this interim he was determined to be a stranger and a pilgrim in the land (Heb. 11:13). Abraham never settled in Canaan; he lived a nomadic lifestyle. Likewise, if the Israelites wanted Jehovah's blessing, they would need to follow Abraham's example of faith and sanctification. The Jews were God's covenant people and, thus, were to be separated from the nations while they waited patiently for their final rest to come.

The second reason Abraham's life was emphasized in this message is that the location in which the God of Glory confirmed His covenant with Abraham was the very place the Israelites now stood – Shechem (Gen. 12:6). Historically speaking, Shechem, situated between the mountains of Ebal and Gerizim and at the crossroads of central Palestine, has been a place of decision. It was at Shechem that Jacob chose to follow the Lord and purge his household from idols (Gen. 35:1-4). Some fifteen to twenty years before the present scene, the Israelites had assembled at Shechem to choose between obedience and God's blessing or disobedience and God's judgment. Centuries later, Shechem would be built up by Jeroboam as a stronghold that marked the division of Rehoboam's kingdom; ten tribes would choose to forsake Jehovah at that time and enter into paganism (1 Kgs. 12:25). Now, at the very location where Abraham had been rewarded for his faithfulness in leaving idolatry, Joshua charged the nation of Israel to do the same.

F. B. Meyer explains the third reason Joshua invoked Abraham's past exhibition of faith as an example to be followed.

> It would appear that the people largely maintained the worship of household gods, like those which Rachel stole from Laban. This practice was probably perpetuated by stealth. But the germs of evil were only awaiting favorable conditions to manifest themselves, and Joshua had every reason to dread the further development of the insidious taint. The human heart is always so willing to substitute the material for the spiritual and where the idol takes the place of God, man forfeits the only antagonistic force strong enough to counteract the workings of his passion. Thus, in every nation under heaven idolatry has sooner or later led to impurity.[1]

Conquest and the Life of Rest

Abraham left the idols of his family in Ur to have communion with the God of Glory in the land promised to him; the Israelites must do the same. Joshua voiced a passionate appeal to the people to put away the gods of Terah and other ancestors. It is the same warning that the delegation from the western tribes in Joshua 22 delivered to the other tribes when they reminded them of the consequences of their idolatry at Shittim, when some joined with Baal-peor. The apostle John echoed the exhortation not long before his death, warning fellow believers, *"keep yourselves from idols"* (1 Jn. 5:21). The bottom line is that fornication and idolatry walk together. Those who do not fear God will not obey His commands for holy living. This is why John sternly admonished Christians to be idol-free; misplaced affection leads to unchecked lusting and eventually immorality. Anything that robs God of our love is an idol. Joshua acknowledged his determination to follow Jehovah and pled with the people to deliberately set their own hearts and minds heavenward, for to revere earthly things results in self-destruction:

> *Now therefore, fear the Lord, serve Him in sincerity and in truth, and put away the gods which your fathers served on the other side of the River and in Egypt. Serve the Lord! And if it seems evil to you to serve the Lord, choose for yourselves this day whom you will serve, whether the gods which your fathers served that were on the other side of the River, or the gods of the Amorites, in whose land you dwell. But as for me and my house, we will serve the Lord* (vv. 14-15).

At this declaration the people thundered back, *"Far be it from us that we should forsake the Lord to serve other gods ... We also will serve the Lord, for He is our God"* (vv. 16, 18). Although the people said they were going to follow Jehovah and even accredited Him with all their progress and success since their sojourn in Egypt, Joshua sensed insincerity. He responded with the following words: *"You cannot serve the Lord, for He is a holy God. He is a jealous God; He will not forgive your transgressions nor your sins. If you forsake the Lord and serve foreign gods, then He will turn and do you harm and consume you, after He has done you good"* (vv. 19-20). To this the people again affirmed their loyalty to Jehovah, declaring *"We will serve the Lord"* (v. 21); they even called themselves as witnesses against themselves before God on the matter, meaning they had nothing to hide (v. 22).

Perhaps Joshua was hoping for a similar outcome to the time Jacob cleansed his household of all their strange gods; he even got rid of their earrings so they would not have the provision to form new images in the future. (Melting down earrings was an easy way to construct a new idol in those days.) But it was not to be. There was no repudiation of sin, no piles of profane idols gathered and destroyed. The people gave allegiance with their lips, but lurking in the recesses of their hearts were secret sins and rebel affections.

The burden of the Lord was upon Joshua, and a third time he plainly rebuked the people, pleading with them to come clean: *"Put away the foreign gods which are among you, and incline your heart to the Lord God of Israel"* (v. 23). To this the people replied, *"The Lord our God we will serve, and His voice we will obey!"* (v. 24). The Jews had consented to the same at Sinai and had failed; now at Shechem they again affirmed their fidelity, and again they would fail. Whether people seek to justify or to sanctify themselves through self-effort, the result is the same – failure. We may have the most excellent intentions, but all of our best energy will never bring us closer to God; we need resurrection power to flow through our members and the mind of Christ to control our thoughts.

It is with this final declaration of allegiance that Joshua stood up a stone before the tabernacle as a memorial to the pledges the people had covenanted to do. After writing down and rehearsing with the people the words of the Law, Joshua dismissed them to their homes. He had called on them to repent, but they had not; now, there would be no defense and no reprieve from judgment if they continued in their idolatrous practices. While Joshua and those elders who saw the wonders of God in Canaan lived, the nation served Jehovah; sadly, however, in the opening chapters of Judges we learn that the next generation departed from the Lord.

Two deaths and three burials draw the book to a close. Both Joshua and the high priest Eleazar died and were buried in Ephraim. Joseph, whose body had been embalmed in Egypt over two hundred years earlier, was finally laid to rest at Shechem. Joseph wanted to be buried, not in an Egyptian tomb, but among his people and in his inheritance (Gen. 33:18, 50:25). Moses honored that request and brought Joseph's remains out of Egypt during the Exodus (Ex. 13:19). The patriarch was now laid to rest in the land of his childhood.

Conquest and the Life of Rest

Joshua was buried in the land of his inheritance at Timnath-serah in Mouth Ephraim (v. 30). This was near Shechem, Joseph's burial location (v. 32). In the resurrection Joshua and Joseph will ascend together to meet the One they both so elegantly typified in life – their Messiah, the Lord Jesus Christ.

As he publicly declared, Joshua had faithfully followed the Lord his entire life of 110 years. It is for this reason that he, like Moses in the opening verses of this book, is now ascribed the title *"Servant of the Lord"* (v. 29). He was never referred to by that designation in life, but after his death he was remembered for his devoted service. At the end of his sojourn on earth, Joshua could inventory his days and rejoice in all that had been accomplished and praise the God who had brought it all to pass. Joshua knew God to be faithful and could thus retire to his grave with the hope of the resurrection yet to come!

Meditation

>"Great is Thy faithfulness," O God my Father,
>There is no shadow of turning with Thee;
>Thou changest not, Thy compassions, they fail not
>As Thou hast been Thou forever wilt be.
>
>"Great is Thy faithfulness!" "Great is Thy faithfulness!"
>Morning by morning new mercies I see;
>All I have needed Thy hand hath provided –
>"Great is Thy faithfulness," Lord, unto me!
>
>— Thomas Chisholm

Endnotes

Introduction
1. Donald Campbell, *The Bible Knowledge Commentary Vol. 1: An Exposition of the Scriptures* (Victor Books, Wheaton, IL; 1983-1985), p. 326
2. J. N. Darby, http://stempublishing.com/authors/darby/EXPOSIT/19027E.html
3. William MacDonald, *Believer's Bible Commentary* (Thomas Nelson Pub., Nashville, TN; 1990), p. 240
4. Warren Wiersbe, *The Bible Exposition Commentary, Vol. 2* (Victor Books, Wheaton, IL: 1989), p. 287
5. F. B. Meyer, *Joshua, and the Land of Promise* (Fleming H. Revell Co., Chicago, IL; 1893), p. 10
6. Ibid., p. 15
7. W. Graham Scroggie, *The Land and the Life of Rest* (Harvey Christian Pub., Hampton, TN; 1950), pp. 9-10

Moses, My Servant
1. *The Christian Friend and Instructor*; 1899; Joshua's Commission (http://stempublishing.com/magazines/cf/1899/Joshuas-Commission.html)

Three Calls
1. James Vernon McGee, *Thru The Bible Commentary Vol. 2* (Thomas Nelson Publishers, Nashville, TN; 1983), p. 4
2. H. L. Rossier, http://stempublishing.com/authors/rossier/JOSHUA.html
3. H. F. Witherby, *The Serious Christian Series: The Book of Joshua* (Books for Christians, Charlotte, NC; no date), pp. 13-14
4. H. L. Rossier, op. cit.

The New Commander
1. J. G. Bellett, http://stempublishing.com/authors/bellett/Joshua.html
2. F. C. Cook, *Barnes Notes: The Bible Commentary – Exodus to Ruth* (Baker Book House, Grand Rapids, MI; reprinted from 1879 edition), p. 354

Rahab's Faith
1. F. C. Cook, op. cit. p. 355
2. F. B. Meyer, op. cit., p. 30
3. J. N. Darby, op. cit.
4. Paul Lee Tan, *Encyclopedia of 7700 Illustrations: A Treasury of Illustrations, Anecdotes, Facts and Quotations for Pastors, Teachers and Christian Workers* (Bible Communications, Garland TX), 1996, c1979

The Token
1. F. C. Cook, op. cit. p. 356
2. C. I. Scofield, *The New Scofield Study Bible* (Oxford University Press, New York: 1967), p. 260
3. Warren Wiersbe, *The Bible Exposition Commentary, Vol. 1* (Victor Books, Wheaton, IL: 1989), p. 296

The Wonders
1. W. Graham Scroggie, op. cit. p. 16
2. Matthew Henry, *Commentary on the Whole Bible, Vol. 2* (Hendrikson Publishers, Peabody, MA; 1991), p. 16
3. H. L. Rossier, op. cit.
4. John N. Darby, op. cit.

Crossing the Jordan
1. F. C. Cook, op. cit. p. 358
2. H. F. Witherby, op. cit., p. 64

The Memorials
1. Matthew Henry, op. cit., p. 20
2. H. L. Rossier, op. cit.
3. H. F. Witherby, op. cit., p. 29

On That Day
1. James Vernon McGee, op. cit., p. 11
2. F. B. Meyer, op. cit., p. 50
3. H. F. Witherby, op. cit., p. 75

The Sign of Circumcision
1. J. G. Bellett, op. cit.
2. James Vernon McGee, op. cit., p. 12
3. H. F. Witherby, op. cit., p. 95

Endnotes

The Divine Captain
1. W. Graham Scroggie, op. cit. pp. 22-23
2. H. F. Witherby, op. cit., pp. 112-113
3. F. B. Meyer, op. cit., p. 65

The Conquest of Jericho
1. http://www.truthnet.org/Biblicalarcheology/6/conquestcanaan.htm
2. Ibid.
3. Bryant G. Wood, "Did the Israelites Conquer Jericho?" *Biblical Archaeology Review*, March-April 1990: pp. 44-58; and "The Walls of Jericho," *Bible and Spade*, Spring 1999: pp. 35-42
4. *Time* (March 5, 1990), p. 43

Utter Devastation
1. Edythe Draper, *Draper's Quotations from the Christian World* (Tyndale House Pub. Inc., Wheaton, IL – electronic copy): Erwin Lutzer - worldliness

For They Are Few
1. H. F. Witherby, op. cit., p. 129
2. Charles Ryrie, *So Great Salvation* (Victor Books, Wheaton, IL; 1989), pp. 59-60.
3. Paul Lee Tan, op. cit.

Sin in the Camp
1. H. L. Rossier, op. cit.
2. H. F. Witherby, op. cit., p. 126
3. James Vernon McGee, op. cit., p. 17

Make Confession
1. F. B. Meyer, op. cit., p. 91

Take All the People
1. Donald Campbell, op. cit., p. 346
2. James Vernon McGee, op. cit., p. 21
3. H. L. Rossier, op. cit.

The Ambush
1. H. F. Witherby, op. cit., p. 139
2. Paul Lee Tan, op. cit.

Blessings and Curses
1. F. C. Cook, op. cit. p. 358
2. F. B. Meyer, op. cit., p. 106
3. H. F. Witherby, op. cit., pp. 148-149
4. Arthur W. Pink, *Gleanings in Exodus* (Moody Press, Chicago, IL; no date), p. 122

Gibeonite Trickery
1. H. F. Witherby, op. cit., pp. 156-157
2. H. L. Rossier, op. cit.
3. Paul Lee Tan, op. cit.

The Consequences of Deceit
1. Matthew Henry, op. cit., p. 54
2. Paul Lee Tan, op. cit.

The Lord Fought for Israel
1. H. F. Witherby, op. cit., p. 161
2. H. L. Rossier, op. cit.
3. J. G. Bellett, op. cit.
4. H. L. Rossier, op. cit.

Step on Their Necks
1. F. B. Meyer, op. cit., pp. 129-130

The Southern Campaign Continues
1. http://www.bibarch.com/archaeologicalsites/hazor.htm
2. Donald Campbell, op. cit., p. 352
3. H. F. Witherby, op. cit., p. 166

The Northern Campaign
1. http://www.bibarch.com/archaeologicalsites/hazor.htm
2. J. N. Darby, op. cit.

The Rest of Conquest
1. H. F. Witherby, op. cit., p. 170
2. F. B. Meyer, op. cit., p. 145
3. W. Graham Scroggie, op. cit. pp. 6-7

Land for Some and the Lord for Others
1. H. F. Witherby, op. cit., pp. 177-178

Endnotes

Give Me This Mountain
1. Donald Campbell, op. cit., p. 356
2. W. Graham Scroggie, op. cit. p. 48
3. H. L. Rossier, op. cit.
4. H. F. Witherby, op. cit., p. 184

A Portion for Judah
1. W. Graham Scroggie, op. cit. pp. 49-50

Two Portions for Joseph
1. F. C. Cook, op. cit. p. 394
2. F. B. Meyer, op. cit., pp. 171-173
3. Paul Lee Tan, op. cit.

Seven Portions for Seven Brothers

Joshua's Portion
1. John D. Currid and David P. Barrett, *Crossway ESV Bible Atlas* (Crossway, Wheaton, IL, 2010)

Six Cities of Refuge
1. F. B. Meyer, op. cit., p. 181
2. H. L. Rossier, op. cit.
3. Paul Lee Tan, op. cit.

Forty-Eight Levitical Cities
1. Paul Lee Tan, op. cit.

The Lord's Faithfulness
1. H. F. Witherby, op. cit., pp. 212-213
2. Ibid., p. 214
3. F. B. Meyer, op. cit., p. 186

The Altar of Misunderstanding
1. F. B. Meyer, op. cit., p. 189
2. H. L. Rossier, op. cit

Joshua's Final Charge
1. J. G. Bellett, op. cit.

Choose You This Day
1. F. B. Meyer, op. cit., p. 203

Overcoming Your Bully

Warren Henderson

"The flesh" describes the natural man. God has no program to change the flesh. Rather He brings in something new: *"and that which is born of the Spirit is spirit"* (John 3:6). A new struggle is brought to our attention. It is no longer the new nature or the believer striving for mastery over sin in the body; it is the Holy Spirit striving against the old nature. The little boy coming home from school was beaten up by a big bully. He was on the bottom, and the big bully was pounding him very heavily. Then he looked up from his defeated position on the bottom, and saw his big brother coming. The big brother took care of the bully while the little fellow crawled up on a stump and rubbed his bruises. The believer has the Holy Spirit to deal with the flesh, that big bully. I learned along time ago that I can't overcome it. So I have to turn it over to Somebody who can. The Holy Spirit indwells believers. He wants to do that for us, and He can!

—from the Preface by James Vernon McGee

A timely book, in a day when many believer's lives, marriages and ministries are being destroyed by being too easy on the flesh. Here is a call to give no quarter to the flesh but to be like Phinehas of old, and Ram the javelin home! Read it, meditate on it, and most of all apply it!   —Mike Attwood

ISBN: 9781926765358 ✦ US: $11.99 ✦ CDN: $12.99 ✦ Pages: 136

www.ingramcontent.com/pod-product-compliance
Lightning Source LLC
LaVergne TN
LVHW051827080426
835512LV00018B/2764